An A

To many people the *Evening Standard* art critic, Brian Sewell, is the most well-informed, articulate and consistently direct of contemporary art critics. Such people enjoy his witty, elegant prose and revere him as a lone voice of sanity in an otherwise crazy world. For others, principally members of the contemporary art establishment, Sewell and his reviews provoke catatonic convulsions because he frequently derides their exhibitions and their favoured artists.

An indication of Sewell's power came on 5 January 1994 when the *Evening Standard* published a letter from members of this group demanding that Sewell be sacked on grounds of philistinism and 'social and sexual hypocrisy'. Thus began a furore which still continues: Sewell and his opponents traded insults on television in the course of which Sewell was described as vicious, ill-informed, misogynist and homophobic. The editor of the *Evening Standard* and hundreds of readers came out in his support, and two months later he won the Press Award Critic of the Year for the second time – no other art critic has won it even once. In 1995, he was the winner of the Hawthornden Award for Art Criticism.

Mongrel dogs, old Daimlers and Michelangelo, Titian and the splendours of the Ottoman Empire, the antique ruins of Asia Minor and the early churches of Armenia – all are the enthusiasms of Brian Sewell, wayward art historian, sometime student at the Courtauld Institute. Christie's, the Royal Collection, the British and Arts Councils, the Council of Europe and the Royal Academy have all enlisted his expertise and given him employment, and he is still the errand-boy for museums in Europe and America. He has a regular column in *Il Giornale dell'Arte*, is an occasional contributor to *Modern Painters, Art Review* and *Antique International*, and for the past eleven years has been the art critic of the *Evening Standard*.

Over the past twenty-five years he has shared his house in London with four women and nine bitches.

An ALPHABET *of* VILLAINS
BRIAN SEWELL

BLOOMSBURY

First published in Great Britain 1995
Bloomsbury Publishing Plc, 2 Soho Square, London W1V 6HB

A CIP catalogue record for this book
is available from the British Library

ISBN 0 7475 2375 4

10 9 8 7 6 5 4 3 2 1

Typeset by Hewer Text Composition Services, Edinburgh
Printed in Great Britain by Cox & Wyman Ltd, Reading

To Tina Brown, first to think that I might have a way
with words;
to Anthony Blunt, who saw the funny side of such
a falling-off;
to Annalena MacAfee, Alistair Hicks, Ian Irvine, John Leese,
John Preston, Alex Renton, Stewart Steven and Roy Wright,
editors all; and to Colin Darracott, wise friend.

CONTENTS

CONTENTS

Introduction

Two common assumptions, amounting to superstitious belief, dominate the art world now; the first is that the artist, however young, ill-educated, inarticulate, inexperienced and technically incapable, however old, burnt out and dependent on habit and hack repetition, is a creature of infinite wisdom, intelligence and perspicacity, to whom, whatever is presented for our contemplation, we must bend the knee as to a saint; the second is that whatever is to be found in art galleries, the new churches and cathedrals of our day, must be art, simply by virtue of its being there, be it dormant actress or dead sheep, be it the evidence of emptied bowels and bladder or the endoscopic exploration of what lies within the vagina and the anus after sodomy and copulation.

The new priesthood, Nicholas Serota and his compliant minions at the Tate Gallery and the officials of the Arts Council and its many subsidiary quangos, a closely interwoven group all sitting on each others' bodies, their number very small and very powerful, their language deliberately obscure and even meaningless, their orthodoxy narrow and intolerant, are now the absolute arbiters of taste and patronage, the experts who decide what shall be seen and subsidised and sent abroad to wave the flag for Britain. As, supported by blind and unquestioning Ministers and stupid civil servants, these self-serving cliques have now assumed implacable authority, the outsider critic is compelled to adopt the role of sniper and take pot shots at their ninepins.

A number of these reviews were included in an earlier anthology; they reappear here only because in any list of frauds, failures, incompetents, pranksters and disciples of Duchamp, their subjects are essential.

An ALPHABET *of* VILLAINS

Afro-Asian Art

THE HAYWARD GALLERY, THE UGLIEST BUILDING in London, has been embellished with the battered remains of car exhausts and bumpers, a bucket, a bicycle, a watering can, a lavatory pan and other relics of society, all crudely painted in bright colours. 'Well, it's Christmas,' sighed a visitor. 'It's nice kid stuff,' said a second, and to others it may seem a witty criticism of the architecture.

It is not a Christmas decoration; it was not put there by a child; and it is not a comment on the brute ugliness of the building. It is a work of art by the Japanese artist Kumiko Shimizu, and was commissioned at public expense by the public servants who run the Hayward Gallery, where there is now an exhibition called *The Other Story*.

The Other Story is the maudlin tale of the frustrated genius of artists working in this country, disdained by collectors and the trade, derided by museum curators and ignored by the education authorities – and all because they are not white. In the visual arts racial prejudice is unchallenged, and even Apartheid would be a welcome improvement on the present invisibility of the black artist in Britain – black is here used as the portmanteau term for yellow and all shades of brown, for India and Pakistan, for China, Japan and the Philippines, and for the Lebanon as well as Africa, the Caribbean, and the Commonwealth ghettoes of Britain.

Are they disdained, derided and ignored? I was under the impression that Britain is to be represented at the next Venice Biennale by Anish Kapoor, an Indian from Bombay, who was a major contributor to the Arts Council's *British Art Show* in 1984, whose work has long been promoted by the British Council, and who is supported by one of London's leading dealers. I was under the impression that the last time I saw Aubrey Williams, from Guyana, he was in full blown white robes as a member of the Arts

Council's Advisory Panel on Art – a position that is omitted from his biography in the exhibition catalogue. Am I in error in recalling that the work of Kim Lim, from Singapore, was included in the Hayward Annual in 1977, and that Lin Show Yu, from Taiwan, was one of the bright lights of the Marlborough Gallery, with work commissioned for the QE2 and exhibited in Germany and America as representative of British painting? Am I deluded when I recall that paintings by Francis Souza, from Goa, and Avinash Chandra, from Simla, once hung on the walls of my own studio, until their mannered emptiness bored me and I sold them for a fraction of their cost?

Glancing through the biographies of the artists in the Hayward exhibition, it is immediately apparent that most have been trained at such art schools as the Royal College, St Martin's, Birmingham, Coventry, Camberwell, the Slade and the Central, that most have won enviable awards, prizes and scholarships, that most have been frequently exhibited at the Royal Academy, the Commonwealth Institute, the Serpentine, the ICA, the Hayward, Whitechapel and Tate Galleries (all hostile bastions of the British Establishment), that their work has been bought by a host of provincial museums and by the Arts Council, the V&A, the Government Art Collection and the Imperial War Museum (more Establishment bastions), that they hold teaching posts and have Arts Council films made about them. Balraj Khanna, an Indian, lists membership of the Arts Council's Exhibition Committee, and of the Art Advisory Group of the South Bank Centre, among his achievements. Gavin Jantjes, from South Africa, was appointed a member of the Arts Council in 1986, and is currently a senior lecturer at Chelsea School of Art.

All this they adduce as support for their argument that they are despised, rejected, ignored and invisible, when they are nothing of the kind.

Let me now suggest that perhaps they should be. Souza's rejection of robust Indian imagery for poor imitations of the School of Paris leaves him now degraded and without substance. Bowling, who thought himself part of the Hockney circle, was once a capable mimic of Bacon, but now paints vast acres of sludge as though attempting to forge late Monet lily-ponds with a dirty palette. Aubrey Williams either mirrors the images of ancient Mexico, or paints blurs that are at best decorative, at worst a mess.

Iqbal Geoffrey, a sometime barrister with Harvard University listed in his CV, plays visual jokes with mousetraps, neckties made of brass, and a decanter containing the ashes of 27 paintings. Li Yuan Chia suspends large metal discs and asks visitors to re-arrange the magnetised objects that cling to them. Rasheed Araeen, who devised this wretched show and wrote most of the catalogue, is yet another prankster, with four short lengths of iron girder, nine bloodstained photographs in homage to the ghastly Gilbert and George, and sixteen red spots on the floor. The vacuous paintings of Saleem Arif are bettered by the background decoration of many an Indian restaurant.

Two artists only must be excluded from this general condemnation. Sonia Boyce matches perfectly the subtle delicacy of pastel to strident colour, sculptural form and robust imagery, so that her work is decorative and profound, sophisticated and primitive, beautiful and urgently political. Donald Locke is a sculptor of exquisite craftsmanship and wicked wit, who can make a black political point with black humour. His *Trophies of Empire*, a cabinet of black and brown phalluses peeping from tankard, chalice, prize cup and candlestick, or spurred and manacled, can be seen either as Imperialism emasculating the black, or as the black's renowned endowment dramatically defiling the institutions of Britain's imperial past. In the end, who fucked whom?

Apart from Boyce and Locke, we have seen it all before. Having either no traditions of their own, or traditions so exhausted that no nourishment is to be drawn from them, these artists parrot western visual idioms that they do not understand and that have been exposed as silly and pretentious. That they should demand serious attention for their third-rate imitations of the white man's cliché must seem outrageous to all who care to judge by quality. Talent in the white west is an extremely rare phenomenon, and most western art is indifferent at best; I see no reason to distort the judgment that damns it so as to praise the work of artists just as bad, or worse, because they make a noisy business of being black.

Evening Standard 1989

Craigie Aitchison

FOR THE PAST TWO HUNDRED YEARS ENGLISH painting has been bedevilled by the primitive and the eccentric. William Blake began the trend with feeble imitations of Michelangelo to illustrate his simple visions and wry rhymes, and the 19th century gave birth not only to a host of whimsical fairy painters, but to rural clodhoppers whose chosen subjects were the gross prize porker and ballooning bull, invariably seen in easy profile. The most extreme example of acceptable insanity is the 'unphortschnitt Edward Lear, a nartist (sic) of skrogfrodious temperament who painted pigchurs for eggzibission' – his words, not mine. Even in our materialist century, together with the ilk of David Jones and Cecil Collins, we have taken to our bosoms Stanley Spencer and Laurence Lowry, because the one was genuinely dotty and the other found it profitable to declare himself a hearer of voices who travelled to Damascus by way of the back streets of Manchester.

We now have another amiably potty painter in our midst, picturesque enough to be popularised in the colour supplements of Sunday papers, a Royal Academician and a man of published interviews. In the catalogue of his current exhibition in the Albemarle Gallery he is asked the question 'Both Victor Pasmore and John Piper advised you to give up painting because they thought you were so bad at it. What made you continue?' To this he answers 'I was not going to stop because of them . . . it would have worried me a lot more if Lowry had said it' – and there's the clue, the appeal of primitive to primitive, of naive to naive, of incompetent to incompetent, the long capricious sideline of the history of art in England.

Aitchison is a man who claims to have graduated from the influence of Van Gogh and Gauguin in colour reproductions, first to Salvador Dali's Crucifixion in the Glasgow City Art Gallery, and then to 'Piero della Francesca and all those painters'. In his tendency to cover canvas with large areas of pink and red with little modulation and not much brushwork, there is still a hint of Gauguin (though only a hint, and that made bright, vile and insensitive to the point of vulgarity), but to claim kinship of any kind with Van Gogh and Piero is blind impertinence, for he has nothing of the real madman's robust impetuous vigour, nor the intellectual grandeur of the Renaissance man – and as for Dali, if only he had a tittle of that man's skill and draughtsmanship, however odious much of his work now seems.

Again and again Aitchison paints the Crucifixion. 'Have you ever used a model for Christ?' asks his interviewer – a foolish question, for no man referring to the live naked male could ever have painted so ineptly any figures as inadequate as these images of God. The answer, to give Aitchison his due, is an honest 'No'. His Christs are usually armless, and in this present batch of unconvincing Saviours he even paints the cross without its cross-piece; his notion of expressing agony is to give Christ the features of a cartoon character caught in a post-prandial snooze – only the balloon with zzzzzzzzzzz in it is missing. And are there Maries, thieves and saints in attendance? No, of course not, for these are far beyond the capabilities of this fumbling Royal Academician, who instead gives Christ the witness of his household pets, the dog and the canary (though even these, unhappily, more resemble an albino ptero-dactyl and a wayward sheep).

Aitchison does not draw. He claims to paint directly 'from the inside out', and uses the curious word 'itch' for his technique of pushing paint as far as he wants it to go towards an edge, which he then defines with a small knife, never knowing when it is right until it is wrong. Alas, it is always wrong, even when he thinks it right, and his assumption of holy innocence as the perfect fool has now become pretentious and deliberate nonsense, a camouflage for incompetence.

To those determined to see virtue in the holy pictures, framed in the Florentine style to invite comparison with the saintly Fra Angelico, I commend attention to the portraits, for these are untrammelled by the spectator's beliefs and associations, and can be seen with a clear eye. They have attracted such praise-words as powerful, serene, compelling, but if the truth be told, their drawing is so weak, their substance so meagre, their sense of the sitter's character so shallow, that were they by some fifteen-year-old in a comprehensive school they'd not get him through an O-level examination.

It is an irony that so much fuss should have been made over such unworthy work simply because its maker is eccentric.

Evening Standard 1989

American Art in the Twentieth Century

THE GREAT EXHIBITION IN LONDON THIS autumn is *American Art in the 20th Century* at the Royal Academy. It is part of the series that has so far examined in some detail and with considerable wilfulness (too many deliberate sins of commission and omission) the art of this century in Germany, Italy and Britain, and is thus, in great measure, the horse after the cart, for in the century's second half, America has been perceived as the great force in contemporary art worldwide. Abstract Expressionism (known in my youth as Action Painting – a happier name for such indiscipline), Photo-Realism, Pop Art, the Colour Field, Reductivist Painting, Minimal and Conceptual Art, Assemblage, Post Painterly Abstraction, the Art of Cultural Violence and many another fad or movement have all invaded the rest of the world from America – though in a strict historical sense some may first have been mooted (as was Pop Art) in Europe.

It was from America that a pile of bricks stormed London, demanding to be accepted as art; all over Europe the idea of dribbling paint from cans vanquished the brush, and neon signs, graffiti, the glamorous advertisement, the photograph, the waxwork hamburger, the seeming oracle of printed messages, the strip cartoon, shattered crockery and the iron girder were all accepted as the authentic means of the expression of the authentic self. Post-war Americans broke down the bounds of all the conventions that had since Mediterranean antiquity governed the development of art and declared a new Renaissance (knowing nothing of the old) always desperately striving to be new: when Andy Warhol spoke of fame for fifteen minutes, he could well have had in mind the rapidity with which American artists replaced each other at the pinnacle of popularity's heap, innovation obliterating innovation. Warhol may, of course, have paraphrased Max Ernst, who in 1950 (or so) had observed in New York that significant changes in the arts 'now take place every twenty minutes'.

The huge and essay-ridden catalogue of the exhibition does well to remind us of Marcel Duchamp's dictum 'Art is produced by a succession of individuals expressing themselves; it is not a question of progress' – though this is nonsense in any art historical sense, and true only of what has passed for art since his dotage. It does not apply to American art early in this century, which was soundly rooted in a European past. Throughout the 19th century America was no transatlantic backwater; American architects and sculptors produced monuments of Neo-Classicism that must astonish Europeans by their scale and purity; American painters joined the great European academies of Paris, Rome, Madrid and Munich, were Romantic, Barbizon, Realist, Impressionist and Post-Impressionist, and were one to search American art for that hackneyed idyll, The Golden Age, it would not be among the great men of drip and detritus, but in the delectable Impressionism of Mary Cassatt (so much more brilliant than Berthe Morisot), William Merritt Chase, Alden Weir, Childe Hassam and many a less familiar name (and dare one mention Whistler and John Sargent too?). If not of a Golden Age, then let us speak of golden pictures – of all those views of Italy by Inness, Gifford, Haseltine and Cropsey, and the last (and very grandest) landscapes in the golden glow of the Claudian tradition painted by Albert Bierstadt on the trail from Dresden to Yosemite, the Rockies and Alaska.

Duchamp was in error; nothing comes of nothing in the history of art (though as much may come from impatience and rebellion as from respect for tradition), and for New York to have been the setting for what has some serious claim to be the most influential exhibition of the 20th century – the Armory Show of 1913 – required a well established popular interest in the arts as well as informed artists, dealers and collectors. Duchamp himself was a contributor to this amazing display of some 1,300 works by artists from Germany, Britain, Scandinavia, America as well as by Picasso, Braque, Brancusi, Cézanne and Gauguin, and though it caused such outrage that newspapers accused it of undermining American democracy, it was a turning-point for American artists, the event that like Picasso's Cubism in Paris (c. 1907) and Kandinsky's abstraction in Munich (c. 1910) drove them away from tradition. As Impressionism died, a cultural gap between Europe and America had opened, and this, made obvious by the Armory Show, American painters hastened to close, absorbing Contemporary European influences willy-nilly: re-jigging, refining and inventing. It is now clear that the post-Armory years were astonishingly fertile in spite of their ending in the Depression, that the long and mischievous presence in America of Duchamp was a vital stimulus, and that he and Man Ray, Stuart Davis, Marsden Hartley, John Covert, Gerald Murphy, Charles Sheeler and others were prescient in ideas and inventions adopted, developed and often enfeebled by post-1945 artists – Pop, Photo-Realism, the flags of Jasper Johns, the geometric shapes of Ellsworth Kelly, ready-made sculptural objects and printed texts on painted canvases are all mooted in their work.

Anyone taking a longer view of American art than just the 20th century must see that it has always been inextricably bound to European art, but the thesis that America was a minor school until half way through this century and that there was then a sudden reversal that made all Europe the rag-bag recipients of powerful American aesthetic impulses, is far too simple. American historians do their 19th-century art no service when they write of it as Barbizon at second-hand and reach-me-down Impressionism, for theirs were painters at least as accomplished as their peers throughout the whole of Europe – compare them with the great bulk of those exhibiting in the Royal Academy and the Paris Salon – and it is only in the adventures of Post-Impressionism that they briefly lost ground.

In the years between the wars – a terrible doldrum for art in most of Europe, even in the Paris of Picasso – American art was vigorous in its exploitation of German and French ideas and their renewal, and New York was Mecca for such energetic young Europeans as de Kooning and Gorky, and a refuge for Mondrian. In the past half century, for all the perceived magnificence of Pollock and Rothko, the furious energy of the COBRA group (working in Copenhagen, Brussels and Amsterdam 1948–51, but exhibiting in New York) must not be ignored in the context of American art, nor, more recently, the pervasive influence of Joseph Beuys. Even now, when the exhausted novelties of American art linger so long in the supposed self-expression of British art students, I cannot see, as Norman Rosenthal (the genius behind the exhibition) would have us believe, that we are 'panting for breath', nor that New York's perceived status as the cultural focus of Europe was ever anything more than a delusion forced on us by the art market there.

The Royal Academy is physically too small to house the whole exhibition, and the unwieldy later part of it is far away in the Saatchi Gallery in South Kilburn – a division calculated to disrupt concentration. The earlier part is far the more exciting, the later far the more familiar from the art market, contemporary exhibitions and the enthusiasms of television's popular generalists, best suited to both those who can take art at a light infantry pace and others who are able to stand entranced by nothingness. For the poor critic, yet again uncomfortably aware of interesting artists omitted and their worthless peers included, of alternative works of greater substance, of a perhaps distorted perspective of American art (the organisers seem inordinately proud of their European view), and of the uncritical stance of most of those who contribute the twenty-five (often tedious) essays in the catalogue, much of the exhibition is less an intellectual marathon than an obstacle course of superficial gimcrack whimsies to which he must return if he is to do it justice.

Evening Standard 1993

Michael Andrews

Michael Andrews is a painter of the now famous generation of post-war British painters that spans from Freud to Hockney, and to those steeped in what is ludicrously known as The London School, he is at least their equal (is that saying much?). His output, however, is much smaller, and this has led his apologists (numbering among them, inevitably, Sir Lawrence Gowing, who sensed a kinship with Piero della Francesca) to promote the notion that none of his canvases escapes the studio unless it is a masterpiece. Rarity has thus become an instrument of hype.

Andrews has no belief in slapdash genius – not for him the trowel-it-on and scrape-it-off business of Auerbach – and in the careful preparation, the prior thought, the organisation of ideas and their thin consequence, comes close to Hockney, though technically narrower and now more intellectually mystical than that prolific and popular hero. A pupil of Coldstream at the Slade, he uses none of the obvious Coldstream devices of grid and measurement, of little ticks and lines to show how careful is his seeing and how diligent his reduction of the things seen to two dimensions with only an illusion of the third – yet the ghost of Coldstream holds his hand in leaden restraint, making the touch tentative, the final resolution of ideas evasive, and the process of painting so slow that many of Andrews's pictures have all but died in parturition on the easel.

He seems not to respond to what is on the canvas as images appear under his hand, nor to savour the excitement of gesture – only to be so deliberately intent on the preconceived pattern that he must use methods and techniques that neuter all that could be impulsive and painterly, that subject serendipitous inspiration to mere accuracy. Perhaps such rigid adherance to the preconception offers him the reassurance that he has needed all his working life – that he is a painter of some originality and distinction, and not merely the wavering imitator of influence whom art historians may one day dub the man who always followed and never forged ahead. At the Hayward Gallery's retrospective exhibition of his work ten years ago the slow drift of his small genius was from Coldstream to Bacon and on to Photo-Realism, with hints of Sickert and the Kitchen Sink, portraiture that derived from Minton and Moynihan, and of the Royal Academic set piece of the family in the garden or friends grouped in a bar or restaurant. None of these things was done with conviction, and all have a nature that is both plodding and irresolute, with all the little braveries either made impotent by indecision and unfinish, swamped by silly tricks and borrowed mannerism, or so close to the photographs from which they were derived that they had scant identity as paintings.

Andrews's work now on view at the Whitechapel Gallery suffers still from all these indecisions, though the influences are less apparent. The exhibition consists of nine paintings of Ayers Rocks executed between 1985 and 1990, but on which he had been brooding since 1983, with one quite unfinished Scottish landscape borrowed dripping from the easel, and one painting produced in 1970, to indicate the whither and the whence. The whither is so quaint a combination of High Victorian topography with the drips and stains of Sam Francis and French Tachisme, over which we were all so enthusiastic in the Fifties, that its inclusion in this condition can only be excused by attributing to the organisers a state of mind akin to that of the Catholic peasantry when confronted by the Turin Shroud. The exhibition's title is *The Delectable Mountain*, Ayers Rock, and it is on Andrews's portrayals of this and other outcrops in the neighbourhood (one of which looks like a gigantic humbug with Mae West's lips) that we must concentrate.

Some of these pictures were first exhibited in 1986; in his brief preface to the catalogue, Andrews then quoted the hymn 'Rock of Ages, cleft for me, Let me hide myself in Thee . . .' and proclaimed that this magical mountain, sacred to the Aborigines, was a radiant incarnation of the verse, metaphor to Christians and fact to Aborigines. A methodist by education and something of a Zen Buddhist by adoption, Andrews is perhaps intellectually attuned to the literal idea of the cleft rock as a safe haven, Freudian though it may be, and to the notion of spiritual salvation through agencies other than the God of the Jewish-Christian-Muslim tradition, even if these be atavistic, pantheist or animist. Whatever we may think of the paintings, we have no reason to doubt the intense sincerity of Andrews when he describes the area of Ayers Rock as an 'Elysian plot for unselfish souls', and his sense there of some transcendental experience is one that all worthy travellers will recognise. The trouble for me is that it is in his words, not his paintings, that I recognise the grip on Andrews's soul, the spirit of the place.

The paintings are large. The largest, with the length of fourteen feet, assumes the proportions of a billboard and has a billboard's flat, shallow, photographic brilliance, the darkening sky broken by scraps of white cloud as though it were the ceiling of a night club in the flicker of a disco light. Catherine Lampert, the Director of the Whitechapel Gallery, is at pains to dismiss the photographic quality as a deceptive impression, a minor thing overwhelmed by the sheer physical presence of the paintings – but the photographic quality is as much part of the physical presence as the paint, and cannot be so naively denied. The paint is meagre stuff largely blown on by a spray-gun, and the crisp outlines of the Burra-shaped mounds are those of stencils blanking the mists of colour. The ghostly grasses in the foregrounds, uncanny in their sense of the photographic negative, realism in reverse, are the result of more deft work with the spray-gun on dried trophies brought back from Australia. The one painting of the Rock that enlists the aid of oil paint (all others are acrylic) suggests that Andrews is not just a man of technical trickery; but the one canvas on which he attempts to enrich the texture by mixing with his paint the real earth of the Rock, results in such a heavy sag of dark material that it destroys all pictorial logic.

How slow all this business was is demonstrated by *Evening, Katajuta*, exhibited in 1986 as a painting in progress, but seeming finished: in the intervening years Andrews has brightened the sun on the horizon, lengthened two faint lines of scrubby bushes, added two small emphatic trees, changed the position of a kangaroo in the foreground and added another in the middle distance, and lightened the long grasses a little – all very deliberate tinkering to give scale and distance, anchorage and direction to a drifting view, and firm evidence of his integrity as a composer of pictures. Andrews, however, is no Turner, recreating and uplifting landscape in the dramatic turbulence of paint; he is no Constable, using the sensual substance of paint with sensuality; he is no Bierstadt, the Düsseldorfer who in equal wonderment applied the sunset glow of Claude to the Rocky Mountains of America. Andrews is none of these, but a minor post-Pop painter on a major scale, who mistakes size for intensity and, utterly failing to communicate his troubled response to Ayers Rock, gives us a railway poster rather than an icon. One late scrap of watercolour by Turner in the Alps makes empty nonsense of his vast enterprise.

Evening Standard 1991

Art and Language

A<small>RT AND</small> L<small>ANGUAGE WAS ONCE A COOPERA-</small>
tive enterprise of as many as thirty artists and theorists, but it is now
reduced to two, Michael Baldwin and Mel Ramsden, Midlanders in
their mid-forties. From earlier discussions it emerged in 1968 as a
press that in 1969 first published its journal *Art-Language*. As far as
one can tell, so convoluted is the language and so minimal the art,
Marxist ingenuities lie at its foundations, and its functions were and
are to question and subvert the established patterns not only of art,
but of art history and the art market, of museums and galleries, and
of aesthetics and criticism – no bad thing, one might suppose, and
even agree, were one able to understand their arguments. Their
basic premise (I think) is that all visual art is conceptually dependent
on language.

The book accompanying their current exhibition at the Institute
of Contemporary Arts is evidence of fine practice in the art of
printing – the type face is the classically handsome Times Roman,
the paper substantial, the layout elegant – but the language of the
limp volume is largely inscrutable and I have scant idea of what
much of it means. I sense that Baldwin and Ramsden tell me what
to think and that I must decide nothing for myself – but perhaps that
is the way of Marxists? As with many a left-wing tract the
vocabulary is the weapon of thought suppression, the cosh, the
whip and the water-cannon that converts lively intellectual exchange into the chanted statements of *Animal Farm*. What are we to
make of the 'art of pseudo rigour' and 'the universality of
pseudomorphisms'? – of 'malapropisation' and 'perlocutionary'?
– of 'individuated iconicity' and 'the Boojum word'? For this
last I turned to Edward Lear's *Wurbl Inwentions*, but found nothing
between blomphious (which means absquoxiously) and the oddly
apposite boshblobberbosh (particularly foolish foolishness). If not
Lear's invention, then Boojum must be Lewis Carroll's – and so it

is, as a species of Snark, of which the hunters 'softly and silently vanish away'. Is Art and Language then an elaborate joke? Have we been seduced into high seriousness over a childish nonsense while our seducers slip away to wank behind the cricket pavilion?

The cricket pavilion looms large in many of the paintings offered us by Mike and Mel. These are views of poplars on the boundary of a pitch, each with a broad sector in plain colour that began as the verandah post of the pavilion; it acts as a formal device to establish foreground and distance, and is at the same time a necessary reminder that Baldwin and Ramsden are utterly modern painters, for the poplars, seen at different times of day and different seasons of the year, might otherwise seem only crude imitations of the series paintings of Monet and Mondrian. It is intriguing that they should at once refer to the most popular of the Impressionists and the most arid of early abstract painters – another little joke, perhaps? Over these paintings is drawn a grid, and enhancing the graph paper impression are outlines that seem to resemble the ground plans of large buildings, but which are, in fact, outlines of the letters SURF, often confused by changes of style and size.

SURF is the Boojum word; according to Baldwin at a point when he is concerned with the material nature of what he himself engagingly describes as 'the mess under the glass', he confesses that 'Surf is an abbreviation, conceivably, for surface. It's also an abbreviation for nothing.' I am tempted to suggest surfeit instead, for one can have too much of this foolishness, and nothing comes of nothing.

Many of the paintings have been deliberately spoiled, for the literal representation of landscape is not the objective of Mike and Mel, and they do not want to make an icon of poplar or pavilion; they are more concerned with the paint itself as the icon. They have in the past even attempted portraiture in the abstract expressionist style, which means much paint and little in the way of eyes and noses, but in these latest works they assert the nature of the paint by squashing their landscapes under a 'shiny unregenerate slab of glass' to which more paint has been generously applied like half smeared blobs of butter in a sandwich; the effect, combining elements of the Rorschach test and the palimpsest, rhubarb and custard, mustard and ketchup, all oozing and melding as the glass weighs down on it, is remarkably unpleasant. Mike and Mel are quite right to take such risks if they consider the taking to be a work of art, a happening of sorts, an action painting at a remove perhaps, but the rest of us must be allowed to reject these glazed sandwiches as an art form, preferring the conventional painting of Titian and Michelangelo, whom Mel and Mike, in their display of intellectual cacafuego dismiss as comedians.

On other works they impose narrow strips cut from paintings of different subjects, much like the abstract affectations of wretched art students who contrive to enliven the dull vastness of an eight foot canvas with a little shock here and there – the art of the cattle prod (imagine Turner's *Rain, Steam and Speed* bandaged with bits of *Dido building Carthage*). Sometimes, although Baldwin argues that 'You cannot read and look at a scene simultaneously. Your attention is split', this is precisely what they attempt, but they only prove his point when they superimpose printed statements on their paintings; at worst the images are obscured and the messages confused; at best the message is victorious, and in its pretence of portent convinces us that Mike and Mel are more skilled in the manipulation of language than in any practice that might be described as art.

Art and Language deserve an amused footnote in the history of conceptual art, but as writers, not as artists, for theirs is an intellectual juggling worthy of French art criticism – that indulgent literary form that allows the scribbler an ostentatious display of sensibility, letting him conjure the ghost of Baudelaire, plunge deep into the obscurities of Wittgenstein (whom we now know to have been mad), and be Marxist, Catholic, whimsically poetic and quite untranslateable all at the same time – indeed many of the Delphic utterances of Mike and Mel read as though they might well be poor translations from the French. The trouble with this sort of bosh is that the intellectually insecure *want* to believe it and find refuge in it, and too many curators feel they ought to have representative examples in their cure, so that willy-nilly it becomes established, even to the point of being short-listed for the Turner Prize.

Those tempted to take to their bosoms the particularly foolish foolishness of Baldwin and Ramsden should remember that among their iconicities, solipsisms, derogations and ontological concatenations, lurks Lewis Carroll's Boojum; it is just possible that Art and Language is a hoax.

Evening Standard 1991

Frank Auerbach

Marlborough Gallery

FRANK AUERBACH, BORN IN BERLIN IN 1931, found himself as a boy of eight suddenly in England, cruelly uprooted from his Jewish parents and his language, new hates, new loyalties expected of him. Now, fifty years later, he is perceived as a grand old man of British painting, a pillar of what is presently promoted as 'The School of London', our painterly ambassador to the Venice Biennale, the darling of the Saatchis, of the Arts Council, of the Establishment, and now of publishers, and a blue chip on the golden pavements of the art market's square mile.

Two men, and only two, played any real part in this – David Bomberg and Auerbach himself – the one a disagreeable Jewish genius of sorts in a wilderness of his own choosing, the other his pupil, determined on a kindred course that blinkered him to fad and fashion, driven by integrity. They met when Auerbach was seventeen and Bomberg fifty-seven, teaching evening classes at the Borough Polytechnic; now that Bomberg has been made famous after decades of neglect, all sorts and conditions of painters claim his tutelage, but in truth only Auerbach understood his use of a loaded brush that dredged and marked its strokes, stressing the material substances and translucence of the paint, and it was upon this quality that he established his own stronghold, pulling up the drawbridge against all the ephemeral forces of photo-realism, hard edge, soft edge, drip, splash and all the other mercenaries engaged in the Byzantine wars of critical esteem and market exploitation. Bomberg not only taught him to paint, but impressed on him the fundamental use of drawing, both as an inventory of things seen and as the means by which the mind and eye are cleared of clutter and preconception, by which, in black and white, tone and colour are established, form implied, ideas and images pared to essentials. It was Bomberg who took the boy back to Cézanne and the notion that nature should always be newly perceived, the raw material as fresh on the canvas as it should be in the cooking-pot, nothing reduced to trick, mannerism or false formula; were he inspired to refer to other painters (and he was – to Soutine and Sickert, Constable and Tintoretto, as well as, obviously, to Rembrandt), he must evolve from them, not merely colonise and imitate.

Auerbach's unremitting honesty has not made painting easy for him, nor are his pictures immediately easy on the eye. As Alfred Brendel searches his piano for some particular timbre in Schubert, playing the same phrase again and again until the wistful note is caught, so Auerbach paints the same subject on the same canvas perhaps thirty times before the unhindered speed and assertion of his handling melds perfectly the specific observation of a townscape or a face with the material nature of his paint. As each irresolution is scraped from the canvas, it leaves a ghost to force on him a palimpsest, a growing chorus to inform the spirit of the final version. Little of this palimpsest is to be read – a few vertical disturbances to a mass of horizontal strokes, or an unlikely undertone – only Auerbach knew its nature before the final version buried it beneath the tempestuous unity that suddenly, violently was manifested from a web of gestures; the historian is left to wonder what evidence is lost to history; the critic wonders if Auerbach's self-criticism is invariably right.

Even as a young man, Auerbach saw each good painting (by others, as well as himself) as a creature not constrained by rules and rubrics, but operating by laws unique to itself. For him, repeated painting was the exercise through which an idea, a geometry, a form, an icon might become a fact anchored in paint, as is a fly in amber, caught in an attitude, a tone, a colour, a mood in which it was the painting, not the painter, that cried 'Halt'. He has been accused of obsession and fixation, so often has he painted his now native heath of Primrose Hill, so often particular nudes and portraits – but these are the known starting points for the exploration of the unknown, triggered by the ever altering evidence of light that in new angles and new qualities of tone and intensity utterly changes form and colour, introducing new urgencies, breeding new images from old, resolving the paradox of representing mass and shape and place with gesture and a blob of paint.

The problem with so limited a range of interest so much repeated is that it induces weary numbness in the spectator. One willingly responds to the emotional resonance of Auerbach's colour – if only Mornington Crescent were really the topsy-turvy typhoon of reds and purples that he sees. One willingly responds to the thickness of his paint – with a wry misgiving that this is perhaps not to the 'tactile values' identified by Bernard Berenson, but is instead a reversion to the infant's interest in his own faeces. One willingly sees him as heir to his declared heroes, and as a match for some of them – but I wonder whether *Zeitgeist* and his German origins play some unconscious part, and if we ought also to see him as instinctive heir to Nolde, Rohlfs, Schmidt-Rottluf and other Expressionists of their genuine ilk, rather than to the false Abstract Expressionists of America. Accepting all that as evidence that the man is a substantial painter, there is, nevertheless, a more than niggling misgiving that his achievement is, in mountaineering terms, a first foothill, and that the peril in his path is a muddied bog of paint.

Crossing the bog with a brave and structural stroke of paint is not enough. Portraits that might as well be of prize porkers as of people are not true portraiture – this is Topolski's bravura without the old Pole's wit and accuracy, the grotesque coincidence of paint and feature quite without humour and humanity, and all abstract interest in paint as paint destroyed by the claim that the image is of so-and-so when all that can be seen is vague caricature.

After all these years the brave beginnings of this once consider-able painter have been hacked into failure, and trick, mannerism and formula now dominate. Those inclined to dispute this assertion should spend a little time with the felt-tip and crayon drawings on view at Marlborough Graphics as well as with the recent paintings that hang in the main Marlborough Gallery. Auerbach's is the saddest falling-off, for it was blind integrity that pushed him; he needs another Bomberg.

Evening Standard 1988

Blasphemies, Ecstasies, Cries, or Anguished Baudelaire

THE CATALOGUE OF THIS EXHIBITION IS covered in purple and gold – a mischievous reference to things ecclesiastical, lacking only a cross, hinting at blasphemy. It resembles in size and layout the limp leather-bound volumes of poetry and whimsical prose so popular in our grandparents' young day – Patience Strong, Wilhelmina Stitch, and *Poems of Passion* by Ella Wheeler Wilcox; as with these, the edition, numbering only 1,000, hints at rarity and preciousness. On each left hand page lie lines from a new translation of Baudelaire's *Fleurs du Mal*; they keep company with the reproduction of a painting, photograph or drawing printed on the facing page; neither lines nor images are identified.

The presentation of the exhibition itself was equally old-fashioned, but less genteel. The walls of the Serpentine Gallery were divided into planes of matt colour, occasionally interrupted by a triangular extrusion; the jostling of eau-de-nil and housemaid's pink, archi-tect's sludge and alizarin carmine, resembled nothing so much as the then daring designs for parti-coloured sitting-rooms promoted as high fashion in the early Fifties, but seeming now both restless and dreary. Against each plane, and isolated by it, hung a single picture, its nearest neighbour the text from Baudelaire. The presentation of these texts was perfect; each was a monochrome photograph of the relevant printed page, greatly enlarged, the nature of the paper and its lively edge enhanced without blurring the elegant type face; the chosen lines were strongly lit, the rejected lines allowed to slip into shadow; the tone of the photographs was matched by uniform frames in dull grey, their general tonality blending into the background and at no stage competing with the pictures.

This exhibition was, it seems, both a rejection of art history and all its disciplines, and a protest against the museum formulas of white walls and uniform frames. At the same time it was a revival of Roger Fry's notion that it is less important, when confronted with a work of art, to know its origins and circumstances, than to maintain one's spirit 'in a condition of tense passivity, a state of passive receptiveness . . . alert to its appeal, ready to vibrate in harmony with it'. Fry, no doubt, would have blessed this exercise in aesthetic apprehension, for it attempted to remove all the ordinary clues to identity – artist, date, subject, medium – and cue a response only with a quotation from Baudelaire, whose reputation as an art critic informed by the sensibility of a poet has never been assailed.

Problems were immediately apparent. It was impossible to render anonymous those pictures that were signed and those from the public domain that were in labelled frames; such old contemporaries as Bacon, Auerbach and Carel Weight have long been too familiar and repetitious ever to be rendered anonymous, and such younger contemporaries as Gillian Ayres and Therese Oulton could scarcely be cast back into the limbo of obscurity after exposure in the Academy, the Tate and the profitable purlieus of Bond Street; of the twenty-seven catalogued images, no more than ten could have been mysterious to habitual visitors to the Serpentine, and of those the age was immediately apparent – a first stage in the art historical discipline of establishing identity. The premise that this should be an exhibition without clues was thus swept away by the curator himself, seduced into a popular choice. For a successful experiment in the rejection of the *catalogue raisonné* and of Vasari's view of art history as a steady progress, he required wholly unknown painters and a wholly ignorant audience. Both could be found in London's larger prisons, but having taught in one of these, I am inclined to aver that prisoners without conventional education often demonstrate alarming acuity, and, not to be patronised with aesthetic nonsense, they demand clear answers to their who? when? why? and what? – Vasari is very much their man.

Andrew Brighton, who devised this exercise in Frydian passivity, should have recognised the Koechel urge in most of us, the need of the developed mind to categorise and record in order to assist understanding and sympathy – for from that sympathy comes the connoisseurship that informs the activity of the historian, the collector and the curator. Brighton, a comparatively inexperienced claimant to the laurels of the art historian, appears to have been too long in the company of such clerks as Christopher Wright, and believes that the *catalogue raisonné* is the be all and end all of art history; were this the case, I might join him in his iconoclasm, but it is not, and the only excuse to be offered for Brighton is that he has never sat at the feet of such historians as Frances Yates, Wittkower, Blunt, Wilde, Mahon or Denys Sutton, has never been humbled or inspired by teachers of their intellectual and cultural range, and believes that the image of art history is perfectly embodied in the present active membership of the Association of Art Historians. I commend to Brighton and all that benighted crew, Pope-Hennessy's plea for 'controlled intuition' and Offner's statement that 'If a document fails to agree with what I see with my own eyes, then the document is wrong'.

It was shrewd of Brighton to choose Baudelaire as his prop. The painters invited to contribute pictures were flattered to keep company with a critic who towered over his contemporaries, who believed in the integrity of art as a means of individual expression, and who, rejecting all the outworn assumptions of his peers, tried such men as Delacroix, Ingres and Courbet at the bar of his own sensibility. To those who know nothing of Baudelaire as a critic, the choice is seductive, for since antiquity the poet has haunted the painter and exploited him for ekphrastic purposes, and the rival claims of poetry and painting formed much of the *Paragone* to Leonardo's *Trattato della Pittura* (who better then than Edward Lucie-Smith to be an art critic?). Those who know Baudelaire only as an impotent syphilitic with an Oedipus complex, a masochist with piles, a hypochondriacal drug addict, a posturing dandy, an anguished adolescent and a middle-aged misogynist, will immediately recognise him as a hero well suited to today, and his *Fleurs du Mal* as a suitably erotic, satanic and blasphemous text, just as Brighton must have recognised (though he does not acknowledge) the germ of this exhibition in the first few paragraphs of his hero's review of the *Exposition Universelle* in 1855.

The choice of images and their relation to the text was inconsistent. The three drawings by Epstein were executed as illustrations to *Fleurs du Mal*, and the most specific, the *Gruesome Jewish Whore* (not illustrated in the catalogue), was the most telling of all the images in the exhibition, but it required its text to turn it from the merely nasty (Henry James's translation of *Mal*) into a pathetic statement of Baudelaire's impotence. The Rodin too, of arse-licking, mischievously dedicated to Will Rothenstein, is an illustration – one of several by the caprine sculptor. With willing interpretations of the text it was possible to discern some relevance in the pictures offered by Kitaj, Bacon, Greenham and Auerbach, and in those by Sandys and Watts chosen by Brighton, though the choice with these was illustrative rather than illuminating; a real Rubens to pair with a line beginning 'Pillow of flesh . . .' might have amused us, but seen at a remove in a copy by Fantin-Latour, the choice seemed wilfully enigmatic; the dapper billy-goat by Abraham Begeijn chosen to run with 'Ecstatic fleece that ripples to your nape and reeks of negligence in every curl' introduced humorous elements of which Brighton was no doubt unconscious. The quality of works contributed by such young painters as Arturo di Stefano, and chosen from the oeuvre of such older men as Wyndham Lewis, did not induce Fry's harmonious vibrations.

This exhibition told us nothing of Baudelaire, and served only to demonstrate the fatuity of Fry's notion of aesthetic osmosis. If Brighton's only alternative to white walls is a disorderly patchwork of colour, then let us retain the quiet anonymity of white. The logical extension of Brighton's idea that no text should inform the spectator, is that no text should inform the reader of his catalogue; alas, logic escaped him, and he offered us a lengthy essay on *Baudelaire the Anti-Modernist*. He is unable to distinguish not only between verbs transitive and intransitive, but between verbs and nouns, and his prose is littered with the vagaries and infelicities of jargon popular in Polytechnics – *exampled*, *specificity*, *marginalised*, *fictive*, *professionalisation*, *polyvalence*, and the much repeated *paradigm*. The essay bears no resemblance in style or argument to his review, *Anselm Kiefer*, in the fourth issue of *Modern Painters*, and appears to be the work of an altogether less educated mind, if not one quite undone by confusion. Few will grasp the muddled arguments at the first, or even the second or third, reading; those who take that trouble, and who know anything of Baudelaire, will discern only an emotional display of learning that is mere camouflage for the author's profound incomprehension.

Modern Painters 1989

Cecil Beaton

It is not surprising that Cecil Beaton responded so enthusiastically to the Bright Young Things of the Swinging Sixties, for it was the decade when class and education barriers tumbled, and any adolescent who had wit, thrust, figure or face could turn a tiny talent into a fortune. He himself, as a Bright Young Thing of the Roaring Twenties, had not had it quite so easy, for behind his schooldays, suffering the bullying Bloods at Harrow, lay the embarrassing spectre of his self-made father, a speculator in the timber trade. Cecil felt compelled to invent a tree tracing his family back to the only distinguished Beaton he could find (a Lady-in-Waiting to Mary Queen of Scots), and at 22 he confided to his diary the unwholesome ambition to dine at the Eiffel Tower restaurant because 'the people who go there are smart, arty, and the set I must get in with'.

He got in, on and up pretty quickly. Beneath the often effete exterior, the occasional transvestism and the sexual ambivalence, was a tough, tenacious, self-seeking and self-promoting climber, and the camera was the instrument of his ascent. The English seem always to have had a vain streak, prepared to sit like puddings for the face-painter, and Beaton was willing and eager to exploit it, pointing his Kodak at any candidate for the pages of *Tatler* and *Vogue*. Through his shutter the Aristocracy became the Photocracy, and as he snap-snapped away, his ambition crystallised into the need to become the successor to Van Dyck and Reynolds and Gains-borough as the master of the icon of Royalty.

And he achieved it soon enough. He posed the Queen Mum as a Venetian Baroque confection by Tiepolo, as Mistress of the Faeries, and in the classical Roman image of Charity. He put the newly-wed Wallis Simpson and her Duke in a window of the Chateau de Candé, unhappily suggesting imprisonment in a tower (and making every man's mistake of top-lighting the tip of Edward's nose). Marina of Kent he posed in the peasant costume of a Greek shepherdess – perhaps with irony, for she once asked him how on earth one got to Ascot if not in a carriage down the Royal Mile. Perhaps no man did more to consolidate the position of the Royal Family after the Abdication (with the exception of George and Elizabeth themselves), and to turn them into a rallying-point for loyalty after the outbreak of war.

His royal portraits now seem imbued with nostalgic romanticism, the work of a courtier on bended knee. In the safer purlieus of Bohemia, the upper crust, and even the lower slopes of Mount Royal, he could be mischievous and waspish. Lady Diana Cooper poses as a painted plaster saint, and Edith Sitwell plays the harp as a superannuated angel in an ancient allegory. Mrs Patrick Campbell's noble profile is thrown away in favour of her button-eyed peke in pudgy full face. The poetaster Auden, languid with cigarette, might be advertising Craven A. Rough, tough Picasso is portrayed as a burly businessman, and Rex Whistler, naked on the rocks, as fallen Icarus. He bedded Lord Mountbatten in the mirrored room of a Delhi brothel, the pair of them reflected like the Hollywood floozies of Busby Berkeley, Beaton himself far the more prominent of the pair.

This is perhaps the key to the man – Narcissus. He used mirrors to steal his sitters' thunder – there they sat, thinking themselves the object of his interest, when all the time it was on his own image that he lavished attention. His was indeed a career devoted to self-promotion (even his oldest and closest friend recognised the 'self-created genius'), treading a careful line between comment and adulation so that he would never be denied his chosen world. His photographs give no insight into their subjects, and they rarely reveal what Beaton thought of them; they demonstrate only that he was prepared to manipulate for effect whoever and whatever was at hand. He borrows brilliantly the ideas of painters, and with the change of medium the references are often unrecognised. He confuses themes and their treatment, so that wild Arab tribesmen in the real desert are tamed as Valentino's extras, and the Sahara wastes that witnessed Montgomery's war are no more sinister than pretty sets for *The Desert Song*. You will search in vain for truth; whoever said that the camera cannot lie, did not know Cecil.

Suffering the chronic infection of good taste, the stagey images are repetitive, and the clever contrivances soon bore. The only surprise is the total absence of good taste from the presentation of the show – and the old arbiter must be rolling in his grave. Never have I seen such disgusting gilt frames, such a litter of gigantic polka dots, such a plethora of plastic ivy – and whose loathsome idea was it to surround the photographs with wide mounts of flowered chintz? If the intention was to make the visitor experience the combined effect of a bit-part in *My Fair Lady* and This was his Life, then it fails, for the obelisks and knick-knacks scattered among the acres of ghastly white greens and milky terracottas are bleak, deflated camp.

Nothing could or should diminish Beaton's reputation as a stage designer, even if the frivolities of *Gigi* and *My Fair Lady* were his only real successes, rather than *Turandot* and *Traviata* – but he was no artist, and his paintings and drawings are frankly feeble. Nothing can take from him his stature as a shrewd and honest diarist. But the organisers of this exhibition have done enough to knock him off his perch as a photographer – if ever there was an example of over-exposure, this is it.

Evening Standard 1986

John Bellany

ON EASTER SUNDAY, THE DAY ON WHICH THE Christian church celebrates Christ's bodily resurrection (a pox on the Bishop of Durham), the BBC broadcast a television programme on John Bellany. The choice significance of the date can have escaped few viewers, for Bellany has just recovered from a much bruited liver transplant, urgently required, and is returned from the brink of death. No one has yet claimed his resurrection – they have stopped short with Renaissance, re-birth, with all its splendid cultural overtones.

The programme was less about Bellany as a painter (though in asides he let us know that he has a high opinion of himself as a latter-day Rembrandt and Van Gogh), than about Bellany the survivor of surgery, touching at length on painting as a therapy for a man possibly *in extremis* and certainly in extreme pain. It made valuable points about the blocking effects of intellectual concentration and the physical energy that seems to flow from it, arguing by implication that the ailing poet should not be parted from his word processor, and that the dying engineer might recover if asked to devise an outboard motor for Charon's punt-useful material for a doctoral thesis on the psychology of recovery, but not much to do with art.

Nor has Bellany's latest exhibition much to do with art – we are asked, I think, to treat it as a celebration, and to share his joy at stepping back from Styx's brink. Woe betide the carping critic.

Bellany once painted a masterpiece. He was only 22, a Scottish peasant bred on Celtic mist and Calvinist restriction, who suddenly challenged Goya and Beckmann with a vast allegory of three crucified fish, gutted, bloody and tormented. The Pascal reference to Christ and his attendant thieves is inescapable; the horde of fishermen, porters and gutters crowding below readily assumes the role of Roman soldier and reviling Jew – the fish themselves are Christian symbols old as Christ, the word for fish in Testamentary Greek an acronym for Jesus/Christ/of God/the Son/Saviour. The butchered forms are as twisted in torment as in any Gothic German altarpiece, or as the Christs of Sutherland and the sodomites of Bacon, as hollow as a Rembrandt corpse or carcase, with the sombre mood as tenebrous and brown. The painting is a host of references to established painters, but obeisant to none of them – it is a visionary recognition of the cruelty and suffering inflicted by ordinary men in the pursuits of daily life, an acknowledgement of the inevitable cycle of death and survival.

As with so many English painters (and more Scottish), Bellany burned out in no time. He had but one thing to say, and by the time he was thirty had said it too often; but he had by then also become a mythical hero, compelled to maintain that self-constructed hero's character, larger than life, carousing and rampaging, a violent saint and social commentator, the creator of a crude Renaissance. I suspect that at that stage he was still honest enough to recognise the fallacy, for the rough stuff was confused and muddied in both imagery and handling – as though Carel Weight, his sometime tutor, had been consumed by COBRA, those wild old men of Low Country capitals and Copenhagen (another acronym), and then regurgitated. All that was left of early promise was an urgent need to daub, an infantile regression.

'Drink, and too much of it', as Bellany confessed to the benign Joan Bakewell on my television screen, took over, and 'knocking back the Baccardi' primed his pump of inspiration. As the pictures became more crassly confused and incompetent, pale and greasy, slick and degraded, so the critics promoted their painter as Britain's greatest living figurative artist – what unctuous codswallop of praise for a fumbling hand, a failing eye and a fuddled brain. As his crippled liver drowned in the tide of alcohol, so painting ceased to be a profession and became a therapy. After a succession of collapses, Bellany found himself in hospital awaiting the delivery of another man's liver to save his life, and it is in truth that man's death that we now celebrate.

Bellany's case compels me to consider my ethics and beliefs. My gut reaction to all forms of transplant is of extreme distaste. I am inclined to think that if there is a God, his view of such surgical interventions must be one of disapproval, and that we, if we share the Christian hope of an after-life, should accept that when our major working parts are worn beyond repair, the time has come to leave this life for another. The situation is further complicated if we believe in the bodily resurrection (another pox on Durham's Bishop). This is an absolutist view, and I am prepared to accept, even commend, the charity of donors – it is those who accept or demand the donation whose motives I question. I have no doubt that I find the morals of a man who knowingly and indulgently drank himself to perdition's door, the damage wholly self-inflicted, and then grabbed a second liver and a second life, quite odious. Who died, I wonder, from *not* receiving this donated liver when Bellany's was judged to be the more important life, the extraordinary painter precedent over the ordinary man?

I suppose that for those who made the television programme and who have profited from telling the tale of Bellany's dramatic operation in newspapers and magazines, his repellent self-exposure of such private matters is justified by his latest batch of pictures, much praised and glorified. In truth, they are stale and repetitious rubbish. The paintings that record his weeks in hospital are on a grand tour round the world. Braw braggartry.

Evening Standard 1989

Jeffery Camp

JEFFERY CAMP, AT SIXTY-FIVE, IS A LATE STAR-
ter. That does not mean that he has not always been a painter (he has, since he was a boy of fourteen), only that fame for him was a one-winged angel slow in delivering the laurel wreath. I have been aware of him for a long time – indeed, way back in 1963 I bought one of his pictures, recognising in it the fumbling incompetence that bedevilled my own attempts to paint the Suffolk countryside, and with a measure of sympathy for a man in middle age who painted so badly but so honestly, resisting fashionable fads and treading water in the outmoded manner of the New English Art Club. I have it still.

I think that what I felt then – a response to the freshness and the obvious signs of struggle, and never mind the lack of any serious achievement – is what inspires the extraordinarily sympathetic essay in the catalogue of his latest exhibition, and I wish that I too could see the ageing Jeffery as a latter-day Blake touched by Expression-ism, but I cannot. My eye tells me that the old incompetence is still there, now touched by the ambition to be Academically grand, greatly grown in scale, but still tentative in touch and confused in composition and proportion.

Proportion matters, for his townscapes are enlivened by a giant order of young nudes, who should be lissome but are largely beanpole lank. A neat naked boy presides over a moonlit Somerset House, but the tumbling figure athwart Tower Bridge is a twelve foot length of greying sausage, the buttocks big, the perineum prominent to add a focus and a zoom to the perspective of the fall.

From a man celebrated for an instruction book on drawing (in the real old fashioned *How To* style), the forms are schematic, hacked from a confusion of brush dabs with long sweeping strokes that in some uncomfortable way recall the caricatures of nubile nudes that once inhabited the pages of *Esquire*. At best they are as bad as old Duncan Grant in his dotage, with something of the same mechanical quality and the hint of obsession with lost youth. At worst they are absurd, and no argument in favour of curvaceous line can excuse the tapering grotesquerie: Doris Zinkeisen superimposed upon some lurid Albert Goodwin, as though Camp were designing covers for Barbara Cartland, all ecstatic wind and water.

It is, of course, a pretty idea to combine the nude with an evocation of some London landmark or a view of Venice, two pictures for the price of one. It works well with bridges, where suspension curves and arches take up the lines and tensions of the human body, though I am not sure that much attention can be paid to Tower Bridge when the foreground is largely occupied by the swelling thighs of a young negro whose languorous penis lies dead centre, deftly outlined with a glisten of white to make it an inescapable, unavoidable presence. In a view of Westminster the young negro is turned buttock-up to share the foreground with a hyacinth; beyond them lies a tumbled heap of dismantled female parts of which only nipple and mouth are readily identifiable, and among these is a huge red shape that can only be interpreted as the phallus and scrotum of a Hercules in recumbent contrast to the distant erection of Big Ben; Westminster and all its works appear to be engulfed in fire – and well they might be, seeming here a modern Sodom and Gomorrah.

It is, I suppose, possible to see something of Bonnard in the colour, the touch, and perhaps even in the idea – if the Frenchman could use a whole room as the setting for a nude, why should Camp not expand the notion and use a whole city? There is indeed something seductive in the fancy that the mud banks of the Thames are littered with young lovers locked in the rapture of a Mills and Boon romance, or that the parapets of County Hall are lined with lithe boys about to leap into the running tides. In Camp's hands the results are romantic, not with the full-blown drama of Turner and John Martin, nor with the ludicrous visionary quality of Blake, but with the reticence of the second wave of Romanticism that washed ashore at Beachy Head in 1945 or thenabouts – the mystery residing in the understatement.

When his palette is cool and dry, Camp hints at Ravilious and Paul Nash; occasionally Minton, Tunnard and Glyn Philpot lurk behind his eye, and the later lot of painters at St Ives, particularly Peter Lanyon's gliding pictures, may have released his brush a little from the hesitation of its stroke. It is all terribly old-fashioned, but it would be none the worse for that were it better drawn and less ragged in the painting. When he attempted high fashion, as in canvases of irregular shape or squares hung on the diagonal, he merely imitated his friend Anthony Green without understanding that Green's purpose, the isometric illusion of reality, was entirely different from his own – whatever their shape Camp's images remained fixed in the mould of the English seaside painter, a latter-day Dorothea Sharp or Campbell Mellon.

Jeffery Camp is a Royal Academician, but the ancient worthies there were tardy in inviting him to join their number. They now compensate for the delay by giving him a retrospective exhibition that entirely justifies it.

Evening Standard 1988

Sir Anthony Caro

The Tate Gallery

SIR ANTHONY CARO, WIDELY PROMOTED AS Britain's greatest living sculptor (hardly a matter for much boasting, if we think about it), is not only a Knight (1987) but a CBE (1969), an Honorary Doctor of the Universities of East Anglia, Toronto and Cambridge, the recipient of Honorary Degrees from the Universities of Sussex and Yale, an Honorary Fellow of the Royal College of Art and Christ's College, Cambridge, and an Honorary Member of the American Academy and Institute of Arts and Letters. A year ago he surprised us all by refusing to be elected a Royal Academician.

He was a Trustee of the Tate Gallery from 1982 to 1989, and it is in the great axial hall of that building that the current exhibition of his recent large-scale work is displayed. I observe in passing that we are now required to call the domed area that interrupts this axis 'The Sackler Octagon' – it seems that yet more Americans called Sackler have bought renown in London by dipping into their pockets for the refurbishment of this public building, the quo for their quid residing in eponymy; such immortality for tuppence is a shameful vanity to be eschewed.

Vanity, however, is the order of the day in the Tate Gallery. Were Caro a man of any modesty he would (and should) have refused the opportunity to occupy for three full months the great space that in the past has housed the sculptures of Moore, Rodin, Matisse and others, and was until recently an essential part of the Gallery's permanent display; perhaps now that this institution is in a never-ending state of flux, we should forgive him for following in the footsteps of Richard Long (who occupied the same space a few months ago), but as a past Trustee he should surely have been better aware of the Tate's true purpose as a national gallery rather than as a place for temporary displays – to have refused the exhibition would not only have been a noble gesture in itself, but one that might have brought the Tate's Director to his senses. The proper place for Caro's sculpture is the Hayward Gallery.

This much honoured man was born in 1924 and by the age of twenty had a Cambridge MA in engineering, of which there is little evidence in his early sculptures – lumpy, dumpy things that resemble the distorted forms occasionally adopted by the potato. It was not until 1959, when he came under the influences of Clement Greenberg (an American critic preaching the gospel of irreducible purity and the renunciation of all that is explicit in visual references) and David Smith (an American sculptor of visual puns in rusting and painted iron) that he developed what he proudly called 'a new vocabulary for sculpture' and emerged from the slough of unnoticed mediocrity, or worse.

His new vocabulary was largely Smith's – the iron girder, the rough off-cut of steel plate, the mesh, the rod, the boiler, the bollard, the pipe, the tube – in fact, metal in any form that could be got from steelyard, factory or dump of industrial detritus and assembled in an entirely whimsical way until it suggested to Caro that he had created an abstract work of art and had better stop before he spoiled it. For the past thirty years this Master of the Arts of Engineering has been churning out assemblages of metal, sometimes so gaily painted that they might well be mistaken for agricultural machinery designed to mow down critics, and sometimes so rusty that they could have been fragments torn from the hull of the *Titanic*. In composition they vary from wild three-dimensional scribbles and things that resemble the noisy working contraptions of Tinguely (a Swiss clock-maker influenced by Heath Robinson and quite cuckoo), to collapsing office furniture and weighty and less penetrable confections that could have been pupped through some unseemly conjugation between an old railway engine and a tramp steamer with an over-heated prop-shaft. They invade the floor and bark the shins. Caro's last London exhibition, two years ago, was of three-dimensional composition studies based on paintings by Rembrandt and Manet, whose *Deposition from the Cross* and *Déjeuner sur l'Herbe* he strove to turn into abstract things of nuts and bolts, cubes and tubes, and bent metal that utterly failed to repeat the flowing forms of flesh and fall of drapery – student exercises of a kind that he must have been required to perform in his youth when the common notion was that within every Renaissance masterpiece could be found a wholly abstract structure.

This reversion to adolescence lies behind the largest work that Caro has ever executed – the *After Olympia* now lying in the Tate. It seems that Caro visited Greece for the first time in 1985 – a rum admission from one who claims to be a leading sculptor, but perhaps his 'continuing investigation of the boundaries of sculpture' had been so absorbing that he had had no time to investigate its root and heart; at the age of sixty-one he was surprised to find the experience of Greek art in Greece an inspiring revelation – the revelation merely confirmed his belief that he had been right to borrow other men's compositions, and the inspiration compelled him to make a sculpture of enormous size. The exhibition catalogue reproduces the sculpture from the long low pediment of the Temple of Zeus at Olympia, and it is this that informs the composition of Caro's twenty-six yards of bent and crumpled metal – though I did not know this when I first set eyes on it and took it to be some kind of naval war memorial, the superstructure of a battle cruiser after a rough night with the *Bismarck*. It was not my only error – the four objects that comprise *Night Movements* I took to be abstractions based on elephants, *Tower of Discovery* (the structure in the octagon) I interpreted as a variation on a baroque organ loft, and *Xanadu* utterly defeated me, though I thought it might not be out of place among the prehistoric monsters of the Natural History Museum (the catalogue informs me that it is some kind of homage to Matisse, and that the elephants express Caro's admiration for the paintings of Courbet).

I can think of no reason to commend these sculptures, repetitive and flabby as they are, undone by their very scale, absurdity made manifest. Only for *Tower of Discovery*, for which Caro coins the horrid hybrid 'sculpitecture' and in which we are supposed to clamber with childish delight, is there any slight intellectual justification, but even this offers nothing that is not already within the experience of those who have climbed cathedral towers, stood within Schwitters's *Merzbau*, descended a great curving baroque staircase, or played house under the kitchen table – it is, if anything, an unintentional monument to what John Summerson dubbed 'the craving for the aedicula', and ought to be in the children's playground in Kensington Gardens, next to the Elfin Oak, or playing the part of folly or gazebo in the garden of some British embassy in an Islamic state where figure sculpture might be deemed objectionable. The idea already mooted that it should take permanent root in the Sackler Octagon, for which it was specifically designed, must be rejected.

I am astonished that the maker of such monstrous trivialities should have been so loaded with honours, and I am appalled that as a teacher and exemplar he should have done so much damage to the art that he claims to practise. If sculpture is dead in this country (and there is good reason to think that it is), blame is largely the responsibility of Caro, with his expanded vocabulary and extended boundaries − expanded and extended like a burst balloon.

Evening Standard 1991

The Effluvia of Helen Chadwick

As the Colonel Blimp of art critics (dubbed so by Michael Sandle, a sculptor, many of whose works I admire), I am acutely disappointed by Helen Chadwick's exhibition, *Effluvia*, at the Serpentine Gallery. From what has seemed in previous exhibitions to be the loud-mouthed self-exposure of an arrant feminist driven by a childish determination to shock with visceral and sexual references, with raw meat and the mess of parturition, a silly woman in thrall to the obsessions of her American counterparts with menstrual blood, vomit, urine, excrement, pus and all other fluids, flows and fluxes from their bodies, I had expected provocation to a Ruskinade, to a rallying cry to the troops of Tunbridge Wells, but in visual terms the provocation simply isn't there. Alas, the wide-eyed wanderer in Kensington Gardens is confronted by nothing more threatening than a bubbling pool of molten chocolate that is more the artifice of a Jeremy Beadle joke than art, and is undone by the seeming innocence of a multitude of flowers.

Miss Chadwick, short-listed for the Turner Prize in 1987, has regressed since then − unless, of course, the rest of us have become inured to the deliberate scatology of artists for social and political purposes, bruising and battering our sensibilities with constant exposure to the body wastes of urine and faeces and the organs through which they are evacuated. Many a Dutch old master of the church interior amuses us with the defecating dog below the pulpit, and the doctor with the lovesick maiden's urine held against the light; Picasso painted his mistress emptying her bladder, and Eric Gill was fascinated by male organs of drainage in all their functions, but these were small beer and occasional. In more recent years the pace and quantity have increased, with awe and outrage in equal measure the responses to Andres Serrano's crucifix drowning in a stream of urine (*Piss Christ*), and to Mapplethorpe's photographs of intrusions into the male anus of bullwhip handle and human hand; but in America a legion of women unknown here has established the human body as the intellectual territory, material and boundary of the visual artist, breaking down taboos and rejecting hierarchical arrangements that are still the conventions of sex and gender.

Compared with these abrasive Americans, who as long as thirty years ago were writhing naked in a mass with raw fish, chicken carcases and phallic vegetables in every aperture and orifice, Miss Chadwick's explorations of the body are restrained and muted, circumspect and genteel. That her chocolate pool is intended to encourage recollection of the loose bowel is made clear by her title for it, *Cacao*, punning on cocoa and the *cack* and *caca* derivations from the Latin *cacare* (to void a stool, as my school dictionary delicately put it) that are ubiquitous from Poland to Portugal, but she uses milk chocolate, palely lacking in conviction, and the point is lost. The catalogue, written by a female worthy of the Arts Council, refers to a 'phallus girded by the obscene venting of glutinous bubbles', but the contraption (and contraption it is, with all the heaving and groaning of Heath Robinson machinery) more resembles a swizzle stick standing in a cup of cocoa, or a flagpole part submerged in a pool of volcanic mud – no man would recognise this meagre thing as even remotely phallic (is everything upstanding, phallic to a woman?). At a stretch, *Cacao* can be seen as a plastic potty full of diarrhoea, but the

Arts Council exegesis evokes loftier images of 'a sexual high . . . the solitary hermaphroditic earthworm ..,' and interprets the pool as 'the gynandrous fecundity of waste'. Gynandrous is a botanical term used when stamens and pistils are combined in a single column, and contradicts the idea of the phallus – but much of this woman's scribbling is contradictory and obscure, larded with the jargon of computer and cod philosophy.

And there's the rub: Miss Chadwick is less an artist (perhaps not at all) than an illustrator of the ill-digested contemporary philosophies and alchemies that can be distorted into a justification for her work – chicken and egg, egg and chicken, I know, but . . . Fascinated by things soft, red and glistening (the odd liver, or one's internal linings glossed with mucous), she treats them as a photographic subject in much the way of a specialist food photographer, adding an unearthly glow, and then argues a pseudo-philosophical point – 'I am my mass or meat times the power of my light', describing her treatment of flesh as 'a transfiguration of its determined tendency to decay'.

Brains, intestines, tongues, liver and chunks of raw flesh and belly-buttons all glisten in the pages of the catalogue, but are reserved for the next staging-post of this exhibition in Essen (there's a bi-lingual pun). Are we too squeamish for them here? Are they perhaps omitted to save the blushes and the stomach of Princess Diana, lately become Patron of the Serpentine? Richard Cork (my predecessor on this paper) observed of this event that 'Nobody would become Patron of the Serpentine without an appetite for adventurous work', but I doubt if the oddments of the abattoir can have much appeal to the Princess, whose lack of appetite is now notorious. If we, the general populace, are supposed to be repelled by such exhibits, indeed filled with disgust – and there is some point in political scatology if it increases our dismay at pollution and the poisonous sludge of chemical waste and oestrogens that has denatured rivers, lakes and seas – then it is more important that the Princess too is repelled than that she use the Serpentine as her Petit Trianon, art lover instead of dairy maid.

Miss Chadwick's serious text is swamped by deceitful prettiness, and her exhibition is too playful. Were the Princess to amuse the young Princes with a visit, the chocolate pool will please them as of the ilk of Peter Pan and Elfin Oak, its hurdy-gurdy bubbling an engaging asset, and none need make reference to shit and phallus; the carbuncled dildos and fur rings of *I Thee Wed* can be passed off as muffs for curious cucumbers, and the *Piss Flowers*, produced by peeing in the snow (Miss Chadwick squatting still, her young assistant waving his willy in an uncertain circle, both bladders very full), may be mistaken for designer meringues by the dc :n; the landscape photographs, smirched by the computer-generated prettiness of cells culled from Miss Chadwick's body, may be interpreted as homages to Victor Pasmore, and the circular photographs of herbaceous border blooms, even though laden with light-hearted references to human sexual organs and emissions, can be dismissed as decorative trifles fit only for the housemaids' bedrooms in the Palace attics. But if the Princess buys the exhibition catalogue and dips into it for the Princes' bed-time reading instead of Beatrix Potter, she will wish that she'd stayed with Sally Henny-Penny, for with Helen Chadwick and her pell-mell effluvia of urine as a creative force, she will be compelled to explain to the innocents the weighty artistic significance of the vaginal tower, the foreshortened penis, and other inversions of our genitals, of sexual circumnavigation, shit and virtuous liquidity, and prep school precocity will be the dangerous consequence.

Evening Standard 1994

Eduardo Chillida

Eduardo Chillida is a Spanish sculptor of international renown not much known in England. The Tate Gallery owns only one small work, and no other is to be found in any public collection in these islands, yet this is a man who has won prizes for his work at the Venice Biennale and Pittsburgh International Exhibitions, as well as the Rembrandt, Kandinsky and Mellon Prizes. He has had major exhibitions all over Europe and the United States, and the worthies of the Hayward Gallery proclaim him to be 'one of the greatest of contemporary sculptors' (the cynic may murmur that there is little competition). To convince us that we should share that opinion, they have imported lock, stock and barrel the exhibition that Chillida mounted in Venice earlier this year, proud that the works are among the heaviest ever installed in the building – and that must be the oddest claim to aesthetic attention ever made.

Most of the work is in welded iron and steel, and the forms adopted are to some considerable extent controlled by these materials and the methods with which they are handled. Chillida has, if nothing else, a feeling for these metals and exploits their texture and colour, giving them patinas more truthful and more subtle than the gaudy greens and bright browns beloved of present-day bronze casters – he is the only sculptor who gives steel the rich red warmth of unpolished granite. He is good with granite too – and with alabaster, seeing in its depths the same translucency that appealed to medieval craftsmen who magicked from it gentle Madonnas that seemed themselves the source of gentle light.

There is, however, nothing gentle about Chillida's work – only ingenuity and the megalomania of so many modern sculptors. The small pieces are neat enough, like the interlocking sections of a jig-saw puzzle or a Rubic Cube – the sort of thing that on a smaller scale might play the rich man's toy on the polished desk of a television executive or lesser banker. Some rather bigger pieces cut, as it were, from large section guttering or open drains, might serve their purpose to confuse the putters on the mini-golf courses to be found in most Spanish holiday resorts, art in the service of sport, subliminally educating players. The next step in size is to that of the large chimney-pot – indeed the gallery that is reached by the Hayward's ramp resembles nothing so much as a New York rooftop, with a variety of cowls to control the downdraughts and add whimsy and amusement to the silhouettes and forms. The heaviest object (and thus, perhaps, in the Hayward's eyes the most estimable) is a roughly rectangular block of granite more than six feet high that at first I took to be some kind of impregnable telephone box; it is called *What is Deep is Air* – a statement of which I can make no sense either in the context of the block or in isolation, but then I dare say it is poetic and intended to confuse the poorer spirit.

The Tate Gallery's Chillida is called *Modulation of Space I*; I am not sure that I understand even that comparatively straightforward title, though I recognise that the swirling coil of iron tubes, rectangular in section yet forced to arc and curve, seems to embody conflicting forces and to describe movement in space in much the same way as do rapid gestures with a torch in a dark room. Chillida told the Tate that he had 'collaborated with the reaction of the material at determined external forces' – whatever that may mean.

In the film that is now mandatory at exhibitions, Chillida tells us that he has 'a very particular connection with the sea'. Indulgent Basque authorities have encouraged him to mount on wave-swept rocky outcrops gigantic variations of the Tate's small *Modulation*, coiling and grasping like an iron octopus; projecting like some medieval instrument of surgery or torture to pluck the tongue or draw out the bowels of monsters of the sea, they speak only of primitive hostility and aggression. On the cliffs above Gijon he has erected a modern ruin; it is called *In Praise of the Horizon*, but from the sea appears to be an ugly tempietto cut from the carcase of a huge boiler, spoiling the natural line of the cliff and its slow fall. Indeed the larger Chillida's pieces grow, the sillier they seem, arrogant, contrived and arbitrary.

I am weary of the modern abstract sculptor's argument that he explores space by hollowing a block, and defines it by describing an arc or placing planes at right angles, and Chillida's statement that 'the dialectic between the full and the empty is essential' is merely a variation on this limited theme. I see a certain playful elegance in

Omar Khayyam's Tables, even if they remind me of the Morrison shelters that appeared late in the last war, and they must look well enough furnishing a garden – but are they sculpture and not the sort of things to be expected in Harrods' garden furniture department? As an intellectual conceit I enjoy chunks of alabaster rough-rounded to resemble enormous geodes so that one expects the interiors to be hollow and crystalline, as indeed they are, but in a regular and formal sense, like a Cappadocian rock church or an Egyptian tomb – but why call them *Homage to Goethe* and not Schiller, Winckelmann or Mengs? Why not to Roger Fry or Bernard Berenson? Why not call them *Homage to Saint Basil*, who knew a thing or two about hollowing rock?

I cannot see that Chillida is in any way 'one of the greatest of contemporary sculptors' if greatness is a concept that is to retain any meaning or value. His work, though major in scale, is minor in achievement, a mere variation of the sculpture that has no subject and is not an object that has been produced for at least three decades throughout the western world, by David Smith and Anthony Caro and all their feeble mimics, their arrogant placement of materials, devoid of all symbolism, a cultural vandalism sanctified by critics.

Evening Standard 1990

Cecil Collins

'N   Anthony d'Offay Gallery
  OT IN RIOTING AND DRUNKENNESS, NOT IN
chambering and wantonness, not in strife and envying: but put ye on the Lord Jesus Christ and make no provision for the flesh to fulfil the lusts thereof.' I had thought the Desert Fathers, those early minor saints of the Christian Church for whom a rush mat was a luxury and a freshly crunched cockroach a feast, to be long dead. Not so. There is a survivor still. And preaching still – in that desert of the arts, the Tate Gallery. His name is Cecil Collins.

The Desert Fathers, of whom Simon Stylites was one, either lived solitary lives or banded into small monasteries; all wished to be inspired with innocence and live in charity, but now and then one fell from grace – one shed all his clothes and proclaimed himself an angel so that others would kowtow, one was a kleptomaniac, many quarrelled, and more were troubled by outbreaks of unwashed sodomy – but prayer, homilies and visions soon reinstated them on the road to sunlit virtue that is so much the concern of Collins, himself a visionary obsessed with angels, a natural solitary, remote, abstinent and Pauline.

Like Prophets, Sybils and the Fathers of the Church, Collins is given to pronouncements that brook no argument. 'The reality of life is incomprehensible, and the Artist creates an incomprehensible image of it' – I cannot argue with a statement that I do not understand. 'All art is an attempt to manifest the Face of the God of Life' – well, that effectively eliminates all pagan art, all political art, all pre-Christian and post-Christian art, all portraiture and a great deal more, leaving us only with the simpering angels of the irksome Fra Angelico. 'The function of art is to find harmony in the world and not reflect the conflict . . . if you contemplate violence and evil, you are propagating it' – but that is the Gospel according to St Mary Whitehouse, and reduces all art to the level of *The Sound of Music*.

I am moved by sanctity, and I see it in the things that Collins says; I do not and cannot share it, but it demands respect. I believe him when he claims that his angels and his visions are a force that paint themselves, painted in spite of him and not because of him, that he is merely the unwitting servant of an irresistible flow of power, but I am surprised and disappointed that God should choose so feeble a painter as his instrument to reassert the spiritual dimension of the visual arts, for Collins is about as inadequate with paint and canvas as is that dear old dame in Battersea with the piano, and she only claims Beethoven, not God and all his Cherubim, to be jogging her elbow.

Collins was born in 1908, and is England's mystical answer to Chagall. Both reflect the idioms and influences of their day, and are quite clearly creatures of this century though nostalgic for their cultural past; both develop a style that is intensely personal, but which runs dry and has to be cannibalised; both devote themselves to subject matter and that is *ad nauseam* repeated; both experience their inspiration (and that's the rub, for experience adds uncomfortable intensity), and the roots of their mysticism, one Jew, one Christian, are not far apart.

In spite of the unwitting allegiances to Thirties Surrealism and Forties Romanticism, hints of Mervyn Peake, David Jones and Georges Rouault, and the dominant ghost of Samuel Palmer, Collnis's spiritual ancestors are to be found in the remote churches of Byzantium, on the hilltops of Cyprus, in the mountains of northern Macedonia, and cut in the cliffs of Cappadocia. A thousand years too late, with provincial incompetence he paints the Bible of the illiterate poor, adding his own Apocrypha; the world has moved on, too far, too fast, and Collins in his private wilderness cries the virtue of the Saint, the artist, the poet and the Perfect Fool. No one who drives a BMW, excludes the world with a personal hi-fi, reads the collected works of Jeffrey Archer or watches Cilla Black on television could possibly comprehend his saintly simplicity: I wish only that he were, like Titian and Michelangelo, those men of earthly appetites, capable of honouring his divine inspiration.

Evening Standard 1989

Le Corbusier

It would be unfair to blame Le Corbusier for all the ills of urban architecture that now afflict us, for he was but one of a generation of now venerated twentieth-century architects to discard tradition and invent new attitudes and the methods to support them. Nevertheless, the tower blocks that have destroyed the skylines of our major cities, none more hideously than London, and the chicken coops that lie between them, are all to some extent the children of his ideas, and the time has come to reconsider the status of this architect of the future who has so rapidly become yesterday's man.

In defence of this Swiss idealist it must be said that he and his peers were confronted with the aftermath of the Industrial Revolution – that the Europe of their youth was blotted with cities that still preserved their dense, cramped and inefficient cores, but had close-ringed them with heavy industry and the tenements to house its slaves, initiating an urban sprawl that was already obsolete on the drawing-board, and that merely accommodated and perpetuated conditions that were (with the addition of industrial pollution) rather worse than the slums of ancient Rome or the Byzantine stews of Istanbul. But in rejecting the organic growth of cities, Le Corbusier chucked out not only the baby with the bath-water, but the bath-tub too, for he rejected the forms and structures of architecture that had been the European pattern ever since man first prettified the Stonehenge formula of two uprights supporting a cross-piece. There are, of course, physical limits to the column, pediment and architrave – too great enlargement not only takes them beyond grandeur and into Metro-Goldwyn-Mayer absurdity, but deprives them of function, and reduces them to mere gross embellishment. A Giant Order could be applied by a late Renaissance architect to the façade of a lofty *palazzo*, effectively uniting a number of floors of different heights, but the same device used on a Manhattan skyscraper gets us promptly into the world of *Alice in Wonderland* after the silly girl had been mushroom munching, and from the immense length of her neck had lost sight of her shoulders in the mists below. Retention of the more-or-less human scale in the column when dealing with overall proportions that far exceed it, results in other absurdities – Wren managed the front of St Paul's neatly enough with one row of columns perched atop another, and Perrault's façade of the Louvre employs the same device, but go beyond two stages and the architect finds himself scaling the giddy heights of Osbert Lancaster's *Late Wedding Cake* and plummetting into his *Early Water Closet*. Le Corbusier would have none of this, and with clean slate, uncluttered mind, and touching faith in the manipulability of mankind, set off on the road *Vers une Architecture* that was entirely *nouveau*.

He sings the praises of pre-fabrication and man-made materials – good old wood and stone are treacherous with hidden knot and fissure, whereas steel girder and reinforced concrete 'are pure manifestations of calculation' (as though hidden mathematics ever made anything beautiful). He prefers piles (*pilotis* – which is presumably where *Private Eye's* architecture correspondent got his nom-de-plume) to the firm foundation of solid basement and the thick rusticated walls of the grounding floor. And in everything he presumes the grace of proportion, which is just about the only aspect of his thinking that is beyond controversy – "our capacity to perceive proportions, and this alone, determines our spiritual values [Be off with you, Holy Ghost!] . . . the mechanism of proportions cannot operate effectively unless the quantities it regulates are comprehensible, *legible* [my italics]. This is where geometry intervenes, geometry's wonderful symbols of clarity, meaning and spiritual structure in the midst of our muddled vision of nature.'

Apart from some misgiving about the spiritual nature of geometry, never remotely apparent to me in the miserable years before matriculation, I have no dispute with the notion that we are all capable, deep down, of recognising proportional harmony. Le Corbusier sees it as a resonance beyond the range of our senses, the sign of some indefinable absolute operating in the depths of our being. The trouble is that perhaps only architects and architectural historians are capable of thus resonating – there is little to suggest that the average Englishman, cooped up in his pre-fabricated reinforced concrete tower block feels the slightest spiritual elevation in the supposed perfection of its proportions, and his resonating is expressed in his using the lifts as lavatories and the walls for wails of scribbled protest. Le Corbusier thought it possible to devise the proportions for a unit that might then be infectious multiplied *ad infinitum* up or along, and such is the madness of pseudo-philosophical mathematics that architects from India to Brazil fell about in fervent admiration of *Le Modulor* – one even experienced a road to Damascus when in the middle of the night a book on the Bayeux Tapestry fell on his head and he awoke to the revelation that this absurd work of historical adjustment had been conceived in accordance with Le Corbusier's 'admirable harmonies'. *Le Modulor* itself is a system of architectural proportion based on the human figure that in some senses follows the work of such Classical and Renaissance theorists as Vitruvius and Palladio, and even Leonardo; the Classical canons of proportion were obscurely related to the canons of ideal beauty perceived in Greek sculpture – were Le Corbusier's based on Moore and Maillol they would have been ludicrous instead of merely dull and illegible.

Le Corbusier invented 'the machine for living in' as his answer to the post-war need to accommodate large numbers of people in a small space at low cost. In Marseilles in the late forties he erected one vast rectangular block that contains 350 flats in eight storeys; its bleakly repetitive fussy monotony chills the spectator with its recall of Huxley's *Brave New World* – God knows what it does to the people who have to live in it. It was lauded with extravagant praise, duplicated ten years later in West Berlin, and has been popping up hither and yon in ever more degraded form ever since. Given his head, Le Corbusier would have taken greenfield sites, drawn grid plans, and slotted great numbers of such identical blocks into them, leading the eye to a central crescendo of identical towers, every vista regulated by identical features, every road an identical chasm through the concrete. He longed for standardisation – Phidias, he claimed, would have loved to live in a standardised age, and would not have hesitated to repeat the Parthenon (that would at least have put a stop to Melina Mercouri's moaning for the Elgin Marbles). He foresaw the standardisation of the motor car and the difficulties that would accompany it, decoration as the excess of the peasant, and proportion as the quantum of the cultivated man.

He was not a man for gnomes in the front garden – indeed he was not a man for front gardens, or even window boxes; shutters and shingles, gables and gargoyles appalled him, and his English disciples did their damnedest to destroy the homely vernacular of the roadside sprawls from Ealing to Romford and Barnet to Croydon. He failed to recognise the Betjeman in us all – that deep down in the cultivated man there lurks not only the instinctive demand for perfect logic, harmony and proportion, but the monster Sentiment, and that it takes more than the perfect chicken coop to eradicate the heart-felt nostalgia for fire-place, door-chimes, oak beams, leaded lights and the Georgian porch. He was too much the arid theorist, and could never come to terms with the craving for the aedicula – that need for the twee that first emerges in children when they set up house under the kitchen table, and inexorably develops into the ideal home of Mrs Thatcher's Dulwich.

Tatler 1987

Tony Cragg

TONY CRAGG WAS THE WINNER OF THE £10,000 Turner Prize in 1988, and must thus be a man of fame and promise. In the arts, alas, fame is too often thrust upon a willing but unworthy recipient, and the promise that only the artist can fulfil flares and burns out in a blaze of publicity.

Cragg had a major exhibition at the Hayward Gallery in 1987 which led me to think that he was at a crucial point in his career as a sculptor, changing from middle-aged and mischievous *enfant terrible* into a serious artist capable of work imbued with mysterious beauty. There was not a great deal of work to support this idea – only a very few pieces from 1986 and the first months of 1987 – but enough, I thought, to suggest that he had purged himself of adolescent frivolities. He, of course, could never see his work as frivolous mischief, nor even as witty comment on our wasteful society – he is, instead, given to such oracular statements of high seriousness as,

'To be defeated by banality is to be confounded by ignorance' (which puts me in my place), and, 'The nomination of banal objects as carriers of important information has been of great significance. Without this a soup can remains a soup can.' I see what he means when I recall that the Arts Council possesses on our behalf a large and highly coloured photograph of what used to be called 'Ladies' Comforters', arranged in all their lurid pinks to resemble the skyline of New York by night.

I have to confess that I am frequently defeated by banality and have great difficulty in accepting Cragg's proposal that smashing the furniture in the spare bedroom provides the perfect ideas and materials for sculpture. He lays broken chairs and drawers, shelves, boxes, baskets, coat hangers and catapults at the foot of a timber packing case, just as floral tributes may be laid at a cenotaph. I cannot see that it is sculpture. I cannot see that it is art. It may just be acceptable as a gigantic *objet trouvé*, but even for that I think it too contrived, too self-conscious; by chance, the same sort of junk is lying about in the courtyard of the Barbican, where a wine bar is being demolished, and this looks so much more interesting, so serendipitously well composed, that when Cragg talks of making sculptures as 'a self-defining situation', it seems to me that the boys wrecking the bar are sculptors as genuine as he, their work as much worth preserving.

Cragg has made so much use of bits of broken plastic that people now tell him, 'We can never walk down the beach and see the tide-lines of plastic and think of it in the same way.' This is flattering to Cragg, but if it means that the filthy detritus on our beaches is now a blessed art form inducing states of ecstasy in cooing aesthetes, perhaps Mrs Thatcher should be set to work on them like Christ among the traders in the Temple. Cragg's problem is that he has not yet resolved the difficulty of forming a coherent visual language from the images, objects and materials that interest him, and these tend to retain their identities so strongly that they confuse and obscure his ideas and propaganda; plastic, for example, remains resolutely plastic, and all imagery is secondary to its garish colour and greasy texture.

Cragg's other trick is to take some simple everyday thing and reproduce it in the wrong material and the wrong size, often distorting a familiar shape; a bottle eight feet tall cast in rusty iron is only momentarily disconcerting and once that effect has worn off (and the shock can never be repeated) is no more interesting than a glass bottle eight inches high.

In the sad little exhibition that celebrates Cragg's Turner Prize, the Tate Gallery includes a vast rambling intestine of pink drainpipe junctions coiled about a laundry basket, a milk churn and a kitchen table – he calls it, without humour, *George and the Dragon*, but it better resembles a pantomime prop for the Widow Twanky. The most disturbing work appears to have been deposited in haste by a passing brontosaurus, loose bowelled after eating an orchestra. Neither Cragg nor the insecure reputation of the Turner Prize is properly served by this misleading exhibition, pretentious, and absurdly restricted to seven works when the sculptor is still at the stage when his ideas are so meagre that only a large number and a wide range of his so-called sculptures can, with their cumulative effects, engage sympathy and interest.

Evening Standard 1989

Michael Craig-Martin

IN 1991 THE SOUTH BANK CENTRE ORGANISED A touring exhibition called *The Primacy of Drawing*, and sent it to Bristol, Stoke-on-Trent and Sheffield; it was not shown in London, far the largest source of visitors. The eye, experience and sensibility employed by the Centre to choose the drawings and illuminate their purpose, were those of Deanna Petherbridge, a working artist. She, though perhaps little known even among those most enthusiastic in the field of contemporary art, is respected with considerable gravity as an accomplished (even unrivalled) draughtswoman by those who care for the arts and skills of drawing, both modern and old masterly, and rightly so, for she wrote an admirable introduction to the arts of drawing (of which there are many), using her passion as well as her knowledge and practice to open the eyes of those who saw her exhibition and read her catalogue. None who let her be their *vade mecum* could remain in ignorance of the vital part that drawing plays in the development of works of art, in observation, fluency and definition, in form and volume, narrative and expression, as mere necessary exercise in skill akin to daily practice on the violin and, above all, in the multiplicity of processes both thoughtful and instinctive that play their essential part in giving pictorial, sculptural and architectural substance to the idea in the mind's eye.

Henry Meyrick Hughes, Director of Exhibitions at the South Bank Centre, has now invited Michael Craig-Martin to mount a sequel to the Petherbridge exhibition of 1991. Craig-Martin is, of course, as a 'Professor' at Goldsmiths College, a long-term Trustee of the Tate Gallery, the darling of Cork Street dealers and a contributor to innumerable conceptual exhibitions, far more important than Petherbridge, and while her exhibition was re-stricted to the provincial wilderness, his is shown at the White-chapel Gallery – moreover, the Directrice there, Catherine Lampert, 'kindly altered her exhibition programme to make [this] possible . . .' So there we have it: the power and influence for his own benefit of this panjandrum, this Serota side-kick, is so great that one of the capital's most important exhibition spaces, with a programme that we are so often told takes years to plan and fulfill and is immutable when set in train, can at a moment's notice be cleared for him.

Catherine Lampert implied in the catalogue of her retrospective exhibition for Craig-Martin in 1989, that he is an artist of immediate and lasting significance who, though outside the orthodox definition of sculptor, has great influence as a teacher and a 'pioneer of new thinking'. There is, alas, little evidence of new thinking, or any thought at all, in his choice of drawings and his self-indulgent essay on them, other than in his adolescent cleverness (in its pejorative sense) in noticing unlikely kinships – indeed, the whole basis of the exhibition, apart from the self-imposed limitation only to line drawings, is restricted to the naive and shallow perception of these meaningless kinships across centuries and cultures. Though it contains masterpieces by Mantegna, Bernini, Raphael, Ingres and Leonardo, none of these, nor any other, is in any way illuminated by Craig-Martin, for this foolish exhibition is devoted only to coincidence and superficial parallel.

Craig-Martin, whose own drawings are dry commercial things, as unsubtle and deadly accurate as those of engineers, utterly unvarying in weight and width of line, as though transferred from a sheet of Letraset, admits that before he began work on the exhibition his knowledge of the history of drawing 'was quixotic and haphazardly focused'; this exhibition, he tells us, thus did not exploit his accumulated wisdom, connoisseurship and experience, for he had none of these, but gave him his first impulse to explore the great museum collections of which he was in ignorance. How dare Meyrick Hughes be so irresponsible as to offer such an exhibition to an ignoramus of such inexcusable vanity that he, in his own words, 'jumped at it'. As a consequence we are told that the drawings of Rembrandt manifest most strongly the values of today – but what does this mean? We have the oracular statement 'The present influences the past more than the past influences the present', and are then left to ponder the enigma. Craig-Martin accuses historians, critics, collectors, curators and dealers who have looked at drawings of being secondary interpreters, governed by prejudice and unacknowledged agendas, while artists like himself are the only honest and enlightened primary interpreters – but then he launches into the familiar polemic of the art school, in favour only of innovation and individuality, damning those whom he sees as art's conservatives, happy to sacrifice cultural coherence for unprecedented expansion in the means and methods of self-expression.

The visitor is left to make what he can of this inadequate exhibition, for neither catalogue nor labels offer information or explanation, and all is in the hanging – the curvaceous abstract and calligraphic scribbles of Cy Twombly, for example, white on grey, hang next to a finely finished drawing in white on brown by Aldorfer, in which the swirling lines of windblown drapery and river waves are also repeated and curvaceous, and in this superficial similarity of things separated not only by the best part of five centuries, but by perception, ability and purpose, we are expected to recognise Craig-Martin's wisdom and, astonished, genuflect. The triviality of this pursuit is wearisome and intrusive – Rodin paired with Klimt to show how each deals with a woman's genital divide, Modigliani with Guston (but is this to demonstrate a similarity, or to show that Guston's hand, unlike Modigliani's, trembles and is utterly insensitive?), Brueghel with Van Gogh (but what is to be learned from that?), Polke with Botticelli, Man Ray with Dürer, Craig-Martin himself with an anonymous Egyptian of 3,000 years ago: compare and contrast, he seems to urge, but this foolish exercise merely obstructs proper contemplation and perception.

Craig-Martin plays a silly game, an aesthetic crossword puzzle, and it is deplorable that for such a vain, frivolous and flimsy exhibition the resources of the Ashmolean and Fitzwilliam Museums, the Courtauld Institute and, above all, the British Museum, should have been plundered. The Trustees of these institutions found it, no doubt, difficult to refuse the requests of a Trustee of the Tate, but they had a duty to examine his credentials, of which, by his own admission, he had none, and if they had the slightest misgivings, refuse all loans. This is an exhibition that should not have happened; if these Trustees see it and read his meagre catalogue, they should hang their heads in shame, for the treasures in their charge should never have been put at risk for so puerile a purpose.

If a third exhibition is to follow, then let Meyrick Hughes enlist an able eye from among the many historians, critics, collectors and curators of drawings whom Craig-Martin so despises, and let him test their wisdom and connoisseurship against the ignorance of an artist early among those who assert that art can be found anywhere and made of anything, and who is most notorious for declaring a small glass of tapwater to be a full-grown oak tree.

Evening Standard 1995

Richard Deacon

THE TURNER PRIZE OF £10,000 WAS GIVEN IN 1987 to the sculptor Richard Deacon. As the jury announced that it was rewarding him for 'his fresh, inclusive approach to ideas and materials, his vigilant self-appraisal and his intellectual curiosity', it is for these three qualities that we should perhaps search in his current exhibition at the Whitechapel Gallery. The first is present in abundance, though I am not convinced that it is fresh; of the other two there is not the slightest hint.

Deacon makes no claim to be a sculptor, preferring to call himself a 'fabricator'. At school he studied A-level physics and mathematics – an unlikely grounding for an artist. At St Martin's School of Art he was more concerned with performance and collective activity (what's that?) than with any solid work as a budding sculptor. In Chicago he attended classes in acting. In his three years at the Royal College he studied Environmental Media – a faculty so whimsical that it has since been closed. In New York he took to potting. With all these lofty qualifications he has been much appointed as a teacher of sculpture, and, no doubt, has had a hefty influence on students in the Central School, Winchester, Sheffield, Bath, and Chelsea, where he teaches still.

What example does he set his students? In 1986 this self-proclaimed non-sculptor threw down a challenge with a travelling show of his work called 'For Those who have Eyes'. The arrogant implication was that those who could not see the point of large and bumptious objects in roughhewn timber or sheet metal that bore no resemblance to such enigmatic titles as 'Fish out of Water' or 'Feast for the Eye', must be blind or stupid. The two large works put on view at the Tate to justify the Turner Prize were made for a 'dance collaboration' (artspeak for ballet?), and even an inevitably sympathetic presenter on the BBC's *Kaleidoscope* could find nothing better to say of them than that they resembled 'an upturned grand piano'.

Resemblance, I suppose, is the point, though Deacon only sees the references to other things after his fabricatures are finished. These fabricated objects are the fagged out tag end of Surrealism and the *objet trouvé*, wearily exploiting familiar materials in unfamiliar contexts and alien relationships. Things are often not what they seem and the materials are tortured into cross purposes; parqueted timber is cheap linoleum scavenged from a skip, real timber, crudely glued and laminated with black rubber, is steamed into the tormented contortions of the bentwood chair, sheet metal is seamed like cloth and inflated like a balloon, or sewn like hides and turned into a nomad tent. What might be a bellows or a hideous souvenir Moroccan pouffe, is made of galvanised steel and the vinyl tablecloth from a back-street Brixton café: the Saratoga trunk that ought to grace the luggage rack of some antique Rolls is merely an empty form, shaped in sheet copper. Occasionally Deacon puns – the intestinal 'Body of Thought' is a flatulent construction of air-conditioning ducts, and 'Troubled Water' evokes the ancient primitive pumps of the Near East.

None of it is beautiful in the making – the joinery is crude, the dowels proudly obvious, the timber chipped, scarred and poorly planed, the glues bubblingly obvious. This raw apprentice has much to learn from the riveted bonnet of a Thirties Railton, or the elegant luggage of Louis Vuitton, yet the initial impact of his work in the white space of Whitechapel is of exquisite theatrical enchantment. This merely demonstrates how much a well-chosen setting flatters work but deceives the spectator – these same bits of old rubber, hardboard, vinyl, cloth, carpet, sponge, formica and wax wane into insignificance in any more conventional gallery, in the open air look shoddy, and in any ordinary house would be preposterous cuckoos. These fabricatures are public art fit only for a very few indoor public places.

I have read with care and despair the two gobbledegook essays in the catalogue, from which I learn only that I have failed to recognise as Deacon's 'principal unifying feature . . . his repertoire of . . . organs, orifices and genitalia, and thus, by extension, to notions of speech, hearing and of language'. I cannot imagine to whom this obscure, pretentious, ill-written rubbish is addressed – certainly not to me. Sponsors who fund such exhibitions should perhaps have the right, the obligation indeed, to veto these self-indulgent displays of stupefying artspeak.

Evening Standard 1988

Frank Dobson

FRANK DOBSON IS ONE OF THOSE MANY BRITISH artists whom we claim as great because they mirror the work of peers and predecessors, but who do not even filter through their own perceptions the observed conceits, ideas and quirks of style of others, but merely passively receive them and add nothing of their own. He happened to be a sculptor, but could as easily have been a painter for painting was his first training and ambition, and had he continued with his oils and watercolours there is little doubt that this damnation would have been as true – as it was for many painters of his generation. To wander now among Dobson's sculptures is less to be rewarded with a fine aesthetic lift than to count a lifetime's obvious borrowings and derivations, even from himself, to see at one remove or second hand the bulk, simplicity, fine finish or deliberate distortion of Maillol and Modigliani, Cubism and the Cyclades, Epstein, Gaudier-Brzeska and Brancusi.

Born in 1886, his earliest surviving sculpture is, it seems, a seated female figure carved in oak in perhaps 1915, though a plaster bust of

George V may well have been his first exercise in three dimensions (we know of this frightful object only from a photograph), and there is some evidence that other woodcarvings were executed in 1914. This cramped and ugly, but ingenious, little lump shows awareness of sculpture from all sorts of sources, and it is worth recalling that when Dobson saw the famous Post-Impressionist Exhibition organised by Roger Fry in the winter of 1910–11, it sent him 'scuttling along to the British Museum, where I found Negro sculpture, Peruvian, Egyptian, Assyrian, Polynesian, and, curiously enough, later, archaic Greek sculpture'. To these, as though with appetite insatiable, he was to add Picasso and Matisse as influences, and after a journey to Ceylon and India in 1925 the orient too began to play its part.

As much as he collected influences, Dobson collected influential friends, not only such artists as Wyndham Lewis and Augustus John, Vanessa Bell and all the Nicholsons, but the Sitwells and their cronies, Lawrence of Arabia (much given to dropping in for tea) and Maynard Keynes – and with them came the opportunities for portrait patronage. Portraits, no doubt, paid the pressing bills, but with few exceptions – of which far the most remarkable is the burnished bronze head of Osbert Sitwell, the metal its true almost brassy colour without an added patina, the form a polished punning reference to Brancusi, yet the likeness true to a most polished sitter – these consistently illustrate just how undistinguished his work could be, how ordinary, how kitsch, even how nasty, and the bust of Sir Thomas Lipton made in 1954 is quite as frightful as that of George V made forty years before.

It must have been his inflated female figures, boneless pin-head creatures of great thigh and buttock, swollen with subcutaneous fat, that appealed to Roger Fry and Clive Bell, the premier critics of the day and formidably influential in establishing Dobson's reputation. Fry was much taken with 'significant form' but did not make quite such an ass of himself as Bell, who in 1922 seems to have thought Dobson a finer sculptor than Bernini (just imagine Dobson as the designer of St Peter's in the Vatican), and in 1927 wrote of

Cornucopia (a plain and heavy female, but far less flaccid than the rest, more taut of form and contour, more deliberately stylish, and the owner of such buttocks as might make a man's hand reach of its own volition) that it was 'the finest piece of sculpture by an Englishman since – since I don't know when . . . perfectly equipped . . .' – as breathless and silly an example of criticism as can now only be found on the BBC's *Kaleidoscope*. From another critic of his day, T.W. Earp, Dobson's brother-in-law, there was talk of the 'pure essence' of the torsos, of 'organic structure' and 'natural plastic form', and the proposal that he should be considered Britain's 'first Post-Impressionist sculptor'.

From nonsense of this kind we learn only that effusive critics are responsible for many misconceptions and that, in the end, even they cannot sustain the insubstantial artist (a consolation in the context of de Kooning and Rothko). With Fry's death in 1934 his influence faded, and Bell (Vanessa's husband) was not long after seen to be a gushing fool, and with their decline Dobson's reputation too took to the wane, to be replaced by the bright young generation of Henry Moore. He slogged on, respected for his command of all the sculptor's skills, taught at the Royal College of Art from 1946 until 1953, contributed to the Festival of Britain in 1951 and became an RA in the same year (a decade or two earlier he would have burned it down), but his work for the thirty years before his death in 1963 was all repetition, formula, habit and stale custom.

This very minor figure is now the subject of a retrospective exhibition and a book. The former is at the Courtauld Institute, and one must question the wisdom and probity of replacing the permanent collection there with any temporary exhibition, and particularly with one of such scant interest and importance, even if Sam Courtauld could be counted as once Dobson's patron. The Institute's business must surely be to exhibit the superb collections that are its own, and not itinerant mediocrities. The book poses as a *catalogue raisonné* of sorts: it is chatty in style, with the literacy of a tabloid newspaper and innumerable illiteracies that should have been eliminated by an editor. We are told that Dobson's first one man show took place in both 1921 and 1927, and the execrable Lipton bust as first exhibited posthumously in 1954 when Dobson still had nine years to live. Marred by a lack of discipline that confuses the chronology and by incomplete research, without an index the book is a wretched offering.

I can add a note. There are hints throughout Dobson's life that he was a man of active heterosexual mind. After his death, his widow asked me to help her clear the studio at Stamford Bridge, and I was appalled by the destruction that she wrought, smashing to smithereens small clay and terracotta models, tearing fine drawings in red and black chalk, hundreds of them, burning the fragments in a dustbin, all because the subjects were erotic. I was allowed to save pastel drawings of exotic and rare birds, and watercolours of farmyards and a pastoral life long gone, but for the figures engaged in sexual congress, face to face, head to toe and doggy-style as explicit as any by his old friend Eric Gill, Mrs Dobson would accept no plea that they were beautiful, no argument that they were fired by a quality not to be found in the 'pure essence' of the torsos that survive, and like a ferociously implacable angel at the Last Judgment, she bent to the business of destruction. These were all, I suppose, the private imaginings of his later years, for the studio in which he made his most celebrated works was bombed during the war; had his widow allowed them to survive, his reputation might now have some chance of a rebirth – on what is left, however, it merits no more than modest curiosity (but the book should have been better written).

Evening Standard 1995

Doubletake

DOUBLETAKE IS AN EXHIBITION THAT GOES beyond the familiar frames of reference in art; instead, it digs deep into the common memories of our culture and biology, and extends our understanding of the world around us (or so its promoters would have us believe). This it does with children's comics pasted to picture canvases, with such oracular messages as 'To dream of sailors is to become an entomologist' crudely stencilled in their urgency, with scraps of petit point of Sydney Harbour so execrable that no sane person would use them to decorate even a souvenir tea-cosy, with the enormous colour photographs of unmemorable subjects that are now mandatory in every art exhibition, and with many another whimsy of the contemporary art world, all tediously familiar and aggressively fashionable.

My first response was boredom and weariness of spirit that yet again the panjandrums of the South Bank should expect our veneration for the pretensions of artists suffering severe forms of intellectual arrest. By damning 'the familiar frames of reference' the three organisers condemn what most of us recognise as traditional forms of painting and sculpture, or developments rooted in them, but what they offer instead has long been familiar too, and without the fresh energy of mischievous originality and fierce rebellion, is mere flabby and flaccid imitation, not the 'subterranean universals' claimed by one of them, who heads her contribution to the catalogue '*Epater le bourgeois revisited*' (sic). This is an enlightening title, for it suggests that the main purpose of these chosen artists is to cause affront – but all in all these ageing adolescents are no more than the green-haired coxcombed punks of art, engendering a mild misgiving but no serious dismay in the decent and respectable.

Their stale offerings are presented as icons too sacred even to label – we are compelled to contemplate them in ignorance of artist's name or object's title, and only when satiated with the spiritual uplift to be derived from a waxwork leg projecting from a wall (with real human hair), or yet another of Rachel Whiteread's rubber mattresses, are we supposed to cast about in search of information. There are labels, but it is easier to descend a monkey-puzzle tree than to find them – but then I suppose that in any exhibition burdened with the cast-offs of the Turner Prize one must expect all other elements of Tate Gallery arrogance towards the public. To my complaint that the labels are absurdly distant from the works, the response of Lynne Cooke (an organiser) was a lofty patronising smile, but a worthy of the Hayward Gallery (to whom I am deeply grateful) bothered himself to explain that this exhibition is less addressed to the common man than to the cognoscenti accustomed to spiritual absorption in the object, souls too remote ever to need enlightenment from a mundane label, the mere presence of which, obtrusive, might distract him from his exercise in contemplation. From such a view I gather that the Hayward's visitors should be as ascetic as were the Desert Fathers of the Christian church, hermits hallucinating with hunger fifteen hundred years ago, and more.

Perhaps I am in error in taking it all so seriously, and the exhibition is a joke, a spoof, a hoax. Can a cuddly toy dog on the floor, with an inscribed T-shirt on a rail, really comprise a work of art? – or the innards of a giant music box, tolling away on the roof? – or an entire room walled and floored in the golden varnish glow of pork crackling, containing what I take to be a sacrificial altar built from slabs of white soap? I can read a meaning into this last (disgust at the way we treat food animals – but is it any better for a prize porker to end as a work of art than a pound of bacon?), but no clue is offered by the title (*Passion*), and no exegesis by the catalogue. The catalogue indeed is scarcely relevant to the exhibition and is merely an excuse for Lynne Cooke and those in cahoots with her to weave a fragile web of art jargon to obscure the futility of their ideas, at a length that adds boredom to absurdity. All that these three curators of the Emperor's wardrobe have done is to gather from four of the five continents (at vast public expense) wearisome inflated trifles, and present their random and frivolous selection with all the apparatus of pomp and pretension that we have learned to expect from those who make their livings from the promotion of contemporary art.

This exhibition is without interest or importance, its contents numbingly familiar, and its underlying thesis silly. Only one serious point is raised by its presence on the South Bank – the deplorable waste of public money spent on bringing this dross to London from New York, Los Angeles and Seattle, from Adelaide, Brisbane and Woollahra, to say nothing of Cologne and Paris. It must not be forgotten that the wrinkled dinosaurs of the South Bank are the ancient denizens of the old Arts Council, and that only the name of the zoo has changed – the funding is still from the taxes that we pay; their initiatives are stale, their attitudes to the public arrogant, and they see their responsibility as lying primarily (if not only) with contemporary artists (no matter how incompetent, inadequate and foolish) and their apologists (no matter how bogus, self-seeking and jargon-ridden).

This exhibition is the invention of a self-indulgent committee amused by the flimsiest of intellectual arguments, to whom I commend the rubric printed on page 70 of the catalogue – 'Distinguish sense from nonsense.' It attracted no sponsorship, which suggests that for once the well-intentioned milch cows could see no cud to chew in South Bank ephemera. It should attract no visitors. I have never, in all the years that I have written for this paper, urged visitors not to visit an exhibition (for I believe that no critic should play shepherd to a flock), but now I do just that, with a declaration of contempt for the artists and their work, for the three curators and the waffle of their astonishingly irrelevant catalogue, and, above all, for the relicts of the Arts Council who continue their thirty year long profligacy with our money.

Evening Standard 1992

Fabergé

ONE DISADVANTAGE OF HAVING A MOTHER who knew sad White Russians ageing in the dingy basements of South Kensington and Earl's Court, was that with Gentle Jesus and

Mrs Do-as-you-would-be-done-by, Rasputin and Fabergé were among my childhood myths, the one as terrible as Grimm, the other the Beatrix Potter of the third dimension. I do not now know if the knick-knack animals shown me as a child, carefully unwrapped from scraps of silk or neat-stitched velvet bags, were really by the Russian master goldsmith – I recall only that the dumpy pugs and porkers, smooth and glistening in chalcedony, obsidian and agate, could as well have come from a bag of jelly babies and been the better for being edible; as for the precious flowers in a tiny vase – told that these delicate trifles trembled at the merest breath of breeze, I was deeply disappointed when they didn't, but required the kind of thump that Richmal Crompton's William might administer.

The scales fallen so early from my eyes, I have never been in awe of Fabergé's reputation, and am relieved that not since 1977 has the V&A required me, as it does now, to reconsider my puritanical view that his bagatelles are not great works of art, or even of invention, and am not one jot influenced by the great price that must be paid for them, nor by the great number in the Royal Collection. Great works of art, it can be argued, are the fruit of religious or political zealotry, and through the sublime and terrible, offer refreshment and catharsis to the soul, but the works of Fabergé are the jim-jam relics of an age of arrogance, the futile frivolities of a selfish society carelessly provoking its own *Götterdämmerung*, and illustrate the desperation with which the very rich and powerful once cast about for presents for their peers.

In a photograph of 1907, two dozen of Fabergé's royal patrons crowd into a group in Windsor Castle, the Queens and Empresses of Britain, Germany, Spain, Norway and Portugal rubbing shoulders with princesses and the grandest duchesses, the Kings and Kaisers jostling their heirs and cousins – but in St Petersburg, the Russian Royal Family and the Imperial Court could have raised five times that number for a photograph, and still not have included all his patrons there. There were still more – the royal families of Roumania, Serbia, Greece and Siam, the landless aristos of France and a dozen little Germanies, the Sassoons, Rothschilds and

Cassells, Astors and Vanderbilts, the Aga Khan and assorted Maharajahs. With these patrons, and yet still more panting for his jewelled photograph frames, onyx clocks, nephrite desk sets, and icon altars framed in rococo curlicues of silver, Fabergé needed a huge workshop and the constant flow of ingenious, preposterous and absurd ideas – indeed there are moments when he seems to anticipate the Surrealism of Dali and the fur-lined tea cups of Meret Oppenheim.

The son of a St Petersburg jeweller of Huguenot origin, Carl Fabergé took over his father's workshops in 1872 and worked for a decade in the standard conventions of the French. In 1881 he received the Imperial appointment. In 1882 his brother Agathon joined him, at the age of twenty full of bright ideas and fantasies, and the house of Fabergé moved fast into the field of curios and ornaments, letting jewellery take second place – and thus was the Imperial Easter Egg invented, that annual exchange of precious nonsenses in precious metals, bejewelled, enamelled, triffid-trapped in flowers, from which, at a button's touch, may spring diamond-framed portraits of the Tsar and all his family, or within which, with the lid thrown back, the Tsar's mother might find her seven royal residences and two royal yachts painted on the pearl panels of a dolls house screen. The demand for such work became insatiable; Fabergé employed as many as three hundred craftsmen in St Petersburg and two hundred more in Moscow, brought his three sons and other workmasters into the business as designers, and still could not keep pace – his London showroom alone, open from 1907 until 1917, sold more than 10,000 objects.

The taste of Carl Fabergé was traditional and perhaps a little dry, but that of his brother Agathon was more exuberant, and among the classical columns and *dix-huitième* reminiscences, the workshops occasionally fell victim to the creeping complexities of Art Nouveau. No handsome Doulton pot was safe from Fabergé's embellishments, cameo glass vases were made to sprout as the obscene blossoms of his silver acanthus leaves, and traditional Russian ceremonial drinking cups were converted into monstrous monuments of war memorial proportions. Bad taste abounded; caviar by the kilo was to be scooped from the writhing body of a silver sturgeon, a clock resembles a Kremlin tower cast in raspberry ripple a little above melting-point, an onyx night-light is as nasty a thing as could be found now in an Istanbul airport shop, the toy regiment in silver, sapphires and polychrome are of the quality of chocolate soldiers, and all the cloisonné work is as vile as a Japanese export tea-set. As for the menagerie of mouse, rabbit, squirrel, cat, capercailzie, carthorse et al, et al, these turn Mrs Tiggy-Winkle and Tommy Tiptoes into works of great gravity and grace.

The outbreak of war brought new and strange commissions, for no subaltern could fight without his Fabergé cooking-pot in brass and copper, small enough for a primus stove, perfect for one man's morning porridge. As the weary business wore on, the craftsmen and workmasters were conscripted and the empty Moscow work-shops turned to making shell cases – odd to think of the works of Fabergé bombarding Kaiser Bill, one of his favoured clients. With the Revolution of 1917, Fabergé left for Switzerland, and the firm passed to a Committee of Employees who kept it going for one more year. Fabergé himself died in 1920.

At the exhibition of 1977, queues reached right round the V&A and old ladies fainted by the dozen or broke their ankles in the fashionable gloom. The current exhibition is much better lit, but one is troubled by the triumphant music played non-stop to drown the noisy air-conditioning, and there are no seats for those wearied when crowding the glass cases becomes too competitive – well before midday it had become quite uncomfortable. I have one frivolous admission: that were I the owner of a Fabergé cigarette case, no propaganda for the moral cause would make me give up smoking.

Evening Standard 1994

Ian Hamilton Finlay

IAN HAMILTON FINLAY, A TURBULENT SCOT, IS The Institute of Contemporary Art A man of such fierce spiritual independence that he is not content to be a citizen of that ancient subject kingdom north of Hadrian's Wall, but has declared himself the Despot of Little Sparta, a Raspberry Republic (his words) in Lanarkshire. Now sixty-seven, he has some small international reputation as a sculptor, but he has longer been a poet of sorts, a man of such brief play with words that he leaves his readers wondering what happened to the next line. His concern with the look of words in print, with typeface, interval and placing, edged him into sculpture through inscriptions, and he has developed into something of a graveyard man, a headstone mason, a deviser of plain funerary monuments, and, in lighter mood, a man to decorate a garden with a pastoral allusion cut in marble.

Finlay is essentially a Neo-Classicist, few of whose crisp-cut letters would have been out of style two centuries ago, nor out of place, for he indulges in obsessive hero-worship for the most single-minded revolutionaries of France. Of these, Louis Antoine Léon Florelle de Saint-Just, who, at twenty-seven, himself fell victim to the guillotine in July 1794, companion to the infamous Robespierre, is Finlay's super-hero – a strange choice, for this wretched poet (who stole his mother's jewellery and pocketed the proceeds) was a man of empty bombast and such preposterous proposals as that, at the age of seven, all boys should be removed from parental care and educated as creatures of the state; perhaps what most appeals to Finlay are Saint-Just's fierce tirades against the king, echoing across the centuries to engender kinship between revolutionaries.

Finlay's current exhibition at the ICA falls into two parts, of which the more important is a coherent group of ten bronzes under the title *Instruments of Revolution*. For this he has reverted to the precious customs of the poetry press and published a catalogue that runs to only five hundred copies, on cream paper with brown print, a cover in grey card, a wrapper in pale terracotta, and illustrations in old-fashioned sepia on glossy paper, laboriously tipped-in. No text is bound in the book, but an easily lost essay on a loose fold is tucked between the covers; it is as though Finlay considers all words other than those inscribed on his bronzes as integral parts of their conception and meaning to be irrelevant – each bronze is its own exegesis and requires no interpreter.

The bronzes are simple images that bind together the apparently opposed ideas of revolution and planting the herbaceous border. Most appear to be direct casts of such simple things as garden tools; only the guillotine blade seems to be invented, and only the modern machine-gun strikes a dissonant note, bringing, as it does, the imagery of terror into the present day. The title of the gun is *Flute* – another dissonant note, for all the other pieces derive their titles either from their inscriptions or from their subjects; as flute and gun are, I feel compelled to observe, art's traditional symbols of the male member in its most puissant state, suggesting potency and bravado and the fathering of children, I wonder if Finlay intends to set in train a particularly complicated set of allusions to the bullet as the seed of revolution – a fertilising ejaculation of sorts – and at the same time to suggest a seasonal cycle of death and re-birth that fits well enough with the watering cans and garden spade.

The everyday tools of the suburban garden are removed from the commonplace by being cast in bronze, a metal that has the associations of great sculpture and monumental permanence, the weighty stuff of medals and memorials. Inscriptions hammer home the point; take a sickle – a particularly potent image for most of us whose lives have in some sense been affected by the Russian Revolution – and in elegant classical letters cut into its handle the legend A COTTAGE/A FIELD/A PLOUGH, to be read only by grasping the blade and turning the whole full circle, and you have not only a reference to Saint-Just (who believed them to be the three elements of happiness), but a sculpture that must be examined in the round, and an object that looks like a real tool, yet is the wrong weight, the wrong material, the wrong temperature, is blunt and, like most works of art, quite useless.

Three watering cans in a wheelbarrow represent the Jacobin leaders in a tumbril *en route* for the guillotine; from their severed necks blood flowed to fertilise revolution as does water from the cans, nourishing other revolutionaries, lending strength to other martyrs. It is a neat conceit, this paradox of the great Terror exchanging images with Voltaire's ideal of retirement to garden peace, the axe that lops both the dead branch and the living human head, the spade that both digs the grave and turns the sod for next year's cabbages, but Finlay should be wary of making too many visual puns lest they grow as wearisome as those in his poetry and sybilline statements.

'The steeples fell silent/The guillotine tolled' is another nice neat confusion of images, and looks as though it must be the beginning of a lengthy narrative poem (Longfellow perhaps?), but two lines are as many as Finlay can manage (quite long by his standards). 'Water's edge/Water sedge' is, however, dangerously near the 'Ice cream/I scream' of pre-pubescent wit. Upstairs in the ICA is a collection of his word-plays of which 'The sea's waves/the waves sheaves/The sea's naves' is an example, all carved in little triptychs of pale timber, hinged knick-knacks for the mantelpiece. Such puerile nonsenses undo the seeming seriousness of his larger work (I am tempted to suggest 'Saint-Just/ain't just'), and the wrinkled kelims emblazoned 'Wave/ waev/wvae . . .' and 'Star/star/star . . . steer' unravel him completely.

To complement the exhibition at the ICA, the Victoria Miro Gallery in Cork Street is arranged like a funeral parlour with samples of all that Finlay has to offer in the way of obelisk and arch, pyramid and tempietto, sarcophagus and mausoleum, urn, cenotaph and shrine, all small enough for desk or cabinet of curiosities, all suitable to hold the ashes of a loved one, or, enlarged, to mark a grave. They have something of the character of the utterly useless present that the rich buy for the stinking rich in Asprey's (Scotland's answer to the Fornasetti object), and of the current vogue for introducing simplified elements of classical architecture into the design of office blocks and art galleries; some might well serve as models for conservatories, front porches or garden sheds for mock-Georgian villas on the fringe of Basingstoke.

I find Finlay too sinister in his concerns, too obsessed with violent and bloody death, with revolution and revolutionary heroes, with terror and the terrorism of the state, a man perhaps admiring Stalin and Trotsky as much as Saint-Just – and I do not trust obsession. I am exasperated by his adolescent word-play, by his desperate scrabble to introduce a double meaning – indeed I am surprised that as a maker of cult objects and something of a cult himself he has not made play with the several meanings of IHS and his own initials IHF (*facio* and *figo*, make and fix, useful in this context). I am troubled by the conviction that he does little more than conceive his works of sculpture, and lets others, largely unacknowledged, execute them. I find the puffed portent of his enigmatic statements as irksome as his whimsy, and I suspect that he is carried wayward on the wind of words, his wings of intellectual severity as sham as those of Icarus.

The Evening Standard 1992

Lucio Fontana

SOME YEARS AGO, A DISCONTENTED ART STU-dent entered the National Portrait Gallery and boldly slashed the then fresh and popular portrait of Princess Diana as a demure Chelsea Girl gone up in the world. It was not, alas, a clean cut, but one that left broken fibres whiskering in all directions, not easy to repair; moreover, the paint was acrylic – the adult's equivalent of nursery poster paint, with none of the subtleties of oil – and this compounded the difficulty. Intrigued by the problem, I spent several happy days slashing canvas, piecing threads together, making moulds of canvas grain, and testing the masking properties of opaque acrylic primer; but what had begun as a simple enquiry into conservation and repair soon moved on to more intriguing experiments into the techniques of a painter called Lucio Fontana.

Fontana's works are to be seen in almost every auction of modern art at Christie's and Sotheby's, in the stock of every second-rate art dealer from Vladivostock to Vancouver, in every minor museum from Aarhus to Zagreb, and in every *piccolo salone* in Milan. They are invariably late canvases, flatly painted Reckitt's blue, heliotrope, or some other such unsubtle colour, their immaculate faces disturbed by a razor-slash, or two, or three. They are repetitive and boring, and they do their painter no credit – I wonder now, having discovered how easy is their imitation, how many of them are genuine, for though Fontana died twenty years ago, their supply seems endless. The point at issue is that Fontana was in his way an astonishingly and satisfyingly enquiring artist who, having always blurred the distinctions between painting and sculpture, spent the last twenty years of his working life breaking through his canvases to some imaginary celestial world beyond; his experiments are consistently exciting until the moment when he fixed on the elegant sweep of the long curved cut, freezing at that point into a classicism of his own, in which the gesture is all and must be *ad nauseam* repeated – unless, of course, these empty nothings are not by him.

It is curious, and perhaps significant, that they are absent from the current exhibition at the Whitechapel Gallery, which purports to be a proper retrospective. This is the last show in which the Director there, Nicholas Serota, has a hand before taking over the Tate Gallery – it is scholarly, informative, entertaining, and seductively arranged, and if it is a measure of the standards that we may now expect at Millbank, then, without in any way mocking the old management there, we are in for all things bright and beautiful.

Fontana's later slashes were done with a Stanley knife; the only variations stem from the length of the stroke and whether the cut is made from the back or the front of the canvas, which accordingly curves either in or out, occasionally with an uncanny sensuality.

Nothing but black, suggesting infinite space, is to be seen behind the cuts, and the paintings are invariably titled Spatial Concept.

The early Spatial Concepts are much more interesting, the canvas varies in weight and grain and therefore in response to whatever damage is done to it; rough, thready edges are heightened with colour, and piercings, circular and triangular, far outweight cuts. The canvas is often subtly varied in tone so that it implies atmosphere and the piercings begin to suggest the constellations of astronomy and the mysteries of the black hole. This all grew quite logically from early work in the 1930s in which he painted and scratched white plaster plaques in his first fumbling attempts to break away from the restrictions of a framed picture plane.

He was a deft sculptor in clay, capable of a Baroque explosion of movement; this he occasionally made vulgar in hideous lumps of kitsch pottery, and it was, even at its best, alarmingly old-fashioned, two centuries out of time and not much better than pastiche – but he could see in his rearing horses and ecstatic saints the simple basic element of form in movement and could distil it into abstraction. With such a sculptural feeling for essentials, no surface could be left flat – the canvas must be loaded with paint deep as a relief map, studded with chunks of jewel-like glass, and poked and prodded until it took on a new dimension. With his sculptor's skill, he could as easily do it with sheets of brass and iron.

There is no doubt that Fontana was a showman, Dali-dapper in striped trousers and fur coat, dashing off pictures for an exhibition as easily as a Halal butcher cuts throats. There is no doubt of his knowing that his Spatial Concepts occasionally took on the imagery of female parts, and that he mischievously exploited knicker pink and finger strokes to exploit the similarity. There can be, nevertheless, no doubt of the high seriousness of his experiments, and that in their pursuit, he achieved things of mysterious beauty as often as he descended into deplorable kitsch. As a young man he tagged onto the Italian Futurists and ran parallel with Ben Nicholson; in 1949, aged fifty, he anticipated the extremes of today's contemporary art with a darkened room in which he placed an abstract shape covered in phosphorescent paint; with the Spatial Concepts that first developed in that year, he heralded the conceptual art of the Sixties and Seventies, without ever losing touch as a painter.

No Michelangelo, his work infinitely better in the experiment than in the final resolution, we owe him his niche in history as a science fiction painter, a little visionary. Twenty years after his death he deserves this beautiful and sympathetic retrospective exhibition.

Evening Standard 1988

Fresh Art

'FRESH ART' IS THE TITLE OF A VAST ANNUAL exhibition of work executed by students in a large number of art schools up and down the land. For such stale mimicry 'fresh' is a misnomer, and 'executed' is a word that should in this context be used in its other sense – the firing squad, the axeman's chopper, or the rope. It is a merry coincidence that the first thing to be seen on entering is a life-size hangman's noose.

Would that the worthy woman who invented 'In' and 'Out', and gave us so much fun with fashion and the words that betray class, were still alive, for in the arts of art students there is much such business to be done. Rope is still In this year, though I suspect that its grip on the student imagination is no longer quite secure. Sacking is In, and so is sewing, both with the professional machine and with the long cobbling stitch of amateurs who dislike the chore of darning socks. Wax is In, both as a modelling medium and as a containing surface briefly richer than paint (briefly because it holds the dirt and cannot be cleaned without severe loss). Kitsch and toys are In, and so are printed exhortations and mysterious messages, though I suspect that these are fading from the scene and may be Out next year. Bare wood, the uglier its coarse grain the better, is very much In this summer, and the influence of those who were short-listed for the

Turner Prize last year, or collected by Charles Saatchi, is everywhere manifest in long-dead specimens or plaster casts of bricks. The latex of French letters, so much the medium of sculptors for the past few years, is Out, and the blanket (its use justified only in the work of Joseph Beuys, whose life it saved in Russia) is fading fast. The amateur photographer may be amused to know that a bunched foreskin, or a finger poked into a slack scrotum, constitutes a work of art; and the housewife married to a smoker need no longer be distressed by burnt sheets, for each burn can be a pretty picture.

Some ancient Sixties visual shibboleths survive still in the student body – the plain field of colour, the bull's eye target, the colour sample sheet – but are now so rare as to seem almost as archaic as imitating Michelangelo. The shibboleths to come (for they make so purposeful a showing this year that they can only gain in power and influence) are plumbers' pipes and junctions, piled sheets of glass, ranked coat-hangers, and boxes of knick-knackery that recall old-fashioned cabinets of curiosities; boxes of carpet rolls should perhaps be included in this forecast, for there were so many on the opening day, but it is possible that these were not works of art at all, but the left-overs of those furnishing the display. The most splendidly aggressive piece of sculpture was a shopping trolley bearing an aluminium ladder that I took to be influenced by John Keane's painted recollections of the Gulf War, but this too may have been an accidental contribution by a workman – it is difficult to tell what's what in these circumstances, for when so much art bears the legend 'untitled', it seems perfectly reasonable for it to bear no artist's name and be anonymous.

Among the influences dominant this year are those of the young celebrities Therese Oulton and Rachel Whiteread, the one with her subjectless knotted and knitted paint, the other with her plaster casts of empty fireplaces. I observed hints of Frink, Caulfield and the irksome conceptual trifles of Craig-Martin – art so frivolous and insubstantial that, like King Lear, the critic must snap 'Nothing will come of nothing', and despair of a student cultural perspective so short that it can find no worthier foundations for its development.

With the residue of exhausted smudge, drip and splash traditions, a larding of graffiti, and the blur of the out-of-focus television screen, it can be argued that the visual language of the art student is at best no better than pre-pubescent mimicry of folk heroes, and at worst a self-perpetuating babble as infantile as the gurglings of a baby at the nipple, and meaning rather less. That the art schools attended by these infant boobies should claim the status of universities is an outrageous insult to true scholarship; that the students should be awarded Honours Degrees for work that is so stale and trivial is an absurdity meriting contempt.

The students of the Royal Academy this year asked me to contribute fifty words to the catalogue of their final year exhibition, and, give them their due, they printed my melancholy comment – 'Largely illiterate, ignorant of their cultural background, incompetent in their craft, arrogant in their determination to express empty and silly selves, greedy, and much of their work rubbish, most art students are unworthy of their places in art schools. Rare talent emerges in spite of teachers no better than themselves.' The Academy Schools deserved the observation less than many others, but in the whole of Fresh Art the students of only one school give me cause to think wholesale damnation harsh; in the City and Guilds Art School in Kennington, Mark Curtis is a painter with old-fashioned painterly skills as well as imagination, and Kevin Sansom is a figurative sculptor whose small-scale wrestlers would not look out of place with the table-top bronzes of the Renaissance and the Baroque. Both must, of course, be wary of the trap of history, and both may have nothing more to say and do, and burn out fast – one can never tell with budding artists, more than any other students here today and disappeared tomorrow – but, for the moment, both are worth enthusiastic patronage.

The publicity for Fresh Art uses such words as off-beat, exotic, juicy, weird and wacky, as though it is art's business only to amuse and entertain, and for its exhibitions to be disco-bright and Disney-trivial. In the catalogue I am rebuked for what I said of it last year – 'This exhibition is a severe indictment of the art school system and the teachers within it who fail to teach. Does anyone ever ask how much it costs the nation to keep in schools these aspiring artists whose professional failure is not only immediate but inevitable?' I am unrepentant. Were music to be taught so badly and by such incompetents, with students left alone for weeks to unravel the mysteries of the French horn, the nation's rage would be abundantly expressed, but when art students are indeed left for whole terms without instruction by tutors and professors (professors! – there's a laugh) unable to instruct, there's nary a word of protest.

If the new Minister for the Arts really wishes to change the status of the visual arts within the next few years, to drag them from the wretched slough of infantilism into which they are long fallen, he should sack all art teachers, close the schools, and re-build art education from scratch. Teachers should teach.

Evening Standard 1992

Peter Fuller

FIVE YEARS AGO, THE EDITOR OF ONE OF THOSE pretentious little art magazines so extravagantly subsidised by the Arts Council, sent me a book to review – 'You'll hate it', he said, 'be as spiteful and malicious as you like'. Biting back any riposte to this assumption that my scribbling is informed with spite and malice, I agreed to review Peter Fuller's *The Naked Artist*. Fuller I knew only by reputation as an ultra-conservative observing Christian intent on a Pre-Raphaelite crusade, a man of Victorian virtue inspired by John Ruskin, pronouncing anathema on all art since Turner. If the cover of the book was a surprise – it bore a photograph of Michelangelo's ham-fisted *David* done up in old-fashioned pink Y-front pants, the pouch sagging with the weight of his endowment – its contents were astonishing; the subjects of Fuller's essays ranged from the geometrical rigidities of Poussin to the decorative possibilities of abstraction, yet I could find nothing to support his reputation as the fifteenth Minor Prophet fulminating Lamentations of his own. I found instead a generous measure of kindliness towards half-formed painters with half-grown reputations, a breadth and depth of scholarship and interest far beyond the capacities of those critics whom we have come to regard as the heavyweights of the profession, and a constant vein of amused self-deprecation that suggested mind and attitude anything but ossified and prejudiced. When I told the editor of my response to Fuller's book, he withdrew the commission to review it and went elsewhere in search of spite and malice; I have not heard from him again.

Nor did I hear much of Fuller until late last year when rumours rumbled that he was to edit a new magazine. Rumour, for once, was truth. *Modern Painters*, a glossy quarterly, was launched in the early spring with such judicious hype as an essay by Michael Davie in *The Observer* and a party in the Private Rooms of the Royal Academy, at which the exhibitions secretary of that worthy establishment launched into a virulent attack, thus ensuring more publicity.

The magazine is substantial and beautifully presented – not a creature addressed to the waiting rooms of Harley Street, but to the library shelf. Its articles and reviews may be stimulated by current controversy, but they are measured responses, not mere journalistic back-biting, and the commissioning is shrewd, for Fuller knows exactly what he wishes to achieve as puppet-master; Grey Gowrie was encouraged to suggest that Lucian Freud is a deeply flawed painter, Sir Roy Shaw, the stoutest defendant of the Arts Council and all its works as long as he was panjandrum there, was encouraged to expose the maggotry that squirmed under its respectable stone, and David Bomberg, who for Peter Fuller is a 'much better painter than Pollock or de Kooning', was eulogised by a past pupil – and here's the rub, for if *Modern Painters* has a fault it is that it is the personal instrument of its editor, a chorus never out of tune with his voice.

Fuller is not an art historian and has no scholarly base for his expertise in art. He read English at Peterhouse in post-Levis days, felt a vague sympathy for Marxism and toyed with the New Left, but felt excluded from it; his family background is Baptist, but with a soundly argued theological base, neither intellectually restricted nor shadowed by simplicity. Now 'a devout unbeliever' and far removed from the left, he seems still, at forty, easily capable of reasoned change, constantly reconsidering his ordered views. As an undergraduate excited by the visual arts he felt that his skill lay with words that could be conjured into exegesis, and became an occasional critic in *Varsity*, second string to Richard Cork; they now make an interesting pair – Fuller wide-ranging, intelligent, intelligible, and urbane as often as he is virulent, and Cork (whom Fuller calls 'a weather-vane critic', and who calls himself an art historian) a man of fads, bandwaggons and art jargon.

Fuller has an editorial stance in support of British art that I dismissed as jingoist. I was mistaken, but the sustained invective of his first editorial against tacky internationalism lent my error strength. He rightly disputes the idiocy of Roger Fry's view that nothing worthwhile in the arts happened north of Paris; he rightly asserts the aesthetic bankruptcy of America and attacks the absurdities of international post-modernism; he believes that the driving force of British art has been and could again be the response of the whole moral being. He has considered the fads and fashions of contemporary connoisseurship and rejected them – for him Rothko is profoundly depressing, Hofmann incorrigibly minor, and photography aesthetically negligible. He maintains that some ability to handle paint and canvas within the conventions of historical art is the only sound base for the future. From his profound belief in the worthiness of British art, past and present, he recognised that there might be room for a magazine largely devoted to it, implying nothing in terms of quality, but providing a focus within the context of European culture, and ready to do battle against the pseudo-culture of America.

I doubt, in spite of the all guns blazing aspect of the early issues, if he and his magazine will ever run out of targets, but if Fuller is true to form, the views will modify and the polemic change, for he is above all a thinking, reasonable man. He is an unlikely successor to Ruskin, from whom he borrows the title of his magazine, seeming shy and myopic, with speech mannerisms as lively as a pudding boiled in a sock – but his pen is sharp and the words that flow from it often beautifully ordered. *Modern Painters* must be here to stay.

Tatler 1988

Naum Gabo

I SUSPECT THAT THE RELATIVE OBSCURITY IN this country of the sculptor Naum Gabo lies in our shying away from the pronunciation of an outlandish name. Naum rhymes with the German *Baum*, and Gabo with the great Greta. Neither is the original given him at his circumcision in 1890 – he was then dubbed Neemia (Nehemiah) Borisovitch Pevsner; he chose Gabo, another family name, in order to avoid confusion with his painter brother, Antoine.

He was born near Bryansk, a town of some 25,000 souls, half way between Kiev and Moscow in the great plain of western Russia. Iron-works were the principal industry in the area, and his father owned a factory that produced alloys and machinery – worth bearing in mind, for it is clear that at an early age Gabo was familiar with the idea of working metal. In 1910, after a precocious boyhood in which he had written poetry, painted a little, and got into trouble with revolutionary politics, his father sent him to Germany to study medicine. He spent two years at it in Munich, before transferring to philosophy, logic, and a course in civil engineering, with art history thrown in as light entertainment. His brother Antoine had meanwhile settled in Paris as a painter, and was to introduce this turbulent mind to the work of Picasso, Braque, Gris and the Cubists – of whom Gabo was later to be broadly dismissive.

It is odd that living in Munich he seems to have ignored the brilliant German artists working there in the heady days of early Expressionism; his interests then were entirely cerebral and analytical. The war brought confusion – he fled to Scandinavia until 1917, when he returned to Russia 'only because the Revolution had happened'. He settled in Moscow until 1922, but then began a lifetime on the move – to Germany for ten years, Paris for three, London for four; the second war he spent in St Ives, with that incestuous mob of minor abstract artists stringing the cavities in lumpish treen. In 1946 he took off for America, to a new nationality and the monumental respectability of a professorial chair at Harvard. He died in 1977.

Through all these shifts his self-taught sculpture maintains astonishing consistency. Ignore the few feeble early paintings and the one naturalistic negro head of 1912, and the lifetime was spent elevating the skills of the model maker from ingenuity into art. Any man who has painstakingly assembled wafers of balsa wood and threads of twine into a foot-long Gloucester Gladiator must warm to Gabo; any man who has made a perspex stand to fix it in the attitude of flight, will know the pleasures and frustrations of working in that material.

His concerns were constant, stemming from the metal-working of his childhood and the medical training of his youth; on the anatomist's slab he peeled back the skin and fat of cadavers to reveal the elegant fans of ligament and tendon, the striations of muscular tissue, the ingenious transitions from bone to flesh. The knowledge was not used to inform the body beautiful, but to stand in its own right as a marvel of twists, torsions and tensions, divorced from sensual response.

Work of astonishing elegance developed, with form, movement and the fall of light suggested by a thousand threaded wires on frames of phosphor-bronze; skate-wing curve meshes imperceptibly into curve, volume swelling and dissolving, shadow thickening and light shafting. These abstract sculptures evoke the prison depths of Piranesi and the September nests of breeding spiders; they suggest the flight of rockets, the hum of turbines and the turn of screws;

they assume the fragile forms of flight and the armoured carapace of shellfish. As fountains and piazza fillers they adapt perfectly to what passes for modern architecture. Some even look like architecture as we now, alas, have come to know it, anticipating by more than half a century the follies of the new Lloyd's building.

Success was not uniform in this family of images; there are moments when the shower appliances of Tilly Losch's bathroom, the ship in a bottle, Asprey's belt-buckles and the mysteries of the inner ear spring to mind. When trying his hand with solid stone, the objects are testicular, infelicitous fossils torn from beanstalk giants. Once in a while the innards of the meat-mincer and the gramophone are at no great distance, and the egg-slicer could well be Gabo's creature.

It all grew from Russian Constructivism, the most arid of artistic speculations, and from his own Manifesto of 1920. In this, buried in a wealth of purple, are a few lines that give the clue: tone, not colour, is the only pictorial reality; line does not describe, but is the direction of force and rhythm; depth, not volume, is the only plastic form in space. To these precepts, constantly refining them, he stuck to his dying day. His intellectual probity makes a strange bedfellow for the lush incompetence of Chagall, his equally peripatetic Russian contemporary.

Evening Standard 1987

Gilbert and George

The Anthony d'Offay Gallery

IN THE FIRST INCARNATION OF THE TURNER Prize, in the heady days when it was open to every ancient and notorious nincompoop and not restricted to the unformed braggart young, the principle of Buggin's Turn governed its receipt. It was thus, of course, Buggin's Turn that got the prize for Gilbert and George in 1986 – a fine pair of Buggins indeed. In their latest work, six years on, they revert to the Prize imagery of the naked youth, to themselves naked or wearing Michael Winner's Y-fronts, and always the enigmatic or explanatory legend – *Bum Cross*, for example, is the inscribed title of a compilation of the hairy cleavages between two pairs of buttocks arranged to form a cross. I presume, as they have so often used their own anatomy in earlier pictures, that this is some kind of intimate self-portraiture, a new variation on the speaking likeness, but even to the agnostic it must seem a gratuitous offence to the practising Christian of much the same kind as that wretched and notorious American photograph of urine pouring on a crucifix.

Most of their current imagery is now, however, less extreme than before, and the words more restrained – there are no four-letter brevities from the Anglo-Saxon, or equally brief references to the fore and aft parts and functions of the male at the point of bifurcation, but this is nevertheless an exhibition for those whose politically-correct liberalism compels them to accept as aesthetically uplifting the sagging nakedness of the male in late middle age, balding and bespectacled, or who have a taste for the prominent penis in fluorescent pink, lemon yellow, or as variegated as a slice of cassata.

The technique remains the same – the accumulation, on a vast scale, of photographic images of high pitch and gloss, compelling compliant art historians to draw analogies with medieval stained-glass windows. In one of their works they stand naked in a urinal placed across the nave of a gothic cathedral – an opportunity lost for punning on *anal* and *ogee* (they occasionally use puns – *Light Headed* is a portrait of themselves as screw-in bulbs) – but most of this current batch of factory productions depict the mating of an urban panorama with a foreground parade of figures that perform an entr'acte on a shallow stage. We have all witnessed such stale business in pantomime with the aid of projected slides and disco lights, but stilled in the hands of G&G, and given the air of permanence by usurping the claims and terminology of art, it is deprived even of that tawdry gaiety and is the tedious trifle overblown.

The sheer vanity of this Tweedle-Dum and Dee as they parade

on superhuman scale across their glistering wastes must repel even those who want to like their work, or at least admire their ingenuity. Their vast self-portrait heads suggest that they might, in portraiture, find employment in those states where the face of the dictator must always bear down on an oppressed populace – Iraq perhaps – for their stylistic idiom is close to the old official arts of Fascism and Communism. To the sane and reasonable man, however, the sight, yet again, of the scrotum, perineum, penis, arse and open mouth of Gilbert or George is enough to push him towards acceptance of the current Turner Prize insanities, for even fictional furniture is preferable to such public privities.

Evening Standard 1992

Eric Gill

For most of the thirty-five years of his working life Eric Gill was accepted as an oddity whose eccentricities were based on conviction – as indeed they were. He thought the Roman toga the ideal garment, but having often to climb ladders, he chose smocks for day wear and nightshirts for bed; he even wore smocks to Royal Academy banquets, and beneath them bloomers of red silk. He wrote a book on clothes in general, and another on trousers in particular, on the cover of which there is a reference to 'man's most precious ornament.'

His clothes may not quite have been an obsession, but his penis was. His father, a cleric, taught him that it was no more than an organ of drainage, but, as is the way of boys, he learned soon enough that it could be 'as enjoyable as it is useful', and went on to enjoy it to the end of his days and to the hilt, tumbling in rumbustious sex with his wife, his sisters, a mistress or two, and his three daughters – a diary note records his visit to one bedroom with 'stayed ½ hour – put p. in her ahole'.

Gill was once widely regarded as a great sculptor, a great draughtsman, a great print maker and a great man, thought by Roger Fry to be worthy of inclusion with the Post-Impressionists, by another critic to be the equal of Rodin and Maillol, and by himself to be the superior of Rodin and Matisse; a psychologist observed that he had a particularly strong phallic fixation, and only the psychologist was right. In the first retrospective exhibition of his work since his death in 1940 we have the chance to see if it deserves more praise than that of other Art Deco decorators, and himself some small niche in the pantheon of British art.

It is a depressing exercise. Gill once claimed that his inability to draw naturalistically had been his salvation. It enabled him to develop a series of formulae to solve all artistic problems, and his basic drawing techniques were easily adaptable to every highly stylised source of borrowings. Able only to develop style from style, he was attracted to European Romanesque and Gothic sculpture, and particularly to Indian art; from his friend Ananda Coomeraswamy, a Hindu expert, he learned that art had a sacred function and was not to be confused with usefulness, and that in India it does not reflect the personal inspiration of the individual, but the common inspiration of society; but Gill was also attracted by the sensual and sexual aspects of Indian art, and in the balance between the contemplative and physical natures that are twinned in man, and learned that in his own work he could bring together Christ's Crucifixion and his studies of his daughters in blatantly erotic poses, illustrating his belief that in joining the Catholic Church 'we are fucked by Christ'. He should have learned some honest and poetic delicacy from his Romanesque and Gothic sources.

Continence enforced by his wife's pregnancy in 1909 triggered his first erotic sculpture, and the following year he made for Roger Fry a pair of lovers too frankly pornographic to be placed where delicate sensibilities might see them. So dominant in Gill's work did the pornographic element become that in the very weeks before his reception into the Catholic church, he was busy polishing a marble phallus, and Fry feared that such frank and obvious interest might damage his reputation.

The German friend, Count Kessler, who published many of Gill's prints, was also disturbed by his obsession – once, when discussing illustrations to Virgil, Gill diverted him to an Indian manual commending thirty-four positions for sexual congress – but he put it down to erotic asceticism. Likening Gill to the early hermit saints was too kind – they did not line their lavatories with obscene drawings, illustrate *Lady Chatterley's Lover*, or seduce the local lady librarians into posing for drawings so extreme that even his most liberal friends found them impossible to stomach. The really distasteful aspect of all this is that Gill, incestuous adulterer, was rantingly illiberal towards the moral dilemmas of others, particularly homosexuals and those who supported birth control.

His political attitudes were no more logical – as a wet Fabian in his youth he embraced notions of family self-sufficiency, but when he graduated to Communism he could not recognise its conflict with his adopted Catholicism. Perhaps all his beliefs were no more than the irresponsible innocence of schoolboy enthusiasm; it was no doubt the schoolboy that had him photographing Epstein nude in the back garden, and it may well have been a late attack of penis envy that had him at the age of 42 wrestling naked on the lawn with the blond Irish giant Robert Gibbings.

Wyndham Lewis thought Gill 'obtrusive, eager and clumsy'; Michael Sadler, a most distinguished collector of Gill's work, thought him 'a fine draughtsman, a vain poseur, a tiresome writer'. Those who organised the current exhibition see him primarily as a saintly medieval craftsman only occasionally drawn towards the secular and frivolous, and very rarely diverted into subjects sexual. All is sweetness, worthiness and beautifulness (the clumsy word invented by Gill's mock-monastic community at Ditchling, where there were no vows of chastity), and the exhibition is thus fundamentally flawed – as one might expect when a woman curator is let loose on so obsessively male an artist.

This exhibition is bowdlerised by its organisers' refusal to recognise that side of Gill that must dismay the Mary Whitehouse faction, and Judith Collins, having done her feminist prating over nudes in the Tate Gallery, now neuters a sculptor who delighted in the nipple, the rima, the testicle and foreskin and all that lies between. If sexual obsession is the factor that nourishes an artist's imagination, then it is imprudent of the prudish art historian to suppress its manifestations; worse, it turns art history into a lie.

The emasculated Gill emerges as an immaculate craftsman, but often so mannered and contrived that much of his work is less art than stylish object, an elegant amusing thing to stand among the flowers just arranged by Constance Spry. Emotion is close-reined by the ever dominant style – Christ's side bleeds in an elegant parabola, crucified thieves stand as languid as spectators at a bathing party, no arrows pierce the perfect torso of Sebastian – all is simple swelling form and sinuous line.

Gill was not a Michelangelo of many masterpieces, but a small talent inflated by great skill; he nevertheless deserves his little niche in the pantheon, inscribed in dog Latin and occupied, not by his portrait bust, but by a polished phallus, of which puzzle posterity may make what it will.

Evening Standard 1992

Robert Gober

The Serpentine Gallery

IT IS A WRY COINCIDENCE THAT AT THE BARBIcan Art Gallery we are celebrating the art of the Swinging Sixties, the decade when we dreamed the American dream that everything there was bigger, brighter and better, but that at the Serpentine Gallery we have revealed to us the nightmare that American art has now become. With photography promoted as an art, we have had in the past few years the swirl of urine playing about a crucifix, the ejaculation of semen as Jackson Pollock up-to-date, Jeff Koons in coitus with La

Cicciolina (wife-cum-prostitute), and the extremes of homosexual paraphernalia and activity; now the Serpentine Gallery offers us wallpaper with scrawled images of penis, rima, buttock and anus, black on white for the rumpus room, and white on black for the intimacies of the master bedroom. Not since donkeys' years ago, when, supplementing my student grant, I worked as a night watchman in Covent Garden Market and as a supply teacher in a girls' school in Islington, have I seen such puerile rubbish, the graffiti in the lavatory of one and on the blackboard of the other.

The designer of this wallpaper is one Robert Gober, born in 1954, working in New York, of whom mercifully little was heard until eight years ago when the first review was written – and then began the swift and inexorable burgeoning of fame, the international bandwaggon harnessed to compliant critics and curators prepared to trumpet this latest manifestation of degraded 'popular' culture with its politically correct attributes of sex, sexuality and AIDS, race, pollution and ecology. The problem with art of this debased kind is that one must, in order to unlock its meaning, have the key, for this is work of no aesthetic value or consequence and is merely a puzzle to be solved; that key is to be found elsewhere.

Add to the sexual icons of the wallpaper the drainholes of the urinal and the sink, bags of cat litter, a giant cigar, ring doughnuts, a pair of buttocks cast in wax, upright candles and a wedding dress, and another wallpaper in which the repeated images are those of a white man sleeping on his belly and a black man hanging from a noose, and you have considerable evidence, not of artistry but of a disturbed mind, either troubled to the edge of lunacy or still cunning enough to exploit the current New York vogue for violence and filth.

This vogue extends to the theatre, where the ranting profanity of sexual politics reveals the dark desires that were once unspeakable, where excrement and menstruation are appropriate to rhetoric, where rape and savagery (both male and female) entertain a veteran audience, now shockproof. On the stage this obscene vocabulary is direct and beyond misunderstanding, but in the visual arts it is obscured by our absurd respect for the ecclesiastical atmosphere of galleries, overborne as we are by the false syllogism that as icons are found in churches, any building housing such images must be a church and be treated with awe and reverence, and then we advance to the third false notion – that everything in an art gallery must be art, and we thus expect of it a loftier meaning than is implied by the mere image. A tired old armchair loose-covered in cheap chintz, much washed, is fit only for the dog unless it is in a gallery – and there, as in the Serpentine, it is metamorphosed into a significant work of art. This temple of the arts, however, is dedicated to false gods, and its priests are charlatans.

At this point the bemused visitor, weary of wax and hirsute breasts and buttocks, may turn to the catalogue for exegesis. In this he will find the artist interviewed by the director of a commercial gallery in New York, and never was hysterical and sycophantic bilge maintained at such a length (no wonder that Gober makes so much of the urinal drain); as the script for comic parody of art jargon it is perfect – the interviewer's comment 'That piece is such a bag of groceries' sets the critical and intellectual tone (try saying it with an all-American whine). We then graduate to a long essay by an art historian devoted to promoting as work of high seriousness all the nonsense of contemporary art, from which those with the stamina to pursue it to its dreary and convoluted end may divine that Gober is a homosexual opposed to sexual stereotyping, and a lapsed Catholic scarred by the trauma of his upbringing under heterosexual and family values; he protests against the primacy of heterosexual bonding and its rituals, and in his attitude to work traditionally the preserve of women, he adopts the stance of rabid feminist.

If, however, we think that at last we have the key by which to understand Gober's images, we are in some cases undermined by his own uncertainty; of the hanged man wallpaper he said, 'I don't understand that . . . I've worked with it for years and it's still mysterious', and his giant cigar is both a penis and a turd (his word). The drainholes, symbols of ablution and of the common emptying of bladders that some men enjoy in public lavatories, are obstructed by a cross – a deliberate reference; the bags of cat litter are another lavatorial symbol; the ring doughnuts, contained in a paper bag inscribed 'Union Camp: made in America', are anal images. Gober's apologist assures us that all these and the graffiti wallpaper 'offer a paean to oral and anal appetites, an affirmation of sexuality's variousness . . . the antipode to . . . normative heterosexuality'.

Paean it may be, but is it art? Is it not rather the stuff of the analyst's couch and the confessional? I am as interested as any man in the effect that Renoir's driving heterosexuality had on his painting, or Michelangelo's repression had on his, or Munch, or Gauguin, Leonardo, Botticelli and a host of others of whose sexuality we know nothing or so little that it offers (where relevant) no enlightenment of imagery, but in the past these private forces were transmuted into works of art that dealt with universal and edifying abstractions. If Gober's spirit is troubled by his homosexuality to the extent that he thinks himself an artist with a cause, he must do better than wear a brassière and sew a wedding dress, do better than offer visual puns for turd and anal sphincter, do better than scribble on a lavatory wall. A case history illustrated for the prurient can scarcely be a work of art.

Evening Standard 1993

John Golding: *Visions of the Modern*

W HAT IN ART IS MODERN NOW? IT IS UNLI-kely that in the last decade of the Quattrocento, with the Italian Renaissance half done, educated Florentines still spoke in awe of Masaccio, Donatello and Fra Angelico as modern, yet in the last decade of this century, John Golding, distinguished art historian, curator of exhibitions and a painter of sorts, offers us as modern Picasso, Matisse, Braque, more Picasso, Duchamp, Gorky, Malevich, Brancusi and more Picasso still, all firmly rooted in the first decade. Readers hoping for a helping hand with Damien Hirst and Rachel Whiteread will find none offered here. Only with Frank Stella and himself does Golding venture into the present day – but Stella he treats exclusively as a fellow lecturer and writer, and of Golding the painter of flaccid abstracts of footnote inconsequence, we must ask how it is that, revealing so sharp an eye and such honest judgement in his discussion of the old masters of this century, he can be so blind to the poverty of his own paintings, daubs that seem merely the therapy of aesthetic masturbation for a man far better employed in intellectual pursuits.

For forty years Golding has steeped himself in the study of Picasso. The obsession began with his doctoral thesis on Cubism, and its present incarnation is the exhibition at the Tate Gallery; its rich fruit is a scholarly and intuitive knowledge not only of all the artists involved with Picasso – Braque, Léger, Gris et al – or with whom he was in rivalry – Matisse – but of the critics and apologists who offered him support, of Tzara, Breton, Eluard and Apollinaire. The first essay in the book is indeed on Apollinaire, the wise, witty and misguided mountebank and showman of Parisian criticism until his death in 1918, whom Golding accuses (amid much praise) of inventing 'the sort of pseudo-metaphysical jargon that is found all too frequently in writings about present day art'.

Golding cannot himself be accused of jargon; he writes with utter clarity, and only a scholar of transparent honesty could observe of Cubist pictures after a lifetime's work that 'I have come increasingly to realise that I do not really understand them, and I am not sure that anyone else does either', which tempts the sceptic to quote Sickert – 'Painting that requires literary explanation stands self-condemned. Here we have the condemnation of Matisse and Picasso, and even of most of Cézanne's canvases.' Golding may protest inadequacy, but his commentaries on the parallels between Braque and Picasso in their Cubist years, on the great *Demoiselles d'Avignon*, on the flowering of Gris and Léger, are passionate in their sympathy, and illuminate with such uncanny clarity that ordinary mortals may well feel that they at last understand, even if their mentor does not.

By far the longest essay is devoted to Duchamp, keyed to his mysterious, unfinished and shattered work on glass, *The Bride stripped bare by her Bachelors*, damaged in transit in 1926. Amid dense argument, Golding admits to unanswerable questions and a labyrinth of ideas from which no thread leads; 'there is no solution, because there is no problem,' claimed Duchamp – but there is a problem, and in failing to arrive at its solution, Golding surveys the whole work of the old mischief-maker, from Mr Mutt's upturned urinal to the almost posthumous *tableau mort* of the naked waxwork woman with her legs spread wide, seeing a cerebral kinship in the wild diversity of style.

Golding writes at a still slower pace and with emotion cooled when he treats of Gorky, Malevich and Brancusi, as though the material has been prepared for tutorials and has adapted uneasily into literary prose – even the death of Brancusi's beloved bitch brings scarcely a spark of life to that essay, and the plodding art historian swamps the connoisseur. Though they are not without merit, the inclusion of such lectures and reviews (if these are indeed what they are) blurs the focus of the book, and at the very end it is blurred still further by the vain inclusion of himself as painter, keeping company far too distinguished. Golding's eye is at its brightest and his pen most passionate when Picasso is his inspiration.

Financial Times 1994

Julio Gonzalez

FOR THE DISPLAY OF SCULPTURE THE WHITE-chapel Gallery is perhaps the most beautiful place in London. The visitor is scarcely aware of it as architecture, for it makes no formal statements, suggests no mathematical perfections, uses no conventional elements of structure and decoration, and (unlike the Tate Gallery's new Turner wing) is not a confusion of fashionable whimsies; instead, it provides a seemingly random sequence of spaces that open and close, or draw aside, lit in varying strengths, some directly, others by reflected light. Everywhere the walls are white, sharpening the silhouettes; everywhere the walls are suffused with light, and yet reflect it, so that the sense of volume in the sculpture is enhanced and even the most meagre form is seen as an element in space, charged with weight and movement. Such a seductive atmosphere lends easy significance to the insignificant.

Julio Gonzalez turned to sculpture in 1910, at the age of thirty-four. Born in Barcelona in 1876, he had in his youth attended evening classes at the School of Fine Art there while working as an apprentice to his goldsmith father during the day. Of the two disciplines, painting became the more important for him, and in 1900, by then the friend of young Picasso, he settled in Paris and soon began to exhibit in the conventional Salons that were the equivalents of the Royal Academy or the New English Art Club. In 1908 his brother Joan, who had also been apprenticed as a metal worker and was with him during these early years in Paris, died – a bitter loss that caused Julio to withdraw from the Parisian art world and made him a virtual recluse. In 1910, perhaps in reverence for his brother's skills and memory, he began to make masks in the traditional Catalan technique of beaten metal, delicate and decorative.

For many years he seems to have been unable to recognise his true vocation as a sculptor, and from time to time exhibited simultaneously as a derivative and uninventive painter and as a goldsmith-jeweller who made decorative objects. Even attaching himself to the Renault factory near Paris in 1918 to learn the skills of oxyacetylene welding did not immediately suggest a new single direction for his work, physical or aesthetic, and the skills were held more or less in abeyance for a decade while he continued to paint pictures and make decorative objects that were far from sculptural. He remained reclusive, his only known contacts Picasso and the Romanian sculptor Brancusi.

The change came in 1927, at the age of fifty. His psychological or aesthetic problems resolved (we know little of their nature, only of their effect), he abandoned both his painting and his decorative fripperies, and throwing himself wholeheartedly into work on sculpture, demonstrated an astonishing artistic maturity. Fewer than fifteen years remained before the heart attack that killed him in March 1942 (in occupied Paris), but in those years he changed the course of sculpture (not necessarily for the better) far more than did Henry Moore (who was essentially a traditionalist in techniques and aesthetic attitudes), and has had much more influence and many more imitators – Reg Butler (for those who recall *The Unknown Political Prisoner* furore), Anthony Caro, Graham Sutherland (not in sculpture, but in the forms developed in his paintings), and in the aggressive vulgarities of David Smith, an American who denies Gonzalez all his subtleties and merely makes large and leaden that which when small is witty and perceptive.

We should not perhaps be surprised that in 1927 Gonzalez turned to the work of Cubist painters for his imagery and inspiration, for the current exhibition at the Tate Gallery is at pains to demonstrate how the art of the first decade or so of this century provided a classic base for the art of the Twenties and Thirties; there is too the point that his intellectual development was gravely interrupted in 1908, just when Cubism was at its most exciting and innovative, thrusting from an African past into a European future, and to Gonzalez it may have seemed logical to return to such a turbulent moment in the history of art and pursue his own course of development from it. Within a year Picasso and Gonzalez were collaborating in sculpture, and though this collaboration is perceived by some as stemming from Picasso's technical dependence on Gonzalez in the translation of his line drawings into three-dimensional constructions, it seems to me that after each had briefly influenced the other, Gonzalez moved swiftly into independent explorations of form, line and movement that were far removed from the mischievous surrealism of his more celebrated countryman.

Gonzalez's technical innovation was his use of iron: 'Today the way is clear for this material to be forged and hammered by the peaceful hands of the artist . . .' he proclaimed, '. . . no longer is it a murderer or the mere instrument of mechanical science.' His handling of the crude material was thus a symbol of swords into ploughshares, and he compelled the sheets and rods of iron, rough, rusty and welded, into extraordinarily refined and elegant forms that he conceived as drawings in space, developing the notion that space itself was a material 'found' by the sculptor. There was no consistent progress: Cubist masks and compositions, surreal linear skeletons (often more than slightly humorous), heavy figures constructed in heavy box-sections, and sensual torsos hammered from thin sheet metal, fractured as though a survival from Greek antiquity, tumbled in disorder from his imagination. Some were severely intellectual, some were pitched only at an aesthetic response, some were frivolous – though so flattering is the light in the Gallery that we risk taking them all to be objects of the same high seriousness.

Among so much that is imbued with the Thirties spirit of Picasso and Miro, his occasional realism is startlingly old-fashioned. His *Montserrat*, the grieving, screaming, hounded woman who was his symbol of the sufferings of the Spanish Civil War, was in some of its forms akin to Barlach, Kollwitz, Meunier and others who had more than a generation earlier concerned themselves with images of oppression, and some of his variations were indeed reversions to his own work soon after his arrival in Paris. In taking his late work out of the context of his whole activity, this exhibition, though beautifully presented, is misleading – but then it seems now to be the nature and purpose of art historians to distort the history of art in order to promote a particular argument.

Evening Standard 1990

Arshile Gorky

ARMENIA, THE OLDEST OF CHRISTIAN COUN-tries, was once a land where art and architecture flourished. It was, like Britain, a far outpost of the Roman Empire, but, unlike this country, did not sink into a dark age with that Empire's retrenchment, division and fall. In north eastern Turkey, and across the border in Russia, are the remains of great churches and monasteries, architectural marvels, mathematically ingenious; in some the paintings that decorated their walls still survive, despite the attempts of Muslims to wreck and ravage, and their ghosts find definition on a smaller scale in manuscripts and miniatures.

The heritage of a great nation a thousand years ago and more laid down patterns that were still current in Armenia in the late 19th century; Christian communities then rich enough to build new churches did so on ground plans and with ornamentation that, at first glance, pass for something built a millennium before; any child with burgeoning talent as an artist turned for his education to the painted images and gingerbread sculpture with which churches were decorated – there were no schools in which to learn the art of easel painting.

Arshile Gorky, who is now perceived to be the last Surrealist and the first Abstract Expressionist, was born in Armenia in 1904, in a village near the city of Van. We do not know to which churches he had access, for many have been destroyed in the course of this century, but on the nearby island of Akhtamar is a substantial example of an ancient church with fine wall paintings and carvings that he could have known. His letters demonstrate how powerful were his childhood recollections, and how much being an Armenian meant to him – 'I respond to modern life as an Armenian from Van. Man cannot escape the sensibility of his time . . .' he wrote from exile in America, and I am convinced that his sensibility was conditioned, if not by the church on Akhtamar, then by the smaller village churches in the neighbourhood, of which some seven ruins survive in the hills near Van.

The traditional images are frontal and hieratic. In painting the proportions are elongated, but in sculpture they are stunted; faces in both are oval, the eyes large, unfocused and deep socketed; what sense of volume there may be is implied by line, and the sculpture is in low relief. These were the formulae that little Gorky carried with him when his family fled in 1915 into the Russian borderland to the north east – he was fortunate, for chance could so easily have sent him on the genocidal marches that decimated the Armenians when the Turks drove them south to die either en route or in the desert near Aleppo. The appalling events that were in some measure the experience of all Armenians during the First World War formed Gorky's mind, larding the ancient images with overwhelming melancholy.

Gorky escaped to America in 1920. He lived first in Boston, and then moved to Providence, Rhode Island, where he began to study art. In 1925, a painter of sorts, he was given a minor teaching job in New York and settled there.

America was hardly the place for a would-be painter between the wars – Paris was pre-eminent, and even London was an intellec- tually livelier place until New York was given its chance by the Second World War – and Gorky was neither well taught in the technical sense, nor exposed to traditions and stimuli that could convert him from a provincial fumbler into a metropolitan genius. He became a mere imitator. As Cézanne was in high fashion, Gorky clumsily and tentatively tried his brushwork and colour without understanding the purpose of either. When he became aware of Picasso's decorative abstractions of still life, reduced to flat patterns, these too he mimicked. In Picasso's large, heavy, semi–classical faces he recognised a character that recalled the sculpture of Armenia, and his response was powerful and emotional – but he broke no new ground. When Picasso developed a mannerism of cool tones and heavy intersecting lines, jagged, triangular, and unrewarding to the point of emptiness, Gorky did so too.

The Picasso paths exhausted, Gorky turned to Miro for mentor, and produced jazzy imitations that lack any merit. He became a Surrealist, though only in the most debilitated sense, and fell under the influence of Matta, a tag end member of that exhausted group. What little originality there is in Gorky's work is in the paintings of the mid-Forties when his landscape abstractions struck an authentic personal note, but had his scribbles and drips not been adopted with enthusiasm by American painters and noisily promoted as Abstract Expressionism, these paintings would now seem as negligible as all the others.

One painting only is worth a second glance, for it tells all – the portrait of himself as a small boy in his best coat, standing beside his mother. Both figures are full frontal, hieratic, the still pose of the photograph translated into an almost religious image; through a series of competent drawings the proportions grew stunted; the heads too hark back to Armenia, but are akin to Picasso, from whose early paintings the soft pale colour comes. Unfinished, it is abundantly clear that though Gorky could draw, he did not know how to handle paint and could not make it work his purpose – no wonder that he eventually abandoned such monumental subjects and took to merely scribbling with the brush.

Gorky had little skill, and nothing in America between the wars could encourage a creative intelligence in him – he was left with little more than melancholy longing, unfulfilled. Had he emigrated to Paris in 1920, the story might have been very different – but as it is, this exhibition reveals only a minor painter in whose faults even more incompetent painters could see only virtue. Willy-nilly, Gorky led the American barbarians into the futile narcissistic nonsense of Abstract Expressionism. In July 1948 he committed suicide.

Evening Standard 1990

John Heartfield

JOHN HEARTFIELD IS A MAN OF SHADOWY REPU-
tation in this country. Born in Berlin in 1891, and christened Helmut Herzfeld, he belongs to that generation of Germans whose work as painters, sculptors and innovative photographers was of scant concern to the British after the bruising experience of the First

World War. Even as a political refugee here, fleeing from the Nazis in 1938, he was interned as an enemy alien, in spite of his obviously anti-Nazi work published in *Picture Post*, *Lilliput* and *Reynolds News*; and in 1950, when he returned to East Germany, we forgot him.

There was a brief reminder of his existence and his work in the Royal Academy's exhibition of German Art seven years ago, but that was only in the context of the political paintings of George Grosz in the 1920s. To my surprise, he was not included in the RA's vast survey exhibition, *The Art of Photography*, in 1989 – yet his standing as an artist lies, not in painting (he destroyed all his pictures in 1915, and, as far as I know, painted no more), but in his manipulation of photography. He was the inventor, during the Great War, of the photomontage – the technique of cutting and wedding into unlikely combinations the images of several photographs (from *montagieren* – to assemble, erect or fit – an engineering term).

At first this was yet another expression of his opposition to the war – he had faked a nervous breakdown to secure his release from the army in 1915, and had bravely (rashly?) anglicised his name to John Heartfield the following year – but as his skill with scissors, paste and retouching increased, it became an end in itself, at least as important to him as the image, and he could claim that 'new political problems demand new means of propaganda; for this task photography possesses the greatest power of persuasion.' It was, alas, to develop into imagery often so complex and so burdened with layers of allusion that the photomontage became the *Lesebild*, the picture that must be read like a newspaper article, not merely seen. The titles were largely unambiguous, but the pictures were not, and as in many cases Heartfield introduced elements of humour, mockery, contempt and amusing paradox, his comments on the horrors to which he drew attention were occasionally confused and now seem little more than clever derision – even Hitler emerges more clown than monster.

I find it impossible to accept the current German view that Heartfield is 'one of the great figures in the history of German art . . .' Scissors and paste are poor tools compared with brush and palette, and the momentary impact of an ingeniously faked photograph is no match for the lasting profundities of paintings by Beckmann, Grosz and Dix. As a political cartoonist Heartfield is of the calibre of Gillray and Daumier, but like their political comments, his extend no further than the immediate subject and have in them nothing that stimulates an imaginative, aesthetic or sensual response (he is no Forain). His pictures are to be read as political polemics, the better for being furiously argued and touched with old-fashioned rhetoric; they emerged from his experience as a leading member of the Dada movement in Berlin, but, conditioned by his parallel experience as a commercial artist and illustrator, he has eliminated from them all the anarchic confusion and childish whimsy of Dada, and they are direct political weapons, as appealing and intelligible to the Communist labourer in field or factory as to the Marxist intellectual – indeed they played their part as a Communist Bible of the Poor; Heartfield joined the German Communist Party in 1918, and was still a member at his death in East Berlin in 1968.

The current exhibition at the Barbican begins with an attempted, but unconvincing (indeed nasty) reconstruction of the First International Dada Fair in Berlin in 1920, that does little to establish the ambience from which Heartfield developed, and the rest of it is a succession of clever ideas and images that only weary the visitor with their constant striving for the same effects. The strength of his emotion is expressed time and again with the same ingenuities, and this too is wearisome, making the point that he was less an artist than a cartoonist, of whom the straitjacket of sameness is always expected. I quite see why, in the memorial speech at his funeral, he was described as 'a wise man and a child, an awful hair-splitting pedant and a very successful artist' – even the devoted East German Communists had their reservations and could not lavish unalloyed praise on him as his coffin was lowered to its grave.

On the Barbican's upper floor can be found some recent British (more or less) successors to Heartfield, though none comes as near claiming his crown as did the absent inventors of Monty Python; the title here is *The Cutting Edge*, but *Blunt Instrument* would suit it better. Apart from Leonardo da Vinci's *Last Supper* turned into a splendid Dada tableau by Spitting Image, with Margaret Thatcher as Christ and Conservative panjandrums as Apostles (eleven only – not even Luck and Flaw could risk identifying Judas among her many minions), the material is too familiar, too leaden, too pretentious, too ordinary, too obscure, too politically correct, or imitates Heartfield too closely to bear the damaging comparison.

The cartoon is a surprisingly fragile and fugitive thing, its wit easily broken by too heavy a hand or too much pretence to art. Karen Knorr, for example, contrives her witless comments in large cibachromes so leaden in effect that we neither know nor care what influence she seeks to have on our opinions; and Art and Language, a pair of pamphleteers in their late forties, are so pretentiously obscure as to be silly – I defy anyone to understand them (if indeed there is anything to understand). Steadman and Scarfe distort, as they have done for many years, and Trog and others of more modest skill stay close to the traditions laid down a century ago and more in *Punch*. With many it is easy to miss the point; one of the exhibits in the Fanny Adams section is a gold box containing chocolate buttons for dogs, a present, it seems, sent to all art critics last Christmas – but I saw in mine, not heavy irony, but the kind thought of some *Evening Standard* reader who recalled my rescued dogs. Now that I know my error, I still do not understand the point. But why is (or are) Fanny Adams in the exhibition? As a band of marauding feminists peddling nonsense to our amused disdain, they must surely be subject to the cartoonist's cutting edge, and not themselves cartoonists grinding an axe?

These two exhibitions demonstrate that cartoons and caricatures are achieved, not by art, but by trick and convention, mannerism and technique; if too complicated or obscure in allusion or imagery, the point escapes us; and if too narrow in their concerns (as in feminist protest) they become the creatures of bigotry and cant. Their humour, irony and rhetoric exhausted in a moment, caricatures have no lasting quality and do not exhibit well; what is acceptable in a newspaper week by week, or even day by day, is unbearably tedious in concentrated quantity.

Evening Standard 1992

Roger Hilton and Julian Opie

THE HAYWARD GALLERY, A FLAGSHIP FLOATING on Arts Council funds, has this year scarcely left its moorings. In January it was awash with the ballast that now masquerades as sculpture; in April, the corpse of Georgia O'Keeffe was brought on board, her coffin packed with studio sweepings; in July, Australian Aborigines ranting of feminism and ethnicity besieged the decks with bedspread souvenirs to sell to the guilty middle classes; and now, the despond of winter deep upon us, this Titanic sinks, weighed down with the trivia of a Sixties never-man and a maybe Nineties boy.

The Sixties never-man is Roger Hilton, one of the several then middle-aged inadequates to steer British art into second-hand abstraction – Heron, Frost, Heath and Scott his fellows. Born in 1911, he settled in Paris in 1931, after two unhappy years at the Slade School, and with an allowance of £3.00 a week, he had enough for lodging, food and frequent dalliance there, and attended independent art schools. Throughout the Thirties his life was one of peripatetic confusion and professional insecurity, exhibiting a little, returning to the Slade to obtain teaching qualifications, teaching a little, returning to Paris several times in his attempt to fit the operatic stereotype of the penniless painter in his attic, sharing flats and studios with half-a-dozen different friends and relatives, and in the months before the war broke out in September 1939, packing bread for the Aerated Bread Company (then the most disgusting bread in Britain).

The war rescued him from the desperation of this doldrum.

What little work survives from the Thirties is embarrassingly feeble and proves that for all his Parisian experience Hilton was quite unformed as a painter. It is always asserted that he was a pupil of Roger Bissière and much influenced by him, but I have a Bissière of 1934 under my nose at this very moment – an accomplished synthesis of Corot, Cézanne and Matisse to which Hilton's wretched little figure paintings bear not the smallest resemblance. His status as a serious student of French painting was not established until after the war (in which, as a Commando in Norway and at Dieppe, he was something of a hero), when periods in Paris were interspersed with teaching, attendance at the Central School (at the age of 34), and as many unsettling peripatetics as before. For years his work indiscriminately reflected the brief influence of any painter, great or small, catching his attention – Picasso, Gear, Braque, Bazaine, Manessier and Poliakoff (all of whom ought to have been represented in this shoddy show) – all re-hashed without sensibility or understanding. In 1952, Constant, the leading Dutch member of the wild and woolly COBRA group, introduced him to the cool grid-like abstractions of Mondrian – and suddenly the path away from his messy little figurative pictures and inept abstract confusions was opened to him, and he could camouflage his haplessness with theory and the jargon that justifies the junk of many modern painters.

'I have moved away from . . . painting where lines and colours are flying about in an illusory space; from pictures which still had depth . . . or space in them; from spatial pictures . . . to space-creating pictures. The effect is to be felt outside rather than inside the picture; the picture is not primarily an image, but a space-creating mechanism.' What twaddle – and what further twaddle it generates in critics even now: 'The greatness of Hilton's paintings in the late 1950s consists in its dynamic containment of the energies of contradiction,' proclaims an introductory essay in the exhibition catalogue but – the only contradiction is between the artist's absurd assertion and the critic's contrary interpretation.

What are these 'great' paintings? After smashing the grids of

Mondrian and distorting his rectangles of red, yellow and blue into random shapes, he turned to large patches of dulled colour pleasantly related in tone – ochre and a greying black, a thin purplish brown on grubby white – enlivened with crude charcoal scribbles that give the lie to all his space-creating clap-trap, for though infantile in effect, they are distinctly sexual in imagery and intention, and assert the primacy of the scrawled figure over unresolved abstraction. His *Once upon a Time* is nothing but a naughty schoolboy's realisation of an upturned woman reduced to buttocks and a rima (most emphatic, unmistakeable), and then, throughout the Sixties, the whole woman, caricatured with flying breasts and ample buttocks, dominates the clumsy abstract patches. The paint is painterly, but rough and slapdash; the compositions are haphazard and the claim that they are space-creating mechanisms laughable; and the drawing, crude and contemptible, is the mere purging of a mind dreadfully damaged by the alcohol that killed him in 1975 and feverish with sexual need. The kinship with David Hockney's work when he was a student at the Royal College is inescapable – and it is worth recalling that Hockney claims to have been aware of Hilton as early as 1957, and to have tried his hand at the older man's abstraction 'for a while, and then I couldn't. It was too barren for me.' Perhaps Hilton later came to mimic Hockney.

It is indeed barren, and pretentious to boot, his declaration that he is 'a seeker after truth' attempting 'to come nearer to the essence of painting' quite absurd, unless, of course, by truth he meant not some aesthetic mystery, but the expression of his personal truths, sex and violent drunkenness. But elsewhere in the Gallery, in most uncomfortable and unconnected contrast, the work of Julian Opie makes Hilton assume the character of old master. Born in 1958, he is not yet an artist of sufficient weight to merit a retrospective exhibition, but for any recent graduate of Goldsmiths' School, such privileges are now inevitable. The work ranges from a funeral pyre of copies after Picasso and his historic ilk, to bleak cubicles that have the high gloss of technology about them, but lack all function, with mechanical paintings of empty motorways that could be mistaken for printed reproductions, models of forts and sandcastles worthy of Harrods' toy department, and out-dated exercises in the humour of Marcel Duchamp — who, I must remind you, said 'I threw the urinal in their faces, and now they admire it for its aesthetic beauty'.

Nothing in any of this extends the boundaries of art (I raise the point because this exhibition makes Opie eligible for the Turner Prize next year); indeed, if art at all, it is the stuff of stale borrowing without giving in return, and of shallow irony, close to commercial art and things seen on computer screens — no wonder we look back to the Sixties as a Golden Age.

Evening Standard 1993

Damien Hirst

Of ALL THE YOUNG ARTISTS NOW CELEBRATED by British dealers, critics and curators, Damien Hirst is far and away the most notorious and, most mocked by the tabloid press, most mystifying to the broadsheets, is both famous and infamous far beyond the purlieus of the London art market, well known to all who enjoy the gossip engendered by professional personalities; though perhaps not quite the equal of Madonna and the Princess Di, he is not far behind in public curiosity. Among his peers, he is, at thirty, the Michelangelo of his day, sculptor, painter, draughtsman, cod-philosopher, polymath and polyhistor, a man of such and so many ingenious ideas that he must run a Renaissance workshop to achieve them, with assistants to construct steel cages, cut sheets of armoured glass, drain blood from slaughtered animals, freeze, unfreeze and cleave their corpses, and, in breathing apparatus and protective rubber clothing, wade in tanks of formaldehyde, for these are the constituents of his most famous works of art — no action painter of the Fifties ever provided so much activity and entertainment. Young Hirst it was who sold Charles Saatchi,

Britain's Maecenas of these modern arts, a tiger shark, a shoal of lesser fish, sheep's heads, the internal organs of eight cows, and a whole lamb, all suspended in formaldehyde.

Not a man of any serious education – indeed, as a schoolboy he acquired the truant's skills of shoplifting and burglary, and achieved only the grade of E in art (he could sink no lower and still pass), and as a man he laboured and boozed in equal measure on London building sites before gaining entry to Goldsmiths' College, the most liberal of art schools, there to scarcely qualify – he is the product of a system that requires nothing of the artist other than the need and the ability to express his personality with the energy of an actor or performer. Saatchi, in converting a factory into an art gallery, showed student artists space on a scale that had never been available before, and in his advertising practice taught them the mentality of marketing. In Goldsmiths,' Duchamp, Dada and Surrealism, Minimalism and Conceptualism were the subjects of re-examination, and tutors there gave students the sense that they could do anything, and that everything was acceptable as art. These factors, combined with an insatiable demand in the marketplace for the young, the new, the innovative, meant that many art students grew from puberty to manhood with the public gaze upon them, dealers and critics vying to be first in their discovery. As a consequence, successful students learned that the traditional skills of painting, drawing, carving and modelling are of far less use to them than a sophisticated use of fashionable art idioms, no matter how hackneyed, and the knowing insincerity that seduces the witless art critic and curator.

When, under the influence of American Abject Art, British students concerned themselves with the fluids, emissions and waste products of the human body, Hirst did a little lateral thinking and declared himself obsessed with death, art his means of coming to terms with it. Serial murder fascinated him, and of Jeffrey Dahmer, whose biography was long his bedside book, he observed without the slightest frisson of distaste, '. . . he has a kind of terrible curiosity to find how living things work, by taking them to pieces', and that is precisely what Hirst did in caging thousands of bluebottles and butterflies, the first with the rotting head of a cow for sustenance, the second with sponges of synthetic nectar, to go about their businesses of living, feeding, breeding and dying. He claims to give spectators access to their nightmare fears, and indeed, whether it be with shark or blowfly maggot, he succeeds in touching on aversions and revulsions, if not terrors, that affect us all – but is this art, and not an old-fashioned freak show of sorts, Madame Tussaud's Chamber of Horrors brought into the present day? Is it enough to present, dead or alive, with not the smallest aesthetic intervention, the creature that induces fear? Is this not the purpose of a natural history museum rather than an art gallery? But here, of course, we encounter the contemporary artist's greatest boon and blessing – the critics' claim that anything and everything is art, provided that an artist has declared it so, and now that art galleries have become the new cathedrals of belief and genuflexion, mere presence within their walls is enough to turn things quite preposterous into icons thaumaturgical.

It is easy to dismiss Hirst, now famous as a wild and heavy drinker, nocturnal clubman, man-about-town in the stews of London and Berlin, as no more than a self-publicist, an outrageous prankster deliberately challenging and demanding, as did Hockney with his homosexual boys, a liberal response, but this is only true in part. There is no doubt that Hirst's way of life and art is intended to affront, and as with Duchamp's upturned urinal basin in 1917, those who accept it as art are damned as dupes, and those who object are damned as reactionary fogeys; those of us who, Buddhist in spirit, feel that the use and abuse of living creatures or corpses from a slaughter-house are unjustifiable and unacceptable extensions of the boundaries of experience, and in no sense art, are treated with amused contempt. Evidence that Hirst was once more than mere prankster, however, lies in the works exhibited at the Institute of Contemporary Arts in London in the winter of 1991, when he was only twenty-six, for in these he seemed to abandon all wish to shock, and chose instead to make a profoundly pessimistic comment on some of the world's ills. These were large black steel and glass cases that suggested bleak laboratories, life support machines and prison cells, with the instruments of both torture and medical survival sharing a cold hygienic kinship, the absence of the prisoner-patient a metaphor for death particularly telling four years on in the half-centenary of our discovering Auschwitz, Dachau, Belsen and a dozen other monuments to the extremes of inhumanity.

The inherited references are clear – to Warhol's electric chair, to the rooms devised by Kienholz, and to the cages in which Bacon trapped his popes and senators, but in these three-dimensional constructions all is order, proportion, placing, precision, each line and interval telling on the next as though to move anything by one half inch would slacken the tension and ease the clinical hostility; horrifying compulsions are implied with elegant precision and economy.

Hirst has not sustained this level of achievement. In his formaldehyde conceits he found one answer to every problem and repeated it, instead of searching for a different answer every time, and one of his most supportive critics sees in them the 'defeat of metaphor . . . they take you to the thing. The thing is the thing is the thing.'

In this he risks not only repetition but self-plagiarism and descent into the quirks of style as old ideas grow stale – just as third-rate Renaissance artists hacked their many variations of one successful image of the Virgin and her Child. It may be that Hirst has devised and done all that he can, and that with the fierce blaze of original ideas extinct, he is wise to turn his lively but undisciplined intelligence to television advertising and settings for the stage. We may well have seen the last of Damien Hirst as a serious conceptual artist; we may soon see the last of him as a fairground barker whipping us to wonder at his freaks; for the new Hirst it will perhaps be enough to be Hirst, the flamboyant personality with the damp, limp handshake, the ebullient nocturnal talker with a felicitous command of parody and Puckish mischief, ripe for television game shows and the chatty host. This will be Hirst in formaldehyde – Hirst the thing and nothing more.

Vanity Fair 1995

Howard Hodgkin

The Anthony d'Offay Gallery

THE POSTSCRIPT TO THE CATALOGUE OF Howard Hodgkin's most recent work is the record of a conversation with one Antony Peattie, who puts the question, 'I was wondering if you would talk about genres?' To such an infelicitous abuse of tenses the reply, quite properly, is 'No.' HH (as he is dubbed in all such material) has been much interviewed of late; by Edward Lucie-Smith, who confessed in his transcript that he was sent away with a flea in his ear – 'I don't really know what you are talking about'; by John McEwen, with whom HH sat in contemplative silence; and by Tom Lubbock, who was reduced to describing the painter's studio and quoting Wagner; and I have no doubt that there may well be kindred adulatory witterings on *Kaleidoscope, The Late Show* and *The South Bank Show.*

I have not interviewed HH; I doubt if he would let me cross his threshold, let alone interrogate him, for I have consistently likened his little pictures to the ghastly painted tea-trays produced in Roger Fry's Omega Workshops (thus pleasing the late, great Peter Fuller) – but I have no wish to do so; for me, as a critic, it is more important to stay detached from painters, to be under none of the obligations of friendship and social commerce, and let their paintings do (or not do) the work of communication and exchange. Dismissing criticism, HH complains that 'nobody seems to be able to respond to art without a gush of words', and I'd be happy to oblige him with omission from this paper were he not recognised by so many compliant critics and curators as one of the nation's great painters and a panjandrum of sorts (a knight of the realm, a trustee of this and that, a winner of the Turner Prize, a D. Litt. and a committee man). To ignore a worthy of such Establishment stature would be quite remiss and would surely displease his dealer.

Alas, neither of us has anything new to say – he as a painter offers the mixture as before, and I as a critic have the same responses to it.

In 1985 I wrote, 'Take a long hard look at a Hodgkin, and what do you find? A piece of timber, grainy, cracked, unprimed, forms the base, perhaps establishing a tone or texture, or even the subject. It may be framed, and the frame may be painted as part of it, performing several functions – extending it, restraining it, giving it a third dimension, establishing its picture plane – part decorative, part structural. Whatever the case, framed or not, Hodgkin will surround the subjects with bands of colour and texture, reducing it to a tiny patch in the centre . . . Painting is now all a matter of "marks". Hodgkin doesn't paint brushstrokes [but, of course, he does], he makes marks. If he likes one mark, he'll make another, perhaps on several panels. He keeps a batch of pictures under development at the same time over a period of years, waiting for their compositions somehow subconsciously to resolve themselves into finished paintings . . .'

In 1993 I can do no better, and nor can HH – indeed he does worse, for his larger pictures falter in their indecisive dabbling, and lack both the decorative immediacy and the hope of the Turner effects that from time to time redeem the small, and the brash small now offend, their palette matched to the vulgar summer clothing of the Costa Brava, in orange, acid green and beachboy blue. His handling of paint, once always swift and deft, is now occasionally leaden, lifeless and opaque, even repellent, rousing the stomach to objection. His dependence on the leopard's-spot effect is too much repeated – 'Oh, that's a dull patch', I hear him say in some imaginary conversation with the battered panel, and dab, dab, dab go on the blobs of colour, as though he were designing rainwear for the common prostitute; it is an effect (all Hodgkin's work is a matter of effect) exploited more timorously by Ben Nicholson, from whom, I imagine, HH took the idea, just as he took so much of his brushstroke sweep and pattern-making from old Ivon Hitchens. Like Nicholson, he declares that he wants us to look at his pictures as 'things', but goes further, likening them to pieces of furniture with different functions; why then should he so object when I see in them the lurking tea-tray?

I cannot blame HH for believing that he is important, for two decades of sycophancy from critics and curators must have a corrupting effect on even the most saintly soul, and at the age of forty or so, his need of flatulent reassurance must have been desperate when at last, after decades of fumbling and bumbling in the wilderness, he hit upon an easy formula of borrowed ciphers striving for effect that with twenty years of practice has become his own empty thing of mannerism and deft gesture. At sixty, HH is no more than a vain conjuror of time-worn tricks.

Evening Standard 1993

Rebecca Horn and William Heath Robinson

THE TERM 'HEATH ROBINSON' MAY NOT YET BE in the Oxford Dictionary, but it has for at least half a century been English usage as a definition of unwieldy and unreliable contraptions in the house, of incompetent repairs to motor cars, and of any machine or installation subject to hiccup, spasm, breakdown, fit and tantrum, or of cat's cradle confusion and exceeding ingenuity. William Heath Robinson, who died fifty years ago this month, is to plumbers, electricians and mechanics what Priapus (the divine runt in a permanent state of sexual arousal) is to gardeners – the household god – and his name and image should be inscribed over the door of every would-be handyman, and laid in gold leaf like a Latin motto on the Ford Transit vans of British Telecom.

Among the welter of pedal-powered machines for peeling potatoes, bathing babies and putting out the cat without rising from one's feather bed, we have perhaps forgotten that William was no mean painter in watercolour, often an exquisite draughtsman, and an illustrator the equal of Rackham and Dulac in fantasy and skill. Art of this kind ran in his blood, his grandfather a wood engraver, his father and uncle leading draughtsmen for *The Penny Illustrated* and *The Illustrated London News*, and his two older brothers, Thomas and Charles, were accomplished illustrators and artists as able as their brother, but without his bent for humour and absurdity.

All three brothers went to art schools, not with their heads full of greenery-yallery art-for-art's-sake Bohemian nonsense, but with the business of responsibility to commissions, deadlines and printing technology firmly dinned into them. William, briefly, as a student at the RA Schools, had ambitions as a landscape painter, but these were abandoned for the less well paid but more secure work of illustration. In 1896, at the age of 24, he began to earn his living with work for periodicals and children's magazines, and a year later illustrated the first of many books, among them classics by Shakespeare, Cervantes, Kingsley, Kipling, Poe and Andersen; in 1906 his *Gentle Art of Catching Things* established him as a comic artist, and the mechanical inventions and ideas began in 1909.

Gradually, and inevitably, the humorous work obscured his reputation as the serious illustrator, a man who made books rich, rare and beautiful, and his commissions came more and more from those who dubbed him 'The Gadget King' and saw him only as a mad inventor. The landscape ambitions of the youth were quite forgotten by the funny 'How to . . .' man – 'How to be a Motorist,' 'How to be a Perfect Husband,' 'How to live in a Flat,' et al, et al.

Perhaps it was as well that gadgetry usurped the landscapes, for painters of Devon valleys and the Norfolk coast were legion, and William would have been but one of quite indistinguishable thousands sending them to the RA each summer. In gadgetry he was unique. In art he was a creature of his time, his styles, mannerisms, tricks and formulae those of Brangwyn, Rackham, Greenaway, Conder, Nicholson, May and Sheringham, with occasional hints that he was aware of Dürer, and his pictorial devices were those of Art Nouveau and, eventually, Art Deco.

His mad machines were addressed to adults with an adolescent streak, their humour largely wry, gentle, and of scant appeal to children even in his day, seeming simply foolish to their clear-eyed and uncluttered minds, Gordian Knots to pubescent Alexanders; to contemporary children, nurtured on electronic mysteries, his contraptions are beyond comprehension and his innocent humour as bland as tapioca – only a machine for boiling babies to make mock turtle soup, or some obscenity for fitting condoms after foreplay might crease a smile into their faces, so low has humour sunk. The adult audience now for the plodding ingenuity of his contraptions must be very small indeed – starved readers of *Punch*, *Health and Efficiency*, Richard Crompton's *William* books and *The Oldie* perhaps, who'd be glad of gadgets to collect their pensions, swap their socks and re-charge their pacemakers.

By chance, the Tate and Serpentine Galleries are soon to open a joint exhibition of Heath Robinson's most celebrated imitator, Rebecca Horn, born, again by chance, in 1944, the year of her master's death. She makes films that recall the work of Buñuel, and is concerned too with photography and performance art, but claims with her mad machines to be a sculptress. Driven by electric motors, controlled by clocks and clicking switches, her inventions turn her exhibitions into noisy places loud with thumps, bangs, creaks, groans and other interruptions to the contemplative state, and the upside-down piano suspended from the ceiling, its keyboard cover opening with a crash, its keys reaching on wires like prehensile tendrils before retracting with wheeze and twang, is the most triumphant of alarms to the spectator.

The anarchic concert extends to violins that play themselves, a number of them arranged from floor to ceiling as though performing some Walt Disney drama, not for a sorcerer's apprentice but for some apotheotic *Himmelfahrt* (Miss Horn is German), to sheets of music fluttering, to photographs of cellists, and even to a pair of shoes tapping waltztime on the polished floor. She gives such things inconsequential titles, sometimes brief, sometimes as mystifying and perverse as those beloved by Damien Hirst, and has recently described them as the 'mechanistic and organic symbolization which is impenetrable to understanding, though perfectly intelligible to poetic intuition and emotion'. It seems then that we should not attempt to understand her work, but merely hope that, in spite of the disturbing background of inherant noise, intuition will perform its interpretive task.

Miss Horn offers a few clues in her recorded utterances. She is, it seems, intrigued by bondage and other elements of sadism, by sexual fantasy and the elaborate narrative often required to support it. She has fantasies of loving and wounding, and sees her contraptions as 'desiring machines' and 'wounding machines' (do not, under any circumstances, stand beneath the grand piano – the wounding would be mortal); the intersections of pain and pleasure, attraction and revulsion, are essential, expressed in common fetishes, inspired by 'the essentiality of the erotic will'. To her machines she attributes 'the fetishism implicit in the archetype of the nude'.

Once aware that eroticism, the fetish and the nude inform her images, it is easy to recognise her references to these essentials. Skewbald shoes entitled *Havanna Joe*, slowly filling with saffron pigment, must be a symbol of the sexual commerce of the pimp, though a trifle confused, for the shoe has for centuries been a symbol of the female genitals; *The Nurses*, a play of starched caps and binoculars, must be a reference to the sexual excitement of those male patients who take pleasure in female domination; and *Brush Kiss* is an hilarious caricature of Hollywood big screen passion. In this last, operated by a curiously cut cam, a shaving brush and a large oval dandruff brush perform an action that suggests an extravagant intake of breath before falling into a kissing clinch – except that the imagery is not of the mouth (the oval brush is upright), but phallic, pubic and vaginal. This Heath Robinson exercise in pornographic symbolism is very funny, but I see in it nothing but naughtiness and engineering, not art, and think the repeated humour of it might wear very thin within a week. Aesthetically Miss Horn's machines are no more significant than Hornby trains and cuckoo clocks, and, less art than automata, they ought perhaps to be installed in public places to amuse the witless tourist who waits for Fortnum's clock to strike the midday hour. Her fingernail and feather fantasies are as risible as the costumes of Carmen Miranda and the extremities of Struwelpeter, the tiresome boy who haunts the childhood of all Germans.

Miss Horn's psycho-sexual problems and their illustration with blood, bonds, fluids, feathers, masks, shoes and whip machines, may suggest an intriguing case history, but the pantomime of her personal pornography is swiftly wearying to those who hope for sculpture and see only sexual therapy; the typewriter rigged to write four-letter words to rumba rhythm, however, might be therapeutic in the office of this newspaper, and, but for the words, could well have been devised by Heath Robinson.

Evening Standard 1994

John Keane: Gulf

As WAR HAD BEEN A PRIME SUBJECT FOR THE artist ever since the ancient Greeks first painted pots, the Official War Artist was a very late anachronism, for he dates not from the mists of history but from 1916, long after the camera that had already rendered him superfluous.

The first of the ilk was Muirhead Bone, one of Britain's most popular draughtsmen, so celebrated for his accurate topography and detail that Bernard Shaw described his work as 'too true to be good', his enemies nicknamed him Bonehead Muir (though his friends dubbed him the London Piranesi), and critics accused him of peeping at war through the wrong end of a telescope. These varying views, though expressed over seventy years ago, demonstrate very different expectations of the War Artist, and the dilemma in which he is still placed when he accepts an official commission to record a war. Should he accept that as an official artist he must, to some considerable extent, be part of war's propaganda machine, and appear to support and glorify its purposes? Should he record, simply and with a dispassionate eye, all that he sees, in defeat as well as victory, craven as well as heroic, base as well as chivalrous, without comment? Should he comment and paint a work of art?

The difficulty lies in the word *official*. It is all very well in the context of the artist for whom war is the subject, to talk of Goya and Callot and their bitter, penetrating studies and evocations of its miseries, and claim that, like them, all artists have the right to make an adverse comment, but neither Goya nor Callot was an *official* artist and both were free to adopt what stance they chose. Otto Dix, as a fighting soldier in the trenches of the 1914-18 war, was intellectually free to paint and draw anything he wished, and after the war to collate his impressions into the most effective of anti-war masterpieces, but he held no *official* position. John Keane, however, the young painter chosen by the Artistic Records Committee of the Imperial War Museum to record the Gulf War, did hold an official position, and it was this, much more than foolish misrepresentations of his work, that gave rise to controversy when a few of his paintings were prematurely revealed to the press, for they appeared to demonstrate distaste for everything connected with the relief of Kuwait.

The terms of Keane's commission were that he was to be paid a modest sum for what might be a dangerous stint, and that the Museum would take a selection from the work produced. The Ministry of Defence provided him with the support given to members of the press. The Artistic Records Committee expected 'an historical record' with some 'aesthetic credibility', but such contrary embroideries of these simple and worthy aims as 'comment comes as a bonus' and 'the work should be something of a monument to effort and sacrifice', led at last to 'we didn't know what to expect'.

Perhaps the commission was too loose and Keane felt free of the constraints of historical record – free instead to make the anti-war comment that is the clear spirit of the work. If indeed his mature view of events turned him against the war, he had every right to express it, but not as an *official* artist, for having, as it were, accepted the Queen's shilling, he had a certain bogus duty to perform if he was not to put in doubt the purposes of the Imperial War Musuem as a bastion of history and heroism. As his paintings are based on photographs and video stills, and not on the immediate experience of the war (he left the front a few hours before the Ground Offensive began), he might as well have stayed at home, for, as we are told in the execrable catalogue of his exhibition, he 'is adamant that he is not a recorder, but a commentator' by no means making the eye-witness account of official artists in the two World Wars. My slightly puritanical response to his commission is that if he already thought of himself only as a commentator, he should not have accepted it; if he was in doubt, then there was some excuse for taking the Queen's shilling, but when he returned from the Gulf he should have given it back and let his paintings take their chance without the support of the Imperial War Museum.

I have some sympathy with what I take to be Keane's views. The jingoist may argue that we fought a just war in the Gulf; the cynic may assert that Kuwaiti investment in this country required our heroic response to the Iraqi invasion; and the sane man with a sense of history's confusions can only see it as a war governed by politicians so politically naive and so poorly educated that they had not the foggiest notion of either the short or long term consequences of their intervention. Posthumously (a word much associated with corpses) we know that high technology failed us and that, for fear of Arab and Islamic mistrust, we let slip the final victory.

Keane in his way makes all these points, not only in his chosen subjects, but in his use of real dollar bills, Saudi riyals and pages of the Koran pasted to his canvases. It is a pity that he did not use the Bible too – perfectly justifiable in the paradoxical context of Christian soldiers onward into battle in the land of the Prophet – for this might have muted the Islamic response to his pictures. It is odd that far away in the Gulf we fought a war supposedly for freedom, but that here in London freedom of expression is censored because we are in thrall to a violent section of our multi-cultural community: the painting in which Keane employed pages of the Koran has been withdrawn from the exhibition by no less a man than the Museum's Director, Alan Borg, timorously anxious not to offend a 'bruised' religious minority – though 'bruising' might have been the truer word. To this the only response must be that if ours is indeed a multi-cultural society and not some neutral cultural sludge, then newly-arrived minorities must learn to respect our long and deeply valued traditions of free speech, and must not seek to impose their views on a majority that has fought for that freedom and is now accustomed to it. Those who worship Mecca in this country must accept pages torn from the Koran as a metaphor for a devastating war between Islamic nations, and not see them as an insult to the Prophet – indeed, in a broader sense, they must accept that figurative art and allusive imagery were the fundamentals of European art long before the birth of the Prophet, and must learn, in Europe, not to protest grave offence at cultural patterns far older than their own.

As for John Keane's paintings, they work very well on a small scale (indeed I would have bought one had it been affordable), but his deft and painterly touch becomes a desperate dabbing and filling on a large scale, and what in small is direct and immediately to the point, enlarged is often empty and laboured. The weakness of his drawing is not camouflaged by the evident speed with which he works (he is no Topolski), and the technical shocks of drip, dribble, collage and scribble amount to no more than an impetuous display that quickly stales. I suspect that if Keane could escape the impulse to perform fast (his brushwork is proof of dramatic gestural performance), he might sustain in the large paintings the integrity of the small; he could do with a touch of Bonehead Muir's meticulousness, just as Bonehead would have been much improved with a dash of Keane's emotional response.

Evening Standard 1992

Kitaj

FOR THE PAST TWO WEEKS OR SO IT HAS SCAR-
cely been possible to open a magazine or broadsheet newspaper
without finding in it some lengthy article on Ron Kitaj, an exegesis,
or an interview with this American expatriate in England, friend
and contemporary of David Hockney, and inventor of the term
'The School of London'. All part of the juggernaut of publicity that
the Tate Gallery now so expertly sets on a thundering progress
whenever it mounts an exhibition, these scribblings hammer home
the man's proclaimed position as 'one of the leading figurative
painters in the world', his revitalised faith as a Jew, his concerns with
sex, history, philosophy, politics and poetry, his friendships with the
famous and his artistic relationships with the old masters of the past,
Masaccio to Matisse, Uccello to Cézanne, Giorgione to Degas (I'd
like to add Carpaccio's Venetian tarts).

The exhibition catalogue continues in like vein, with an
introductory essay by a panjandrum of the Tate, from which we
gather that Kitaj is a painter who not once in his life fumbled,
bumbled or lost his way with a picture, every one a work of
absolute perfection and himself a creature of constant genius; the
same panjandrum then interviews the artist (the fifth interview I've
read – there may well be more), enabling the horse's mouth to
confirm all that his apologists claim for him; the Director of the
Tate, the eximious Serota, contributes a foreword larded with
expressions of the low kow-tow – 'We are delighted . . . we owe
an immense gratitude to Kitaj . . . it has been a privilege and
pleasure to work so closely with the artist . . . we are indeed deeply
grateful', all this in one page – and a famous philosopher
(philosophers, I observe in passing, are as foolish as psychoanalysts
when they work on the mysteries of art) is allowed to ruminate,
recall, reflect, and conclude that to the question 'What is Art?' Kitaj
is the answer.

'Kitaj draws better than almost anyone else alive,' said Robert Hughes in 1979. So thought I, then, seeing in his pastels something of the sympathy that William Rothenstein put into his subtle portraits of the old, and something of the courage of Degas, the tooth of rough paper biting the soft pigment; but now, fifteen years on, confronted by such a mass of material, very little of it seems to have the quality of greatness – indeed none of it – the kinship with Degas no more than brief accident, the Rothenstein sympathy a matter of one sheet and one only, the study of Degas on his deathbed. Kitaj has in portraiture an unremarkable ability to catch a likeness – no better than Eric Kennington, for example; in many a female nude his erotic response cheapens his sense of form, feature and colour to such a degree that the slightest exaggeration more of eyelash, mouth, nipple or pubic hair would make him the draughtsman of publishable pornography; yet frank images of masturbation, fellatio and congress he occasionally lifts to drawing-room respectability. Of the male nude he seems to have no grasp, and expresses little interest other than the flicker of locker-room curiosity.

In a female nude that is probably considered one of his finest drawings, a girl seated on a buttoned mattress, her back to the spectator and her face in *profile perdue*, the left shoulder and supporting arm are massively out of proportion with the torso, a heavy outline emphasising the disproportion; this dark line descends to silhouette the ribcage, waist and buttock, destroying all sense in the shadowed modelling that it contains – and then one begins to realise how weak is Kitaj's grasp of form and structure, and that he seduces the viewer with the sensual appeal of a young girl's head and neck, and with the tender touch and colour of the pastel crayon. Uncertain in form, uneven in finish, this is a study grotesquely ill-matched in parts, neither competing with Degas nor, I hope, a better drawing than one by 'almost anyone else alive'.

What abilities Kitaj has as a draughtsman are rarely enlisted in his paintings. He began, as did so many in the early Sixties, with all the suddenly fashionable idioms of the day – the drip, the deliberate deformation of painted areas with scratches and meaningless strokes of the loaded brush, and with collaged elements of paper and small rectangles of canvas; he anticipated Hockney's similar mannerisms by a year or so, but with much less bravado. He tried his hand at hard and outlined edges, at flat areas of bright insensitive colour, at American Abstract Expressionism echoing de Kooning, and began to develop the spaceless assembly of half-formed or fragmentary ideas as though imitating in paint the random chop and change of narrative and image in the prose of William Burroughs.

His handling of paint became flat and dull, the colour as bright and unsubtle as beachwear for a Spanish holiday, but so dead and dry, so lacking in surface richness and translucence that it is almost impossible to believe that it is oil – if this is all that Kitaj can make of such a succulent material, he should settle for acrylics. So, for the most part, it remained, though there were such exceptiois as *The Arabist*, in which a sense of texture suddenly emerged with the use of one colour over another, though both are opaque and the effect is derived from stippling; and occasionally it seems as though he has sought to learn something from the watercolours of Burra (in handling the subject too, as well as the medium), and from the dry surfaces of Michael Andrews.

In recent work he has taken to extremes the habit of drawing with the brush that first appeared ten years or so ago; it has the quality of urgency, whether it is the sweeping line, the piecing together of broken scraps of line, or the staccato stabbing of bright colour in short touches, but urgency is its only quality, for Kitaj now cares for nothing but his need to express piecemeal and pell-mell his ideas for fusing the influences that he picks up from the cinema with those that come from Cézanne or Uccello, and produces thoroughly bad pictures at a prodigious rate. The pictographs and ideograms of earlier paintings have been replaced by graphic tales half told, as though from pages stuck together or by breathless incoherent children with no sense of time or order, their titles enigmatic and subject to change. He offers clues to these narratives, but with the disintegration of his uncertain talent his drawing has become so incompetent and careless, so caricatural, so childish and so ugly, mated with a quality of paint so coarse and insensitive, that the viewer is repelled by what seem no better than overblown frames from crude strip cartoons.

It matters not a damn that Kitaj claims to be the heir of the spaghetti western and the Italian Renaissance, invoking the ghosts of Giorgione and John Ford, of Peckinpah and Lorenzetti, of Huston, Wilder and Uccello, if what he now offers us from these masters is wretched adolescent trash unfit to hang with the works of Otto Dix, Max Beckmann, Balthus and Chagall, the true twentieth-century masters of the veins he seeks to mine. A pox on fawning critics and curators for foisting on us as heroic master, a vain painter puffed with amour-propre, unworthy of a footnote in the history of figurative art.

Evening Standard 1994

Yves Klein

Y VES KLEIN'S WORKING LIFE AS AN ARTIST WAS short, and merry enough to finish him with a heart attack at the age of thirty-four. Born in Nice in 1928, the son of a Dutchman who painted Babycham pictures, his French mother was a by no means negligible abstract painter, but even with the smell of paint and turpentine for ever in his nostrils, he himself came late to painting. He had no formal training, and his first tentative activity as a painter occurred only in 1949, with plain colour applied to scraps of fine white card – the abstract colour fields for which he was to become notorious.

With little academic prowess as a schoolboy, and scant aptitude for art, his first job was as a salesman in a Paris bookshop. He knew something of Surrealism and Parisian abstract art, but all his intellectual energies were given to the then fashionable Existentialism, Spiritualism, Zen Buddhism and, of all such cod philosophies,

Rosicrucianism, for which he held a particular enthusiasm; he spent hours in rapt concentration on the moon, and fasted to the fainting stage; blue, the colour with which he is most identified, began to play its spiritual part, and with his signature he laid claim to the sky as his 'first and biggest monochrome'.

Rosicrucianism, a mock medieval hotchpotch of Christian and eastern mysticism, secret signs and hidden meanings, larded with alchemy, the occult and pseudo-science, its overtones Masonic, informed the rambling and utterly undisciplined apologias with which, too frequently, he explained his activity as an artist, for though the philosophy itself was eventually abandoned, the wayward thought processes that it engendered remained. Nothing that Klein ever said made sense. His other dominant activity, obsession indeed, was judo, on which he wrote two texts, and for the technical improvement of which he spent months in Japan in 1952. At this stage, having composed poems and written essays on Utopian ideas (as do most young men of reasonable intelligence), and devised the concept of an infinite present, he had no clear ambition or intent (other than as an expert on judo), and his only work as an artist was still concentrated on small paintings in plain colour on rectangles of card.

He was intrigued by pure pigment, dry, its powder not suspended in the gloss of oil, for in its particles he perceived an intensity and depth that were destroyed when saturated or held in a fixative. Discovering a synthetic medium that though it dried very quickly and could not be reworked, retained the optical quality of dry powdered pigment, in 1955 he embarked on a new series of monochromes in pink, yellow, violet, vermilion and other emphatic colours; of these he spoke in terms of primal freedom, fields of silence, the work of art de-objectified, and a colour field as a window without bars. In the summer of 1956 he began work on an exhibition in which everything was to be in one colour, his intention to release the public from their intellectual imprisonment in 'a learned way of seeing', and to offer an alternative to their past experience of looking at pictures. His choice fell on his favourite blue.

.

This blue is always described as ultramarine, but its tone is closer to the intense and unpleasant blue that those in their dotage may recall from laundry blue-bags, and Klein himself dubbed it 'International Klein Blue'. He continued to apply it to paper, but now in large sheets laid down on canvas, to canvas itself and other fabrics, to reliefs of sponges and pebbles, and even to ready-made souvenir multiples of such sculptures as the Winged Victory in the Louvre. Blue became an obsession that Klein explained as an attempt to depersonalise colour and give it a metaphysical quality instead of its traditional resonance and symbolism. Blue, he maintained, not only has no dimensions, but is beyond dimension, suggesting only the sky and the sea, while all other colours are limited by their innumerable and inescapable associations.

Klein's talk of paintings de-objectified when a stretched canvas is painted plain blue not only on its surface but round its edges too, to hang without a frame on a white wall, is nonsense, for this is in fact the deliberate reduction of the painting to mere object, particularly when, without imagery, the purpose of this painted thing is to act as point of departure for the contemplative in an act of self-delusion or self-induced hallucination. Klein protested that his blue works, sculptures as well as pictures, were not aesthetic objects, but it is inconceivable that his *Forest of Sponges*, all painted blue and mounted like toy trees on metal rods sunk into discreetly rough rocks of different stones that carry semi-precious connotations, was conceived without some trifling aesthetic intention in the wake of Fabergé. It is, indeed, this decorative sensibility that distinguishes his work from 'the space of black' that so intrigued Casimir Malevich in his black-on-black paintings, or the pure aesthetic feeling of his white-on-white canvases of 1917–18, and it deprives Klein of the intellectual rigour of Mondrian's abstractions.

It must be admitted by those who see Klein as an influential genius, the great opener of gates through the conventional boundaries of art, that he was little more than the child of his time, with Duchamp, Beuys, Fontana, Magritte and the Zero and Lettriste Groups, with Arte Povera, Performance Art, Environmental and Conceptual Art, part of the sea change that separated for ever the artists of the present day from etiolated ancestral traditions. He may well have been the first to compose a *Symphonie Monotone*, a single note sustained for ten minutes, followed by ten minutes of silence (1947); he may well have been the first to exhibit an empty gallery, a room with all its features blanked with white paint (1958); he may well have been the first to cover with pigment (blue, of course) chosen parts of naked women, and let them imprint themselves, crawl, or be dragged about on canvases laid on the floor (1960); but if he was indeed the first in these and other such extremes, he was soon imitated, and was himself extending through a new Dadaism ideas and activities that had been in strong evidence no more than thirty years before, nourished between by the lunacies of Dali and other performing Surrealists.

There lies the paradox with Klein. His early activity may have been informed by the muddled sincerity that is so often evident in adolescent boys (not girls), but he grew into a tiresome showman and himself became the work of art. This does not mean, however, that the response to his paintings should be contemptuous, for there is, if nothing else, a freshness about them, a sponteneity, a zany sparkle that makes the spectator realise that to be early in the field of exploration beyond the boundaries is quite wonderful (even if the exploration proves to be in error), and that so much of what has been done worldwide since Klein's death in 1962, is stale repetition growing mustier by the day. A blue painting, fourteen feet long, made in 1960 by women on their hands and knees, is as good an abstract as any of its year on either side of the Atlantic. Another, much smaller (No. 82), is astonishing and beautiful in its references (even if unconscious) to European old master drawings and oriental calligraphy. A blue painting deliberately left in the rain is transformed into a landscape that combines the vision of a Turner watercolour with the touch of an Impressionist. A large abstract in gold leaf is a bold barbaric reference to the small gold leaf vulgarities of the Japanese Edo period. And if Klein's activities with a flame gun at the test centre of Gaz de France in 1961 seem no more than a flamboyant performance for the television cameras, consider the effects achieved by charring paper, for some of these huge 'drawings' offer a terrible beauty, as though Rembrandt in a rage could find no image and turned to abstract gesture.

For an art critic compelled to read so much extended rubbish in exhibition catalogues, the most engaging of Klein's works are the slim volumes that he printed in 1954, the model art books; the illustrations are rectangles of plain colour, and the texts are composed only of ruled lines with not a word of sense. I see them as a damning comment on the art writers of the day, but forty years on, it still applies to the commercial drivellings of critics in thrall to Cork Street and the Arts Council. For these little books alone I'd warm to Klein.

Evening Standard 1995

Franz Kline

ABSTRACT EXPRESSIONISM IS THE PORTMAN-teau term invented to embrace the New York artists who in the late Forties appeared to play Pied Piper and lead their peers world-wide into a realm of unpremeditated spontaneous improvisation. Suddenly there was no need to know what to paint or how to conceive a painting, and the artist was not driven by idea or concept, but merely hoped to find it as the random mass of paint mated on the canvas and spawned abstract suggestions that pleased the painter's searching eye. That their work was largely abstract is true (though de Kooning remained loyal to cyphers of the human figure), but that it was expressionist in any intelligent sense is an absurdity, though it is certainly intelligible as an expression of the drunken temper tantrums for which it was a useful therapy. The more appropriate term Action Painting, coined in 1952, seems to have fallen into disuse – more's the pity, for it is a fair description of their practices.

No uniformity of style and handling tied the group together – Jackson Pollock laid random lengths of canvas on the floor and poured and dripped paint onto them with incantations and a rhythmic sweep. Others remained loyal to the easel, more or less, Motherwell with rough-edged rectangles, Guston with myopic mosaics of colour, Francis with patterns of drips and stains that have an art nouveau elegance, and Franz Kline loaded the housepainter's brush and at arm's length raked the canvas with a gesture. But lack of coherence could not deter critics from compelling these uneasy companions in time and geography into a group and enthroning them in art history's Valhalla as the first American artists to lead the world. They have had thrust on them a mythical importance, outdoing even the Rosicrucians in mystery and awe, and the words Abstract Expressionism are now the shibboleth to be uttered when the impudent dare to question the merit of contemporary painting, as a remonstration to bring them into line or exclude them from the pale, words with which to bless the bucket and slosh imitators of Pollock who now abound, and justify the gestures of Howard Hodgkin and his ilk.

Some of these New Yorkers adopted contemplative procedures before painting, and, helped by tobacco and alcohol, Zen Buddhism and Japanese calligraphy, sat far into the night waiting for the great Unconscious to launch them into 'psychic improvisation'. They harboured the misgiving, if not the conviction, that art was dead, and that as the aesthetic language of the Greeks and Romans, of the Renaissance and Romanticism, of the human form and its secular moralities and spiritual aspirations, was exhausted, they must invent an entirely new language to replace it. This new language, they thought, must liberate the artist through a process of self-discovery – though it was a precarious assumption that their precious selves were worth discovering. They threw away the dictionary, jettisoned the maps and charts, and abandoned all traditional concepts of composition, volume and perspective; they rejected the subject, yet insisted that their paintings were not devoid of content, arguing that the very action of applying paint to canvas should be taken for content, the materials themselves willy-nilly an image of sorts in a pictorial space that had no structure and no limits. The physical action of putting paint on canvas, by whatever means, dominated the new pictorial language and demanded an empathic response from the spectator – 'join in,' it said, 'conduct this music of the brushstroke and the action', and colour assumed a vague insistent resonance that was ambiguous in place, plane and implication.

This then, bucket and slosh, gestural sweep, drip, splash, stain and accident, circle and square, rhythm and staccato stab, monochrome and ill-matched colour, was the new language of painting – the grunt of the gorilla lauded by critics and curators as a new totality of art and aesthetics. With Zen and the Unconscious to support them in their exaggerated sense of destiny, the inventors of this new language, convinced of its internal logic, shouted their messianic messages and the critics took them for Messiahs, and have done so ever since.

Franz Kline, often promoted as the most intelligent, remote and mysterious of these New Yorkers, enables us to see through the myths of Abstract Expressionism. Born in 1910, destroyed by drink in 1962, he had some small ability as a conventional painter of still lives and townscapes, and, had he been English, could well have exhibited at the Royal Academy. At the age of forty or so, he took to painting pseudo-oriental ideograms in black on white, as though exploring and clumsily enlarging Japanese characters, but they had no meaning and were accidental and unconscious – 'I paint what I don't know.' A series of these characters on pages torn from telephone directories are, we are told, 'an astonishing record of . . . a total reconceptualisation of his art'; alas, they are no more than doodles, uncertain excercises to free the wrist for fluent gestures, practice to make the brushmarks deft, and to see them as great art is to proclaim the five finger exercise great music. That such exercises were essential is made clear by the earliest abstractions – halting imitations of Gorky and de Kooning, the fat paint slowing the brush and bulking the abstract forms – and the facility derived from them gave Kline the courage to increase his canvas size and write his nonsense large.

A single Kline in black, on white canvas six feet high, can seem a monumental thing, an abstract architecture of strains, stresses and supports, but a dozen and another dozen suggest that his unconscious was not invariably the best of guides, that he often did not know quite when to stop the gestures, and in adding more and more merely buried what may have been initial elegance under a turbid mass. Occasionally, in the overlap of black stroked onto white, or in the corrections of white on black, the excitement of the brush is clear, and when he can restrain his colour to a single dominant red or purple, the huge canvases assume a theatrical presence – but much less substance, much less intensity, much less beauty than a late watercolour by Turner. With a multiplicity of colours, the confusion and the palette are detestable.

Kline, like Pollock, Rothko, Motherwell, and all the others of this New York school, emerges as the minor painter of a minor theme, a man of signs and symbols without meaning, their tedious minor variations writ too large. That he and his peers should have for so long been eulogised, now seems astonishing, for this is empty stuff, always on and too often over the edge of failure, too often flaccid, fumbled and uncertain. These overblown symbols were not the signposts to a new Renaissance, but to the Nowhere and Nothing of art in art schools now.

Evening Standard 1994

Willem de Kooning

WILLEM DE KOONING, PRINCE OF ACTION Painters, Abstract Expressionist Extraordinary, is, it seems, '. . . the supreme painterly painter of the second half of the century and the greatest painter of the human figure since Picasso . . .' If there is

any substance in this declaration, then it is right that the Tate
Gallery should exhibit these icons of the female figure, and that we
should bend the knee to them; if not, then this exhibition is still
justified, for de Kooning's claim to be considered Michelangelo's
successor is so frequently reiterated that we have the right to debate
it and perhaps declare ourselves iconoclasts.

De Kooning's last exhibition at the Tate was in the winter of
1968–9, a travelling show that sought to establish his reputation
well beyond the purlieus of his adopted New York, but it was not
altogether favourably received, and was even described by the critic
of the New York *Times* as 'by and large a disappointment'. It
contained 92 paintings and 42 drawings; the current exhibition
contains no drawings and only 83 paintings, though 26 years on the
old boy is still alive and reported to have churned out, at least in the
early part of that quarter century, a painting a day. Pared of the
drawings, we are not aware of the very young Willem's academic
prowess with the pencil in his native Holland, sketching the sort of
crocks that it pleased Vermeer's cook to use, nor of Willem in his
late thirties dabbling in the sort of wide-eyed portraiture that can
convert the most grasping Manhattan harpy into a demure and
wistful waif; and pared of the early paintings we are compelled to
take for granted the intelligence and sensibility claimed for his
exercises in the shadows of Picasso, Léger, Miro, Masson, Ozenfant
and others that we are not allowed to see. He is, instead, conjured
for us fully formed only as a painter in 1940 and thenabouts, aged
thirty-six that year and working on drab figures derived from
Arshile Gorky in a fashionable olive palette – there is, indeed,
something drearily 'Festival of Britain' about them, so akin are they
to Robert Medley and Prunella Clough in 1951, Colquhoun,
MacBryde and Vaughan (something mephitic in the *Zeitgeist* no
doubt). Picasso lurks there too, ill-digested hints of the Pink Period
concurrent with the devices and distortions of the Thirties.

In the mid Forties, after toying with grotesque female figures in a
palette briefly risen to mustard yellow and bright green, with eyes
staring and nails varnished scarlet (one of several fetishes enjoyed by

Willem), he turned to fragmented abstracts, at first in the same greens and yellows (of which one is a fantasy of free-floating penises and testicles), and then more or less in white stroked onto black, or black onto white, as though haunted by Picasso's *Guernica* (as, indeed, he was), with odd variations in yellow and red. In these he comes closest to the work of his rival for supremacy in the burgeoning New York school of Abstract Expressionism, Jackson Pollock, whose friends damned de Kooning as an opportunist, a bully and a drunk (Pollock's death in 1956 left the field clear for this paragon). Abstract painting did not hold him for long, and he returned to distorted images of women crudely painted and more crudely drawn, obsessed with the fetish elements of feet and shoes, mouths, teeth, bulging bosoms and phallic references.

Willem was by the mid Fifties an irredeemable alcoholic, given to sudden violence and much random sexual activity, and for a while the women vanished from his canvases, to be replaced by abstract compositions, dense and confused, referring to no subject, with no space or volume, no beginning and no end, offering nothing but gesture, handling and material. From these, eliminating all the agitated fuss and fume, emerged a short series of large landscape sketches, bold but accurate in the placing of bravura strokes, beautiful, and very European, sharing something of the sensibility of Ivon Hitchens at his best, until again, in 1963, his work descended into confusion, and he removed his studio from New York to East Hampton.

On Long Island, perhaps through separation from the ready 'art tarts' who kept him warm in bed, women returned to his easel, sloppily painted as though in flavoured yoghourts, sagging, dripping and dissolving on the canvases, the work of desperate and frustrated obsession; in these de Kooning carries Renoir's claim to have painted naked women 'with his prick' to an extreme, seeming less to have ejaculated on the canvas than to have raped it with the utmost violence. And again the work repeats the cycle of descent into confusion without image.

Now comes the mystery faced by neither the Tate's exhibition nor its sycophantic catalogue. In 1976, after some twenty years of separation, Willem's wife, Elaine, herself a wretched painter, returned to him. He was by then, it has been elegantly put, 'drifting on the quicksand of senility', Alzheimer's Disease a powerful reinforcement to the fuddling work of alcohol, and for some time he had been dependent on the help of studio assistants; of these, Elaine replaced the most faithful with her brother, Conrad Fried, another unsuccessful painter, and from Willem, cocooned with nurses, all old friends were excluded, while a sunburst of new paintings was produced. These his dealer, Xavier Fourcade, declared to be 'from the mind of a genius' and as great as any late Turner or Rembrandt.

Is it possible for a man whose mind is so lost that he cannot recall yesterday, to remain a creative genius, if indeed he ever was one? The late paintings were at first little different from those that preceded Elaine's return to Willem's side, their increasingly curdled confusion a quite logical extension of the growing disorder of his handling already obvious as early as 1970; but in 1982 an extraordinary change was announced, and we were confronted no longer with thick and clouded paint and the scrapes and scarifications that made of it a palimpsest, but with spare white canvases on which danced delicate ribbons of red and blue. We were expected to believe that de Kooning, deep in dotage, had devised a new technique, a new handling, a new gesture, that Elaine's return had wrought a miracle a match for Lourdes – the critics (with one exception) were as credulous as ever and poured out their souls in ecstasy (and so too did the dealers and the auctioneers). By the time of Elaine's death in 1989 a second development had occurred, in which smoothly organised forms, abstract, but with a clear sense of volume and structure, largely in green and brown, were dominant; these, for reasons not explained, are excluded from the exhibition and are not mentioned in the catalogue.

There are those who view all these late paintings with grave misgivings. Conrad Fried filmed de Kooning at work on them, but the old boy seems only to scrub a little colour between the flowing lines, his movements with the brush very short and tentative, and much repeated long after the bristles are dry; if he tackles a long line, it is only to follow one already there and seem to make adjustments that are imperceptible. We are compelled to face the possibility, even the probability, that very little in these late paintings was invented or put there by de Kooning himself, and that almost all pigment, perhaps every fleck of it, was applied by others, with not the smallest intervention by the master.

Was de Kooning a master? It is certain that his reputation was first founded by his wife and her busy bedding of critics in exchange for favourable reviews – Clement Greenberg, after a night with the tigress in 1953, panted that Willem was a figure painter in the great tradition of Leonardo, Michelangelo, Raphael, Ingres and Picasso; and it is certain that American politics found it convenient to use de Kooning as an instrument of cultural authority in an impoverished Europe and lent support to increase his fame – to the rage of French critics – and he represented the USA in 1954 at the Venice Biennale. It is certain that once these bandwaggons began to roll, curators, dealers and collectors all took on a vested interest and with their money turned this very late starter into 'The American Picasso'. Wandering round the Tate, however, I wonder at the awe and adulation expended on this man, most of whose paintings reveal not the slightest merit. The exhibition proves only one thing – that a poor painter's greatest asset is a clever wife going about her business in a critic's bed; without Elaine's determination in that quarter, wretched Willem, now in a rocking chair mumbling to his television set, would be a forgotten minor figure in a scarce remembered school.

Evening Standard 1995

Lawrence of Arabia

LAWRENCE OF ARABIA DID NOT IN ANY WAY resemble Peter O'Toole. Very short, his meagre trunk stood on skinny shanks and was topped by a large head of which the most remarkable feature was its disproportionately long and heavy lower jaw. In photographs he has the cast of a boy among men, an adolescent never quite gangling his way out of immaturity, a perpetual runt.

The scars of flagellation marked his body, and his confused homosexual soul bore the cicatrice of sodomy at the compelling hands of Turkish soldiers. He was torn between a monkish reticence and the desire to draw attention to himself, between literary scholarship and flamboyant self-revelation, between the dull plod of Near Eastern archaeology and the political splendour of work as the architect of Arab kingdoms, conjuring from desert sands new states and Hittite shards. He was illegitimate at a time when bastardy bore the stigma that would stultify a man's ambitions and stunt his social life; like many bastards he bore authority no respect and sought to prove himself superior; and like many bastards his volatile emotions were riven by insecurity.

To the editors of tabloid newspapers and that curious body of jingoist literature addressed specifically to boys in short trousers, Lawrence was the perfect hero. On wild Arabian steed and racing camel, in white windblown robes and fluttering burnous, brandishing the dagger so perfectly curved for ripping livers and sickling testicles, his Lee Enfield rifle puffing smoke, he was the Nijinsky of the desert war and the Rudolf Valentino of his day. Of this genre, the film of derring-do with Peter O'Toole more resembling Flora Robson *en travestie* than little Lawrence in full fig, was the apotheosis.

To the Turks Lawrence was a Scarlet Pimpernel. To the Arabs he was the political force that would retrieve their ancient freedoms from the Turks. To the international statesmen who carved the Ottoman Empire to pieces at the Paris Conference of 1919, he was a man whose pretty promises to the Arabs must be broken under the rolling spheres of influence. To the highfalutin' officers of the British Army he was an irrelevant jack-in-the-box in fancy dress. To the soldiery that had slogged a wearying and unrewarding war against the Turks in Mesopotamia, Gallipoli and Palestine, he was the thief of thunder.

From time to time such little Alexanders must be re-assessed. The literature so far suggests that Lawrence divides his examiners into those who see him as a cleanlimbed white knight, and those who take him for a prancing clown. Biographers have been wary of such matters as his illegitimacy, not wishing to offend the long surviving members of his family – his stern missionary mother died only in 1959, just short of her century; they have not enquired too deeply into the nature of his relationships with such young Arabs as the water-boy whom he brought home to Oxford; they have tended to ignore the moment in his multiple rape when he smiled at the corporal in charge, enjoying the 'delicious warmth'. These biographers found it impossible to defend Lawrence from the implications of his own statements, and thus would not accept that their imperishable champion of all that is noble, pure and true, could self-indulgently expose himself as a homosexual masochist. Lawrence was, after all, the friend or familia of famous men, of Bernard Shaw, Thomas Hardy, E.M. Forster, Augustus John, Winston Churchill and half a dozen desert kings, to say nothing of Nancy Astor, and in their context such things could not be acknowledged.

The truth must be that Lawrence, intelligent, intuitive, emotional and romantic in both the heroic and amatory senses, was conditioned by the restraints and customs of parents, society and class, to suppress the homosexuality that fired him. A generation later he might have taken the conflict in his stride, but, too early, it vitiated his actions, and explains the instinct for self-destruction that dominated his life in later years.

Much of this is now celebrated at the National Portrait Gallery with the kind of centenary exhibition that is done so well in that Pantheon of public images, even though the display is an absurd attempt to reconcile the purposes of a gallery with the illusion of a desert ravine, a carpeted tent, a barrack room and a garden shed.

The life of Lawrence is chronicled in photographs, clothes, letters, memorabilia and major works of portraiture. The boy is evoked by a velvet suit with a Van Dyck collar, and the student by his photographs of French castles. The young man digs among the Hittite remains of Carchemish on the Euphrates, and the warrior destroys the railway to Arabia's heart and gallops his gallant ragamuffin bodyguard into Jerusalem with Allenby. The peace-time misfit writes *The Seven Pillars of Wisdom* and curses the lubricious barracks humour of the Tank Corps. The Brough Superior motorbike on which he was killed is black Pegasus tamed in glass case. The posthumous image of nobility, Lawrence as medieval tombstone knight, is a ridiculous truth, life size.

Documentary and dispassionate, the exhibition avoids the pro-motion of these relics as objects of superstitious awe, and merely uses them to chart the life. There is no special pleading for Lawrence as good, great or heroic – he is merely a once famous figure, now a hundred and become historical, whose turn it is under the micro-scope. The almost admirable catalogue, itself a worthy relic and much more reliable than most biographies of Lawrence, is tedious only in the detail with which it treats the convoluted genesis of the various editions of *The Seven Pillars*; had it attempted to define Lawrence's political hopes for Arabia and Jewry, it would have been more useful; it would certainly have been more amusing had it included an essay by a Freudian analyst, for there is no doubt that Lawrence was a suitable case for the carpeted couch at No. 20 Berggasse, Vienna.

Evening Standard 1988

Fernand Léger

Cubism as we now understand it is the invention of art historians – men who, by and large, have little idea of the mysterious process by which a vision in the head becomes a vision on the canvas, and who prefer the neatly ordered pigeon-holing of developments to the realities of ebb and flow, flux and reflux, mainstream and backwater. The accepted statement of Cubist principles and aesthetics was written by two wholly negligible Cubist painters, Gleizes and Metzinger, in 1912, some five years after Picasso had completed *Les Demoiselles d'Avignon* in which Congo barbarism raped two thousand years of classical tradition and pupped Cubism; it is the blatantly obvious rendered pretentiously obscure by clap-trap of the kind that only the French can write, and I cannot for the life of me see that it offers explanation or exegesis. With it for *vade mecum* it is no wonder that Cubism fragmented into Orthodox, Heretical, Cézannien, Scientific, Physical, Orphic and Instructive, and for once the art historian must be forgiven for re-arranging this cabinet of curiosities in little Cubist boxes logically labelled Analytical, Synthetic and Hermetic, even if the two latter seem more than likely to be misunderstood; in this re-ordering of developments I greatly regret the loss of Pre-Cubism with its suggestion of foreplay, Cubo-Futurism, and particularly the Crumbling Cubism conceived by Fernand Léger's friend Blaise Cendrars. Gleizes and Metzinger are less remarkable for what they write than for the painters whose work they choose as demonstrations of Cubism – their own, of course, in quantity, along with one Picasso, one Gris, no Braque and two Laurencins; now any man who can write a book on Cubism omitting Braque carries carelessness to an extreme, but one who includes Laurencin can only be wilfully perverse, utterly stupid, or totally ignorant, even if the wretched woman did go through a phase of knocking sense into her revolting ice cream maidens by drawing heavy and insensitive lines all over them. Fernand Léger, however, is given five plates (as many as they give themselves) and this suggests that they held him in high esteem.

Léger is not mentioned in the text, larded as it is with such statements as 'Cubism is painting', 'Let the picture imitate nothing', and, 'It is by consummating ourselves within ourselves that we shall purify humanity'; they quote Leonardo da Vinci as a defender of Cubism, but on their peers they are infuriatingly coy, naming neither those whom they dismiss as *tricksters*, nor those whom they laud as great mystics for whom constraint is the vestment of fervour (whatever that may mean). I cannot see Léger as a mystic, and his considerable fervour was never constrained, but he was no trickster. As for the constant references to *taste* made by Gleizes and Metzinger, these cannot have taken Léger into account, for his Cubist work was invariably a robust statement of his intellectual and painterly independence (his late ceramic relief murals, mosaics and sculpture are remarkable only for their crass vulgarity and the offensive arrogance of their scale). To those who know Léger only from the dross that too often surfaces in Bond Street and in private (largely American) collections – the immediately recognisable heavy outlines, the flat, hard abstract patterns of colour unrelated to the busy subjects, the piling of Pelion on Ossa in the compositions, the contradictions of volume, space and picture plane, the scaffolding of girders and ladders, and the simplification of human form – the epithet *Tubist* in place of Cubist is readily acceptable.

I cannot agree with Peter de Francia, who argued in his recent book that the late works in which these coarse and clumsy characteristics flourish have been unjustly neglected in recent years; they may well reflect Léger's left wing position in the politics of art, and his views on matters social as well as cultural and aesthetic, but that makes them not one whit more acceptable, for they are megaphone art to match the megaphone speeches of his Communist friends in the trade unions. Were they merely pictures they could be ignored, immured in museum basements and forgotten among dealers' stock, but they are vast assertive public statements for public places, in unforgiveably permanent materials, and not even I, imbued with the spirit of iconoclasm, would wield a seven pound hammer against his ghastly ceramic sculptures and reliefs, so they are with us for ever. His *Jardin d'Enfants*, twenty feet high, resembles a decapitated bunny and a hand of bananas, and four hundred square metres of mosaic and ceramic embellish (can that be the word?) the façade of his own museum with three detached hands reaching for a ball, and an androgynous figure engaged in an unfortunate relationship with a bicycle – I know that it has a respectable root as the last fling of Ozenfant's *Purism*, but it is enough to send me rushing back to the early works for a measure of intellectual substance and some true painting, convinced that the degradation of this once lush talent was self-inflicted.

Of his earliest pictures we know almost nothing other than that they were vaguely Impressionist, for Léger destroyed most of them after a Damascene revelation at the great Cézanne retrospective exhibition in the autumn of 1907. By 1909 he had evolved a simple rising perspective of softly generalised forms fused in tonal unity – *Nudes in the Forest* is a beautiful example in which what is represented in the mechanical forms is entirely subject to a sombre mood and the conventions of pictorial structure, and only after acceptance as a landscape of formidable emotional power does the viewer begin to see the lively interest of Léger's intellectual experiment with Cubism. The shallow rising perspective was to stay with him all his life; at first he brought the elements back to the surface at the top of his pictures, asserting the picture plane, but eventually he denied the picture space altogether and merely made shallow patterns of symbols. The Cubist work does not conform to the Picasso formula, and is inconsistent; invariably exciting, both as experiment and as finished picture, it reaches towards Italian Futurism and some aspects of German Expressionism – he may fragment forms, but he does not synthesise what he knows to be there with what he can see, and nowhere does he attempt to make us see round a figure. I believe that at no point at this stage in his work did he neglect to make his pictures beautiful, no matter how pressing the intellectual problem with which the disciplines of Cubism confronted him – indeed in many ways I find it difficult to see him as a Cubist, even though Douglas Cooper (with whom no one should ever dispute for fear of haunting) promoted him as one of the four great *Essential Cubists* (thus devising yet another little art historical box). He was instead a man greatly but not overwhelmingly influenced by Cubism, who retained a poetic and painterly element that prevented his degeneration into the formula painting of Picasso and Braque at their most arid.

The Great War gassed him, but did not kill him off – that was left to Le Corbusier and his loony side-kick Ozenfant with their silly magazine *L'Esprit Nouveau*, in which they promoted the already old hat machine aesthetic. Once hooked on that, there were no more beautiful and exciting pictures from Léger's brush – only work to rule and the rubric of *Tubism*. He turned to words. Against the political and intellectual background of an unremittingly turbulent period embracing the two World Wars and the growth of Communism in France, Léger performed as commentator, theoretician and teacher, always on the Left. He took to the theatre, cinema and the circus – his 1921 designs for ballet costumes must be among the most exciting of the period, and his kinetic set for *Le Pas d'Acier* of 1948 would even now still be strikingly modern and minimal. His was an acute mind, its capacity for the examination of ideas never diminished, his sensibilities always usefully functional. However much one may dislike the late work, one cannot help liking the man – and he was the only Cubist to make Cubism sensual.

Tatler 1987

Annie Leibovitz

T HE WORK OF ANNIE LEIBOVITZ, CHILD OF THE National Portrait Gallery 1994 American Sixties, pop chronicler of the American Seventies, glitzy annalist of the American Eighties, and on-the-spot opportunist of the Bosnian Nineties, photographer most extraordinary and extravagant, is on view in the National Portrait Gallery.

Extraordinary and extravagant? Worth 50,000 dollars a day in fees, a million dollars a year? The darling of American Express for her celebrated (celebrated? – by whom?) 'Portraits' campaigns devoted to the fit and famous of athletics, stage, screen, popular culture and unpopular politics? The sweetheart of *Vanity Fair* for her winsome icons of those whom its sometime editor, Tina Brown, in her despairing moments described as wall-to wall nobodies? Am I alone in never having heard of this suddenly lionized wielder of the Kodak Brownie? Am I alone in thinking that it is not the business of our National Gallery of National Portraiture to flatter her by showing us her photographs of those many who have perhaps been famous for fifteen minutes on the far side of the Atlantic? Am I alone in knowing nothing, nothing at all, of Roseanne Barr and Tom Arnold, rolling like Rubens cherubs in deep mud? – nothing of Peter Sellars, who has acne and electric hair? – nothing of Jodie Foster, who has prominent nipples and a scarlet dress? – nothing of Kirby Puckett, whose genital bulge is of such prominence as to make his surname seem misspelt? – and nothing of a hundred other of her sitters?

I might not feel so grouchy about this exhibition if the work of Miss Leibovitz seemed in any way original or remarkable, if her eye seemed fresh and clear – but it does not. On the contrary, her eye is cluttered with borrowed imagery, and her aesthetic achievement is no better (and often worse) than that of many a sound commercial photographer whose witty advertisements for billboards and magazines have long been familiar. Dennis Hopper in multi-coloured motor-cycling leathers is a far less intriguing image than many presented as a BMW promotion; Bruce Springsteen in free fall against a backing of stars and stripes could well be advertising popcorn; the naked torso of Randy Travis and leather jacket of Willem Dafoe require nothing but printed titles to turn them into advertisements for the spaghetti western or the cinema of the homosexual underground.

Miss Leibovitz borrows from Magritte – the Surrealist source of so many startling advertisements – her double portrait of Isabella Rossellini and David Lynch, in which his face is completely covered by the turtle neck of his black sweater, very much a Magrittian conceit, and David Byrne in a Peter Pan jacket of ivy leaves (unless this is a pun on Ivy League status) is pure Magrittian semi-metamorphosis. In 1979 Miss Leibovitz saw Bette Midler as one of Alma-Tadema's ancient Roman prostitutes smothered in red roses, just as that Victorian academic's painting of an historic orgy was gaining fast in fame and price. In her 1981 portrait of Yoko Ono in Central Park one is again compelled to consider the possibility of images culled from Victorian paintings as their auction market rose into the dollar millions, from William Dyce perhaps, and having lit so successfully upon such a Ruskinian image, she repeated it with one of Philip Glass, of Peter Matthiessen cowering in Tiggy-Winkle undergrowth, and of David Bowie framed in a Pre-Raphaelite mandorla of dank ivy. Is it preposterous to suggest that the Douanier Rousseau inspired the photograph of a nude Mark Morris, his genitals clamped between his legs for fear of the surrounding Triffids? – that Lucian Freud lurks in the portrait of Morris with Baryshnikov? – and even that behind the silhouetted image of Sammy Davis stands Annigoni's first portrait of the Queen? The sculptor Christo she portrays Lazarus-like as one of his own wrapped sculptures; Steve Martin in white evening dress daubed with swathes of black paint, strikes a pose before a matching abstract picture (the intrusive gallery lights are a mark of slovenliness in detail); and the Keith Haring nude, again all white and black, part of and camouflaged against a room environment of his own painting – none of these is her original idea.

Miss Leibovitz works to useful and particular devices. If framing a millionaire in the back seat of his limousine is deemed successful, then the pose will do again for Joan and Jackie Collins. If contrasting the great height of overfed American soldiers with an undernourished Philippine peasant is thought a telling image, then let her do it again with basketball giant and jockey at his hip. With Warhol and Richard Avedon we have the tired old trick of the photographer photographing the photographer in action, and then, by extending the image to include her lights and other paraphernalia, she uses and re-uses the visual synecdochism to photograph herself. She likes nudity and mud – Lauren Hutton lies in it wet, mustard and cress growing in her pubic hair, and Sting stands on it dry, patched with it from top to toe, modest hands clasped at his groin, strongly lit but strangely shadowless. For such bare-skinned athletes as Carl Lewis, Schwarzenegger and Magic Johnson she prefers the old straight formulae of *Health and Efficiency. Ad nauseam* we see the blur of cigarette smoke, the boot-level distortions of the figure that are the grotesque exaggeration of the lens but never the experience of the human eye, and all the other tricks of the photographer who with contrivance strives for attention but knows nothing of the intuitive perceptions of the painter.

As for her lauded work in Sarajevo – the newborn babe, the bloody dead, the hapless on the operating table, the swimmers in the summer sun – these photographs are surely no more distinguished than a thousand others snapped by jobbing journalists, and are the fruit of chance, of simply being there. And I have worked with enough hardnosed photographers to be utterly sceptical about the economic elegance of a tumbled bicycle and serpentine of blood as serendipity, for so telling an icon is too easily arranged while one's companions carry the shattered body of the boy who rode it to die on the back seat of one's car. I am sceptical too for with a finger always on the trigger a photographer can shoot a hundred exposures in a trice and, back in the darkroom, discard all but one – and that one drastically doctored to get the best from it. In Sarajevo any fool could take fine photographs.

I am in two minds about such work. I suppose that such Sarajevan images may spring the well of charity in uncharitable politicians – though there is little evidence of this – but I could not have photographed that bloodstain in the road while the child whose blood it was died in my car; had I been the millionaire Miss Leibovitz my hands would have been better occupied, hopelessly no doubt, but with more human warmth. What was the woman doing there? I have a neoconceptual image in my mind, in which the camera lens is replaced by a gross black phallus of the kind found in sex shops, for I see the photographer of such terrible moments as a spiritual rapist; I shall make this black obscenity and call it *Leibovitz*.

Evening Standard 1994

L.S. Lowry

The Barbican Art Gallery 1988

Laurence Stephen Lowry died in 1976, a mythological master to match the Douanier Rousseau, a romantic recluse, a natural primitive, a visionary, an obsessionist, a preacher whose voice had not been heard until too late, the Gully Jimson of the North dimly perceived among the mephitic glooms of Manchester. The Royal Academy promptly gave him a retrospective; critics likened him, not to painters, but to Pirandello, D.H. Lawrence, Beckett and Ionesco, and Marina Vaizey was promptly and irrevocably convinced of his genius; only John McEwan cut through the nonsense, examined the pictures in the context of European art, and got to the truth – 'His pictures, even with the help of the myth, looked amateurish in technique. There is no subtlety in his use of paint at all, and he constantly appears to be striving for illusions of depth which he simply has not the expertise to attain . . . They are of no symbolic or more generalised interest, as it is to be expected from such a profoundly provincial man . . .'

Lowry spent the eighty-eight years of his life in Manchester and its purlieus constructing, developing and polishing a fantasy about himself. To be blunt, he lied, and lied with cunning persistence, adroitly keeping apart those friends who might compare notes and find fallible their separate oral traditions, gulling worthy journalists with tales of the tenor that they most wanted to hear, though distant from the truth.

The truth was too dreary to be tolerated by a man who affected naive modesty but craved success and adulation. He talked of himself as a neglected but well-trained professional artist pottering along in modest independence on an inherited private income of £200 a year, protecting himself from accusations of failure by suggesting that in having an income he did not need to sell his pictures. The truth is that for fifty years he was an office boy, an insurance clerk claiming shorthand at eighty words a minute to his credit, a rent collector and a cashier, and retired with a pension, as men do, at the age of sixty-five; his training was a matter of evening classes protracted over a period of seventeen years, and though it may well have begun in a genuine spirit of enquiry, I suspect that it soon developed into a convenient and habitual avoidance of the amatory conventions of the society in which he lived – 'My God, you're ugly,' commented the doctor whom he consulted on the failure of any biddy to be attracted to his bed. As ugliness has never been an obstacle to sexual success (look about you for abundant evidence), there must have been more to his celibacy than the Caroline ears and long nose that feature prominently in the portrait that he painted of himself in 1925, for in this the twenty-seven-year-old has a wide and generous mouth, frank grey eyes, an engagingly troubled brow, and the clean-cut jaw that in the Twenties was an essential attribute of manliness; when this face fell with age, keeping its cap of silver hair unthinned, it was certainly no worse than those of the politicians and divines who litter the benches of the Lords, or even Jonathan Miller. Lowry's friend James Fitton, fellow student in the Manchester evening classes and, as an adolescent of fourteen, half Lowry's age, maintained that he was neither homosexual nor neuter, but merely unobservant; others suppose that he was inhibited by relentless devotion to his clock-collecting mother. That's as may be, but if the libido was lively, then it had to be suppressed, and what better numbing activity could the poor wretch pursue than trudging the streets of Manchester on a stomach filled with tripe to spend evening after evening crouched over his drawing board contemplating the sagging nipples and meagre posing pouch of a middle-aged male model?

If the popular life of Lowry is now known to be only a palimpsest of autobiographical confections, what should we make of his paintings and what he says of them? The myth is that he sprang fully-formed from the brow of Minerva and painted more or less the same picture of urban dereliction eight hundred times after a Pauline revelation in a park in Pendleton in 1915 – his converting angel said, 'Look', and, looking, Lowry saw that grime was good.

Again the truth is prosaic; in 1912 Lowry saw a production of *Hindle Wakes*, a tedious proto-feminist play, and was influenced by the set – dim light, rooftops and mill chimneys – the first time that a stage direction has sired a painter's work; and if in these early pictures there is some pathetic attempt to tackle tone and its attendant tenebrous subtleties, then the art critic of *The Manchester Guardian* was responsible for turning him away from it and proposing the formula and technique in which he worked from 1921 until his dying day – the plain white ground upon which everything is silhouetted; late in life Lowry changed the tale of sudden inspiration to one of missing the train to Manchester and drawing a mill for want of something to do while waiting for the next.

I wish that I knew what books he had, for I do not believe the myth of fecund isolation. Though he exhibited at the Salon d'Automne in Paris from 1928 to 1933, he never went there, and indeed never left the country or went much further afield than Lytham St Annes for a holiday with dear Mama (but how did he know about the Paris exhibition, or who suggested that he should submit to it?); without travel, books and magazines must hold the answer to a number of small mysteries that cannot be solved by pointing to pictures in galleries that he can never have visited. Julian Spalding, Director of Manchester City Art Gallery, ever a brave critic, has poked a hole in Lowry's immaculate conception by suggesting that Adolphe Valette, the sub-Impressionist painter marooned in Manchester's Municipal College of Art, influenced him, and that Lowry had some sympathy for the Camden Town Group, picking Malcolm Drummond as an example. I have long believed that the abiding influence was Charles Ginner, in the urban subjects, the often wayward perspective, the clumsy over-booted figures outlined and silhouetted, and in the texture of the paint; I think that he must have known the late work of Robert Bevan and taken from it greedily; and the origins of those ghastly lake landscapes that are so proudly owned by the City of Salford and the University of Manchester must lie in the schematic horrors of that member of the Group of Seven, the Canadian Lawren Harris. It is inconceivable that Lowry's more ectoplasmic and slug-smooth figure drawings were not borrowed from Max Beerbohm and witlessly re-hashed. Looking further forward I wonder about the urchins of that over-exposed flash in the pan Bernard Buffet, and looking further back, think it possible that Lowry owned one of Gustav Glück's popular books on Pieter Breughel, sharing that great master's interest in the crone, the cripple and the beggar, in children's games and adult idiocies, borrowing from him the perspective of the sixteenth century *Weltlandschaft*.

I have no patience with the Sunday painter, the therapeutic or the primitive when the impertinent claim is made that they are part of the great stream of European painting that flows from the Renaissance; I do not accept that they are even eddies and backwaters; they are merely self-serving in their search for intellectual and emotional releases that are of more interest to the psychologist than the art historian. Lowry needed to paint as other men need to mow their lawns or fiddle with their motor cars, and is an amateur who gives us nothing but tricks and mannerisms that support a formula, in dry paint straight from the tube, chalky for want of the varnish that he forbade. He deserved the neglect that dogged him to his dotage – the mystery is that the London art world, for which he proclaimed such scorn, should ever have been seduced into recognising him as a professional. He was an official artist at the Coronation in 1953. The Royal Academy appointed him an Associate in 1955 and elected him full member in 1962. Harold Wilson offered him a knighthood, and Edward Heath wanted to make him a Companion of Honour. The Queen and the Tate Gallery were among his earlyish patrons, and at least four hundred and forty of his tedious, repetitive, lacklustre and stereotypical works are to be found in the kingdom's public collections, such is our philistine English enthusiasm for the half-baked amateur.

Tatler 1988

William Morris

I DREAD THE THOUGHT OF 1996, FOR IT IS THE centenary of the death of William Morris, and will be the excuse for all sorts of arty-crafty shenanigans larded with pie-eyed socialist nonsense about the inherent virtue of the working classes. Morris believed, or promoted the belief (I am sufficiently cynical to doubt his sincerity), that the craftsman is an artist and the artist a craftsman, taking his lead from the medieval cathedrals in which he could see no distinction between the visible splendours of the saints adorning the façades, and the hidden mischiefs that decked the distant roof bosses and water-spouts.

To some extent Morris was right, and he had Cennino Cennini to support him, though I do not think he knew it. Cennino, none of whose works survives, left a written record of the scope and practices of an Italian artist's studio in the early years of the fifteenth century, which makes it clear that he regarded everything from the grandest altarpiece to a carnival banner or the trappings of a nag as an acceptable commission. What Morris, the blinkered medievalist, failed to recognise was that once the Renaissance had got into its stride, the status of the artist changed from artisan to intellectual, and was never to revert – except, of course, in England, where itinerant portrait painters ate their suppers in the servants' hall, and landscape artists were asked to varnish the carriages and broughams when they put the finishing touches to their views of house and park. Leonardo da Vinci left Florence for many reasons, but salient among them was his sense of frustration that as a painter he was not ranked as the equal of poets and philosophers at the court of the Medici, where the perception of the painter was still as medieval craftsman working either to an accepted formula, or as the illustrator of a text or programme. Within half a generation, Michelangelo and Raphael had swept these restraints aside, the one a moody genius, precursor of

Rembrandt and such Bohemian mavericks as Gauguin and Van Gogh, the other on a white horse, riding with a retinue, knight-like, through the streets of Rome, Rubens and Van Dyck his heirs. Morris was, of course, more strictly Pre-Raphaelite than any member of that brilliant Brotherhood, a real Cennini man who would rather that the High Renaissance had not happened, but with no more than a tittle of their skills, inspiration and abilities, he was an aesthetic Luddite.

For Morris, a member of the very comfortable educated middle-classes, never without a roof over his head, never short of cash, being a Socialist was an indulgence – he could afford to rant and rave and publish his absurd pamphlets, write plodding poetry, translate Icelandic legends, design fake furniture, tapestries, wall-papers and even houses, living a medieval dream in which there were no stinks or plagues, and taking occasional cures at German spas when good living got the better of his body. His level of achievement was pretty low as a third-rate Pre-Raphaelite of the applied arts, and he must bear the blame for the incrusted gloom of late Victorian good taste and the fake Tudor references of street after street of suburban semi-detached houses, to say nothing of Liberty's in Regent Street and every tea-room called The Copper Kettle.

Any man who wrote, lectured, hectored and bullied as much as Morris, coinciding with educational reform, the disgustingly degraded tag end of the Gothic Revival, and a romantic view of Socialism as yet untried in practice, was, riding on the backs of Ruskin and Pugin, bound to have influence. He has it still. The Morris Gospel according to Neil Kinnock is the notion that the British working man is but aesthetically asleep, worn out by the harsh pressures of Capitalism, waiting only for the kiss of Socialism to awaken him to the passionate pursuit of natural creativity and natural good taste. The Morris fancy that art is merely 'man's expression of his joy in labour' has been turned into the assumptions that every man is at heart an artist capable of artistic expression, and that every expression of self is art – it is the justification for treating graffiti as an art form, and for the artists' co-operatives that now spring everywhere, demonstrating little more than inflated egos and blind incompetence. Morris is directly responsible for much current loose political thinking about the arts, and for much that is undisciplined, squalid and degraded in their practice. The worst aspect of his teaching is that it reversed the trend established by Leonardo, Michelangelo and Raphael (and heroically continued by Joshua Reynolds and his henchmen here) that set painting, sculpture and architecture apart from and above the decorative and applied arts, the gap inexorably widening; with Morris we were suddenly back five centuries, persuaded to believe that some wretched waxed wood candlestick has the same aesthetic authority as the Sistine Ceiling – a claim that Cennino Cennini would never have made. God knows what Morris would have thought of Picasso, who only a decade after his death, wrestled with Congo Barbarism to bring art into the twentieth century. In his own practice Morris was a prime mover in the ludicrous Arts and Crafts Movement, which bore even more perverted and exotic fruit in Roger Fry's Omega Workshops in 1913; in Europe, it was a profound influence on the Deutsche Werkstätten in Dresden in 1898, on the Wiener Werkstätten in Vienna in 1903, and on the Deutscher Werkbund in Munich in 1907.

From time to time the moribund beliefs of Morris are resurrected in wearisome attempts to convince us that pottery, painting and petit-point share the same aesthetic and intellectual stature (the Victoria and Albert seems to preach this idiocy more or less non-stop); the Barbican is now exhibiting an artists' co-operative named Material + Form, a group of German throwers and blowers who would have us believe that clay pots and glass bowls can stand comparison with sculpture and painting, claiming in their apologia that they are the spiritual heirs of Old Father William (they throw in Oscar Wilde for good measure). Their work is drearily old-fashioned, attached to the notion of the object as a work of art, and the work of art as object. The pots look much the same as any other craftsman's pots, in no way particularly German, but of a kind to be seen all over this country in every craft fair from Aberystwyth to Aberdeen; a pot is a pot, when all is said and done, and the games that can be played with texture, glaze, shape and function are limited – indeed more amusing and spirited pottery has emerged from every archaeological dig in Anatolia, and the Roman Glass exhibition at the British Museum last year produced far more work that could more nearly justify a claim to sculptural status. Most of what these contemporary Germans offer us is knick-knackery that might have been fashionably amusing in the later Sixties (who now remembers Fornasetti's glossy coffee-table objects?), and it is in no way elevated by the presence of a few paintings, prints and photographs, for once such robust self publicists as Beuys and Baselitz, Penck and Polke have been dismissed (none of them present here), current German painting and sculpture are revealed as bleak, dreary, incestuous and unpromising.

The members of Material + Form show us nothing that we have not seen before, and offer no new insights to illuminate the *Paragone* between art and the bauble. I cannot imagine why they have been invited to display their vulgar uninspired wares in London; even less can I see the point of their later trekking off to Mrs Thatcher's home county to set up shop in Lincoln – except that the Lincolnshire worthy who appends a local addendum to the catalogue (a nincompoop committed to the jargon of *craftsperson* and *craftspeople*) believes that between the arts and crafts 'conceptual barriers have been progressively broken down over the past twenty-five years . . .' Let me assure him that they have not; let me, moreover, draw to his attention the current thinking about all those thousands of black and brown Greek vases that occupy museums from Copenhagen to Nicosia, so long held in awe as works of art – it now seems that they are nothing of the kind, but were mere adjuncts to the Athenian equivalent of the Smallbone kitchen, containers for oil, vinegar and the local brews and vintages, bought from some antique Habitat. A pot is a pot, and always has been. A pox on Morris and all pseudo-medieval dreamers.

Tatler 1989

Rodrigo Moynihan

T*HE TEACHING STAFF OF THE PAINTING SCHOOL at the Royal College of Art* is the one picture by which Rodrigo Moynihan will be remembered. At first glance this life size group portrait seems no more than an evocation of the great studio interiors of the nineteenth century tinged with the melancholy of Euston Road, Courbet and Fantin translated into the drab austerity that was the London of a post-war Labour Government. By chance its closest parallel is Boilly's record of Isabey's studio in the post-Revolutionary Paris of 1798, where the central figures are back to back, divided by an onlooker, and set against an element so powerfully vertical that it arrests the slow rhythms of the frieze – but the differences are more illuminating than the similarities; Moynihan chooses a viewpoint that is high and off-centre, as though the spectator were casually joining the *conversazione*; the space is subtly tilted, angled and made abstract, the elements that define it ingeniously unstable, so that we know neither the shape nor size of the room; most of the figures are congested in a group that seems nervously confined, with only John Minton as the outcast separated by the age-old symbolism of skull and ivy, his miserable suicide eerily predicted; the mastery of tone and subdued colour stems from Picasso's grey and ochre Cubism, the composition distantly from the diagonal slants of Braque.

I see nothing of the 'objective naturalism' with which the painting was credited in the catalogue of *Exhibition Road* (RCA 1988, No. 62). It was one of sixty paintings commissioned by the

Arts Council for the Festival of Britain in 1951, with a stipulated minimum size of 45″ × 60″; Moynihan took from them more than four times that measure of free canvas, and returned to them a composition that is held together by hard work and judicious contrivance, not by some amusing dialogue between planned and accidental effects, and certainly not by random chance. Even though in 1951 my head was full of Titian and the Raphael *Stanze*, I thought the Moynihan a masterpiece. I think so still.

Masterpiece is not the word to use of any other of his pictures. The *Objective Abstractions* exhibited in 1934 now seem astonishingly precocious only in the sense that they were the first examples of the messy, undisciplined, expressionist abstractions that are still mass-produced in every art school in the land by students who know and can do no better – they were muddle-headed then and are so now. The still lives and nudes of the later Thirties were William Nicholson and a dash of Picasso. The celebrated *Short Arms Inspection* of 1943 is quintessential Euston Road – and no room in the Royal Academy's *British Art in the Twentieth Century* could have done more damage to our jingoism than the wretched etiolated offerings of Gowing, Coldstream, Pasmore and their ilk, making a virtue of mannered incompetence. It was the still lives of the Forties that laid the foundations for *The Teaching Staff*, for in these controlled and measured assemblages of conventional domestic objects he came to terms with the requirements of disciplined composition; it could, I suppose, be claimed that he had learned something from the Dutch still life painters of the seventeenth century with their skulls and books and curling sheets of paper (it is indeed with a Dutch *Memento Mori* that he mated Minton), or perhaps from Chardin and Manet, but such similarities may be mere accident for there are as many with the work of Orchardson – Richard Shone lays claim to Goya, Ribera, Zurbaran and Saenredam as his spiritual mentors. Moynihan could not repeat the success of *The Teaching Staff* – its immediate follower, *The Directors of Penguin Books*, of 1952, is unhappily laboured, the stitching of the seams and gussets all too obvious. Turning to abstraction in the middle Fifties, he mirrored Sam Francis, Victor Pasmore and Chinese tachism, and in the mid Sixties eschewed all but extreme abstraction while he edited the magazine *Art and Literature* with Sonia Orwell, John Ashbery, and Anne Dunn. In 1971 he returned to painting the still lives that have ever since been his mainstay, circular, oval and rectangular, sharply observed, more or less restricted to the impedimenta of the painter's studio. He took to portraiture – long bust lengths in which the heads are dominant, the rest of the figure abandoned but for some caricatural note; these are effective records, but fudged painting had occasionally to be clarified with a deftly scribbled line, and his dispute with Mrs Thatcher brought him unwelcome public notice. His portraits of himself suggest some relish for the mirror and the model.

The still lives of the Seventies and early Eighties were astonishing at a time when the art market was still dominated by abstract art in its least disciplined and most aberrant incarnations. Moynihan clearly stated what the sane already knew – that to be effective in an abstract sense no painter is compelled to abjure the identifiable subject – and with a shelf of knick-knacks set about paying homage to Mondrian. When he subdued the line and let the light play about the plastered wall he could produce a match for *The Goldfinch* of Carel Fabritius. These deft, subtle, economic paintings seemed, after twenty years of prodigal hiatus, to be a logical, delightful and painterly development of all that had been intellectually stated in *The Teaching Staff*.

Alas, the Roman spring was short. Moynihan's October exhibition was of a fumbling hand that can no longer tell the difference between plaster, plastic, paper, cotton wool and cloth. He can still *sketch* the nude, but painted, the female figure is a thing of cylinders that, though identified by hirsute crutch and nipple, is denied all sensuality; recumbent, the twisted rigidity of this studio prop is laughable. Intent on painting objects as he finds them, the still lives have compositions, if at all, by accident – all wit and tension gone. From late promise that was so positive the falling-off is lamentable. The concurrent retrospective exhibition of his drawings reached back to 1932, the year after he left the Slade, with a clumsy study of a nude that vaguely recalls Modigliani, but which is damned by a heavy unsympathetic line that expresses nothing of the inner form; much later nudes were equally inept, though caught in that scratchy sketchiness that is characteristic of the Slade tradition of drawing on its deathbed. Moynihan's landscape studies are, for the most part, competent exercises in the centre, surrounded by broad acres of indecision close in character to the flaccid abstracts in which he seems never to have identified his objective, and lets the wash and splatter take their chance. Only in two studies of sleeping soldiers and in the preparatory pen drawings for *The Short Arms Inspection*, does he show any sympathy for the subject or any control of his technique. At his best his subject drawings resemble the worst of Edna Clarke Hall; the feeble abstract watercolours are contemptible.

All this is celebrated in a slim volume of reproductions that is not a *catalogue raisonné* and prints its plates in random order. It has a much bracketed and self indulgent foreword by John Ashbery, an American Professor of Creative Writing whose prose is an example to eschew; the meat of the text is provided by Richard Shone, but it falls into the category of commercial catalogue introduction – fulsome praise and evasion of all things contrary and controversial. Even an indifferent painter deserves a better book than this.

Modern Painters 1988

New Contemporaries and the Whitechapel Open

THE MOST ENGAGING EXHIBIT ON VIEW IN London now is a set of restaurant chairs and tables ready for the hungry visitor. These are not in Langan's Brasserie or any Casa

Vomitorio in Soho, but in the Camden Arts Centre, among the photographs, Wendy houses, builders' pallets, old clothes and post-to-the-point-of-posthumous Dada and Surreal objects and constructions that are now (and have been for too long) the vocabulary of international contemporary art. If we accept Damien Hirst's definition of a work of art – 'it's in an art gallery ain't it? . . .' – then the chairs and tables and their settings must surely be the work of some young Michelangelo of today – and they are indeed the concept of a student at Goldsmiths' College (that forcing-house of notions enigmatic and arcane), born in 1970.

At the age of twenty-four Michelangelo had hacked his sculpture of the *Pietà* from a block of marble six feet tall; on the lap of a Virgin Mary untouched by time lies the body of Christ, collapsed in the weighty inelegance of death, realism tussling with theology; the cutting of the block is deep, the gestures expansive, the Virgin's effort well-defined, anticipating the baroque dramas of Bernini in the 17th century, yet restrained by the decorum of the Quattrocento; it is descriptive in every detail, yet all are subordinate to the controlling composition that compels the spectator to move from side to side; it demands the strong emotional response of grief and compassion, and yet its poignant nobility induces awe.

This grave sculpture is not, of course, controlled by timing mechanisms and electric motors, and does not wave its arms and legs about and utter cries and groans. In this particular, young Milo Garcia has the advantage over Michelangelo, for his chairs slide in and out without the aid of human agency, grinding on the floor, banging the table legs, rattling the cutlery and almost (always almost, so delicately is the impact judged) upsetting the wine glasses. A mild sense of shock dismays the visitor at the first movement of the first chair; he waits for others to perform the little trick – some do, some don't; turning to look at other exhibits in the room, the noise of dragging chairs is an inescapable distraction. He watches other visitors and waits for their reactions – the startled yelp, the quick step to one side, the unsure smile. He sees a purpose for this 'sculpture' as an instrument of farce in Widow Twanky's kitchen, in domestic comedies by Terence Rattigan, or in the supper scenes of *Tosca* and *Bohème* for those who think opera ridiculous, but he cannot see that this ingenious amusement has any place in an art gallery and is compelled to ask the question that is now forbidden by the High Priests of contemporary art on pain of condemnation as a Philistine – 'How can this be art?'

Suppose that one wished in the Tate Gallery to contemplate an abstract in white on white, or plumb the depths of one in black on black – would this cerebral-cum-spiritual exercise be possible with young Milo's chairs scraping the floor in a neighbouring room? Suppose one were a modern Medici – would breakfast, that most desperately humourless of meals, be tolerable with his prandial machine pranking within earshot? And crank and prank it must, for without noise and movement it is nothing. Like so much that is now churned out as art, this is the stuff of temporary exhibitions, not permanent display, demanding attention yet offering nothing but a transitory frisson in return, forcing a glance over the shoulder for a moment, but, in spite of technical complexity, so shallow in content, so arid in spirit, so unrewarding in any aesthetic sense (indeed so contrary) that it cannot hold the visitor.

The mass rejection of the hereditary instruments of art, emotional, aesthetic, technical, by those who teach, those who play apologist, those who claim that anything is art and anyone an artist if he declares himself to be so, and that mere presence in a gallery is the touchstone that turns dull object into art, has destroyed the very arts that they pretend to support. We are told again and again by commercial sponsors that they seek to 'widen access to the arts', or some such gibberish, but does BT, the sponsor of both the New Contemporaries at Camden and the Open Exhibition at Whitechapel, really imagine that they offer this 'accessibility' with bars of soap the size and shape of washbasins, with upturned furniture, with bright postcard views that can be seen from any riparian hotel in southern Cyprus or Cattolica, with the plastic begging-boys of chemists' shops locked behind the glass door of the lavatory, or with mindless videos of mindless artists with appalling accents droning on about the disappointments of America? How can a video of a clumsy young woman clambering about the empty bookshelves of her room make the arts of painting and sculpture 'accessible' to anyone? How can a monstrous screed of scribbled text elicit an aesthetic response from those for whom the arts have hitherto been inaccessible? Do these sponsors really believe that they perform good works in playing Lady Bountiful to the politicians of the arts who impose on us their choice of mock machines and toys for mentally arrested adults, their ink blots on the floor, their over-blown smudged photographs, their light-box art (a large transparency of a young Rastafarian with extra details of his penis in two stages of erection), their vast array of airline tickets and tawdry offerings in plastic bags, and even neatly folded shirts straight from their wrappers?

There is a larger issue. Most of those who make this unbuyable, unhouseable and unexhibitable art (the 2,470 submissions to White-chapel were whittled down to fewer than one in ten) passed through art schools at great cost to the taxpayer, often for periods of seven or eight years, sometimes for ten. Few, very few, support themselves through sales when they leave school, and far too many are still, and will remain, a charge on the public purse, each living at our expense the delusion that he is an undiscovered genius. In the wastes of Whitechapel only two decent painters can be found, Anthony Whishaw and John Copnall, both to be classified as ancient has-beens by Richard Shone, a critic for whom increasing age implies decreasing competence – but both made their reputations without the help of sponsorship, and neither is a charge on the state.

If sponsors of such exhibitions as New Contemporaries and the Whitechapel Open believe that their standing is in any way enhanced, then they are vain; if they believe that they ease an ignorant public into appreciating art, then they deceive themselves; if they believe the advice of the petty art politicians from whom they have so far sought it, then they are gulled and cheated; better that they give their shareholders' money to the destitute, even to the dogs at Battersea, than in their dismal ignorance sponsor such wretched art as this.

Evening Standard 1994

Ben Nicholson

Ben Nicholson's father was the cele-
brated artist William Newzam Prior Nicholson, a painter of
lustrous jugs and pretty flowers, with a plump touch to the
paint. Ben's mother was another painter, Mabel Pryde, much less
celebrated – indeed forgotten, but for marrying William and
pupping Ben – a woman given to putting order into asymmetry
(or perhaps asymmetry into order). With the smell of oil paint in his
nostrils and its smudges on his clothes, the infant Benjamin was thus
destined to become another painter, but the evidence suggests that
he resisted destiny, was no infant prodigy, and had no clear sense
that the brush was to be his instrument, seriously considering the
pen instead. His purpose as a painter was not established until he was
almost thirty.

William Nicholson was only twenty-two when Ben was born in
1894, and was then much less a painter than a man forced to earn his
living with popular posters and woodcuts; he too was almost thirty
when painting became his prime occupation, and at his knee the
boy Ben absorbed enough of this new practice to be worthy of the
Slade School by the time he was sixteen – perhaps, indeed, too
much, for rather than pay attention to his tutor, the tyrannical
Henry Tonks, he preferred to play billiards in a Bloomsbury hotel,
and stayed only for four terms. He had spent only three terms at his
boarding school, Gresham's, and was remembered there for
nothing more than his precocity at cricket, and in later life his
skills in tennis and table tennis were recalled by friends as fiendish; it
seems that the clarity of red and white on green, the swift ricochet,
parabola and googly, the swerve induced by spin, and the under-

lying mathematics of them all as they drew their invisible lines against the rectilinear frames of court and pitch and table, were far more formative than the traditional discipline of drawing nudes and antique plaster casts. Paul Klee's definition of drawing was 'going for a walk with a line'; Nicholson's was playing ball games with it.

In many of his mature works he makes these invisible lines visible, seeming to chart their course in bounce and curvature, but to see only this is to neglect the planes that lie beneath them; these are often scraped and scratched and distressed as though Nicholson has tried to deny the pliant nature of oil paint exploited by his father, and turn it to dusty stone or plaster, bearing the marks, not of the painter's brush, but of the workman's tools. This affection for worn surfaces may have been born of another childhood experience at the parental knee – the sight of his mother impatiently scrubbing the kitchen table whenever conversation turned to aesthetic theory, the pine darkening in tone when damp, the grain criss-crossed with knife marks darker still, or grey-veiled with Vim, the stains of blood and beetroot bleaching pale. Nicholson achieved his frottie-frottage-palimpsest transparent surfaces through sheer hard work that is far removed from the laying-on of paint, and had much to do with his passion for turning paintings into *things*.

To ping-pong and the kitchen table must be added the impact of Picasso. If, as some suppose, Ben's development as a painter was stultified by quiet rebellion against William's undemanding pictures, the stuff of dining room and boudoir – and it is true that he painted very little in the more than ten years of hesitant apprenticeship self-taught after the Slade terms – it was a late Cubist painting by Picasso (thirteen years his senior), seen by chance in Paris in 1921, that released him from his inhibitions; he wrote of it '. . . none of the actual events of one's life have been more real . . .' Thus began a period of 'fast and furious experiment', of which few paintings survive to illustrate the fastidious distillation of influences that interested him – early Italian Renaissance frescoes (another source for his pale and distressed surfaces), Cézanne and Matisse, Braque and Picasso, even Mantegna, who haunts the Lugano landscape that is the rare relic of 1921 – all subtly incorporated into work that over the next ten years (his lack of urgency was quite remarkable) fumbled its way towards the abstraction that at last could be immediately identified as his.

In the 1920s, English influences and friendships came into play – his wife, Winifred, a painter whose work was then much more assured than Ben's, gave him a sense of light and colour that he had been unable to develop for himself, Paul Nash, whom he had known at the Slade, lent him a feeling for design, Ivon Hitchens reassured him as he edged towards the abstract, and Christopher Wood and Alfred Wallis pulled him in the contrary direction of the self-conscious primitive. In works of this last kind we sense Nicholson's intellectual confusion; he attempts a naive approach to the perspective of landscape, deliberately misjudging tone and scale, yet at the same time tries his hand both at a revival (or survival) of the Romantic tradition of English landscape painting (anticipating by at least a decade the Neo-Romanticism of the late Thirties), and at so careless a scribbled sketching with the loaded brush that the resulting landscape is scarcely better than the amateur.

Early in the Thirties, many continental abstract influences renewed and reinforced his intellectual discipline, though many years passed before he finally relinquished his romantic English nonsense. He met Arp and Brancusi, Calder, Miro and Giacometti, Picasso and Braque, Moholy-Nagy and Mondrian – that so many of these were abstract sculptors was due to the close friendship with Barbara Hepworth that began in 1931 (they married in 1938); their effect was not only to confirm him as an abstract painter, but also to turn him into a maker of shallow painted reliefs that were at least as much sculptural objects as paintings hanging on the wall. Some of these were white, complementing, as it were, Hepworth's carvings in white marble, but the paintings after 1934 were closer to Mondrian, even though Nicholson claimed that he did not then understand the Dutchman's work – 'later I valued . . . flat planes of colour controlled to an exact pitch, and the greater tension obtainable by the use of true circles and rectangles . . .'

As the acquired pictorial devices matured and were refined, Nicholson developed mannerisms that grew tedious with repetition; as a self-constructed artist, the artifice of self-construction was often his undoing, for far too many of his pictures and reliefs are the mixture as before or the umpteenth ascetic variation on an arid theme. When they succeed, his works are things of extraordinary delicacy, as economic in means and effect as his abbreviated Christian name (in contrast to his father's multiplicity), serenity and repose or alarming tension their prime characteristics, but when they fail, nothing redeems the sense of dull deliberate contrivance.

Nicholson's place in the history of art is now a subject of debate: is he an artist of world stature, or merely a painter for the Millbank parish pump? I am inclined to put him down as a minor craftsman who through much intellectual anguish and physical effort occasionally produced work that gives dry pleasure; for the contrary view, I commend, not the Tate Gallery's yard upon yard of worthy exegesis, but a brief, sympathetic and convincing essay by Christopher Neave in the catalogue of Bernard Jacobson's concurrent exhibition.

Evening Standard 1993

The Omega Workshops

THE IDEAL HOME EXHIBITION, AN ANNUAL beano for the makers and vendors of furniture, paint and interior decoration, is not well regarded by English intellectuals, and never has been. Interior decorators would not be seen dead at this bottom of the cultural abyss, but Queens are always pleased to attend and give the Gadarene Swine a friendly push. In 1913 Alexandra, her taste corrupted by gilt, took King Edward VII to look at the room assembled by the Omega Workshops, and commented that it was the perfect example of how *not* to decorate a sitting-room.

The Omega Workshops were the short-lived brain-child of

Roger Fry, eximious critic, aesthete, and panjandrum of the arts who coined the term *Post-Impressionism* in 1910 – that he almost fixed on *Expressionism* instead, not knowing quite what he intended to express with the term, is neither here nor there, except that in 1911 it was used by the Berlin Sezession, and the art historical confusion would have been appalling. Quite what he meant with *Omega* is not clear either; in its meaning as *the last word* it fitted with Edwardian slang, implying up-to-the-minute modernity, and as *the end* it fits comfortably with the slang of today. The Workshops were the outcome of Fry's rapidly developing views on the place of the artist in society, and an attempt to relate the fast flowering of the contemporary art of the day to the daily life of ordinary people – the connection to be made through decorative and usable art. The idea was conceived within six years of Picasso's painting his *Demoiselles d'Avignon* and the consequent explosion of Cubist and Abstract Art, of which the ramifications had reached England partly under Fry's wing in his Post-Impressionist exhibitions of 1910 and 1912, and in the Futurist exhibitions of 1912 and 1913. London was not at that time by any means the cultural backwater that it became under post-war desuetude – even Kandinsky had exhibited with the Allied Artists Association as early as 1909. There were, of course, financial and patronage problems for young painters, and these were among Fry's reasons for setting up the Workshops – 'there are many young artists whose painting shows strong decorative feeling, who will be glad to use their talents on applied arts . . . as a means of livelihood . . .' he wrote to Bernard Shaw in December 1912; Shaw gave him £250 for his scheme. Six weeks later he was brooding on abstract art to another subscriber – 'I want to find out what the function of content is, and am developing a theory . . . that it is merely decorative form and that all the essential aesthetic quality has to do with pure form.' This was rather better put by the philosopher and critic T.E. Hulme, friend of Ezra Pound, in an astonishingly perceptive lecture in January 1914, in which he recognised that complicated machinery would influence abstract art, and that 'The geometrical line is something absolutely distinct from the messiness, the confusion, and the accidental details of existing things'.

To improve on the messiness, confusion and accidental detail of decorative design, was Fry's other aim with the Workshop. He was not the first to conceive the notion. In France he knew well the example, and hoped for the collaboration of Paul Poiret's Studio Martine, in which working-class girls translated their observations and fantasies into pottery, furniture, textiles and decorative ornaments; and in England William Morris and John Ruskin had inspired the Arts and Crafts Movement with its belief that 'The true root and basis of all art lies in the handicrafts', and its intention to turn artists into craftsmen and craftsmen into artists. This was romantic Socialist nonsense with rural overtones, based on the medieval guild system; it revived first Gothic and then Queen Anne before subsiding under a wave of Art Nouveau, and its final fling was the country cottage not-quite-genuine antique. Fry loathed it, but the example was useful; his Omega Workshops were to be urban, not rural, in their concerns, cared nothing for the immortal souls of common workmen, put aesthetics before technical skill and achievement, rejected the heirloom aspects of art, and responded immediately to any frivolous impulse.

It was impulse that finished Omega almost before it began. Fry's project attracted the whimsical creatures of Bloomsbury, who saw it as a revolution against custard – if that seems preposterous it must be recalled that Fry dubbed Britain *Bird's Custard Island* (custard was then no longer the delectable confection baked in the oven, but a skin-covered bright yellow sludge made from powder, a by-product of the Industrial Revolution, developed by Jeremiah Bird); it also attracted Wyndham Lewis, Edward Wadsworth and Gaudier-Brzeska, but these and other serious artists seceded from Omega after Fry, on impulse, deceived Lewis over the work to be done for the 1913 Ideal Home Exhibition. This stormy secession after only nine months led to the birth of the Rebel Art Centre, a rival workshop, and by July 1914 the Vorticist Movement was under way with its Manifesto printed in the first issue of *Blast*. If Omega bore any real fruit, it was Ishmael Vorticism – the fiercest intellectual achievement of any group of English painters, and the only one worthy to stand with their continental peers.

Fry was left with the painters he deserved, Vanessa Bell and Duncan Grant, whose facility for mimicry was boundless, and whose inventions were at best humorous or sophisticated, and at worst tasteless and puerile. Others drifted in and out – the American McKnight Kauffer, the South African Edward Wolfe; Simon Bussy and Paul Nash worked for it sporadically, and at some time David Bomberg, William Roberts and Mark Gertler were connected with it; when they needed money they had only to attend Omega and design a rug, a screen, a fan or lampshade, and be paid ten shillings for half a day's work, with a limit of three half days a week. But it cannot have been only the promise of small sums of ready cash that drew these essentially forward-looking artists into Fry's web – they must also have been responding to the idea and the challenge. To Bell and Grant it was the logical application of the decorative talents that Fry had long seen in their work, with a larding of ill-digested Cubist and Fauve influences; to Wyndham Lewis and the impending Vorticists it was an equally logical extension of art into the third dimension, a response to the industrial environment, and a powerful move towards the victory of form over representation.

The designs of this disparate group were often difficult, if not impossible, to translate into being, and the real work was done by a bevy of backroom girls and jobbing carpenters. Fry maintained that the artists must have 'free play . . . in the making of objects of common life', and that they must not spoil 'the expressive quality of their work by sandpapering it down to a shop finish'. In this way he sought to emulate what he saw as the spontaneity of the Studio Martine, forgetting that that very spontaneity would be lost in the repetitive drudgery of producing the work, however spirited the designs might be, for there was little creative joy in painting the legs of tables, tea-trays and 'endless candlesticks for electric light'. If ever there was a crushing indictment of Fry's taste and invention, it lies in that complaint by Winifred Gill, his sometime business manager, in that he could think of no better craft response to electric light than an electrified wooden candlestick. For the artists the absence of rules and regulations was one of the boons of working for Omega – they were free to come and go at will, and to work on whatever project they chose; but for the workers it was a turmoil of slavery amid the vile smell of hot size, and the more bearable odours of wax, varnish, paints and solvents – worse, the inexperienced girls often made much of the work unnecessarily laborious through ignorance of the necessary techniques. This did not trouble Fry, who believed technical skill to be deadening in its effect, hoping that fresh solutions to old problems would maintain a high level of spontaneity. Its only real effects were to reduce efficiency, increase costs, and put the Workshops on the road to bankruptcy. The girls themselves rarely stayed long; the Studio Martine employees were largely working-class, drawn from the sweatshops and markets, but the Omega girls were often graduates from the Slade School (then the best art school in London), often not without a reasonable level of achievement as artists, firmly middle-class, and disinclined to endure the conditions of work imposed on them. When they left they took their hard-won skills with them, and the Workshops suffered from the breaks in continuity.

The only finely finished Omega designs were made by craftsmen outside the Workshops. Marquetry was in fashion; the popular painter Frank Brangwyn, for example, kept the craftsmen of the Rowley Galleries occupied with his designs for landscapes and architectural caprices distantly recalling Renaissance Urbino, and even some very distinguished car bodies with marquetry interiors (including the rooflinings) were designed for Lanchester and Daimler chassis. It was inevitable that rich patrons drawn to Omega would ask for marquetry furniture, and like both Bell and Grant, Fry himself produced designs for it in *papier collé*, in which paper silhouettes in different colours easily imitated the marquetry process. Marquetry tea-trays, for which there was a long and honorable tradition in England, were among the most popular products of the Workshop, but Fry also turned his hand to large-scale furniture. His *Giraffe Cupboard* of 1915–16, now in the Victoria and Albert Museum, is a fine example, demonstrating his taste for opposed pairs of animals as a decorative design – it had also appealed to William Morris, and its origin lay in the distant medieval past, or in Islam. At first glance the design seems as pure as Mackintosh, its bulk stripped of messiness, confusion and accidental detail; at a second glance there is a clear reference in the marquetry to the broken pediment that traditionally tops such pieces, and the ziggurat steps were anticipated in much Biedermeier furniture from central Europe only two generations earlier. It is perhaps no coincidence that the craftsman most employed by Fry was John Joseph Kallenborn, a Polish cabinet-maker working nearby. In more roughly finished furniture – a raw wood cupboard, mass-produced and bought in to be gessoed and painted – a continental influence again seems obvious, and such pieces would not look out of place in the peasant houses of Germany and the Austro-Hungarian Empire.

Textiles were hand-dyed and hand-painted, unless they became the subject of regular order; by May 1913 linens were being printed by the Maromme Printworks near Rouen, which had a London office, but when the works were overrun by the Germans during the war, Fry had to find another French firm further south, now forgotten. Maromme had to satisfy Fry by reverting to the traditional printing method of felt-covered wood-blocks, but their wartime successors used metal lino-type blocks blurred with flock to achieve a hand-made effect. Carpets, for which Grant, Bell and Etchells made spirited abstract designs, were at first hand-knotted in the Workshops, but by mid-1914 the Royal Wilton Factory was producing them, with some loss of the irregularities of weave and surface considered so vital by Fry. Fry himself made the design for the eight identical carpets for the Cadena Café in the then fashionable Westbourne Grove, with the Workshops responsible for the rest of the decoration, from the abstract murals to the flower vases; each rug was an island on the floor, defining the area in which might stand the chairs and tables with Teutonic discipline.

Measured disposition seems to have been an essential part of Omega design. It has been suggested that the appearance of the

Russian Ballet in London from 1909 onwards was a fundamental influence for richness and splendour, but the lush and casual barbarism of Bakst finds virtually no reflection in Omega products and designs, except perhaps in the exotic and eccentric dresses that Vanessa Bell began to make and exhibit in 1915. In contemporary photographs of Omega rooms and displays there is rigid balance, and witnesses recall what can only be described as tonal restraint – the feeling that while individual elements might be exciting, the overall effect was often disciplined and retiring unless enlivened by one of Grant's more daring paintings. It is pointless to extrapolate from Charleston, the house occupied by Vanessa Bell and Duncan Grant until their comparatively recent deaths, for both artists continued to paint and decorate until quantity compelled total disorder, though the tired tonality of it all seems true to the beginning; coming to terms with the present, Grant in his last years painted false fronts for loud-speakers for himself and others, logical descendants of the wind-up gramophone that he had painted for Maynard Keynes in 1926.

There was no aspect of the applied arts from which Omega recoiled – mosaics, stained glass, pottery, embroidery, as well as furniture and textiles; no object was too grand to be left untouched – an early Arnold Dolmetsch harpsichord, now in the Courtauld Institute Galleries, was indeed one of Fry's most successful attempts at decoration, combining almost all the styles on offer at the Workshops, and yet fitting into the Renaissance tradition of painted keyboard instruments. Antique furniture was not safe in Fry's hands, and was often painted beyond period recognition.

If the products of the Workshops had been more professional, they would have been less influential; it was their crude amateur finish that encouraged widespread imitation, and if the Workshops themselves lasted only the six years from March 1913, when Fry took a lease on premises at 33 Fitzroy Square (then the heart of London's Latin Quarter), to the sad clearance sale of Omega stock in June 1919, their influence lasted at least a generation. William Morris encouraged a taste for the fumed oak dole cupboard and gate-legged table, embossed lincrusta dado and imitation tapestry curtains; Omega suggested that it was legitimate to paint Hepplewhite matt grey or dull red, to stencil designs in bright colours on drab jute, and made the gingham-covered tea-chest an accepted article of household furniture. Morris, concerned to bring art within the scope of the working man, merely nipped the bud of taste that he hoped to engender in the artisan; Fry, concerned only for the freedom of the artist's expression, released in the middle classes a flood of primitive talent that seized on every box and jam-jar as an object to be decorated, and that made a virtue of shoddy finish and the hideous clash of colour – in 1916 the *Daily Sketch*, a defunct newspaper that appealed to middle-class women, was ecstatic about the thrill of tomato soup in a black Omega tureen, vivid lettuces and shy (sic) radishes on black plates, and 'amusing' macaroni. 'How long will it last? Will it fizzle out . . .?' asked Fry at the beginning of the Omega experiment. T.E. Hulme answered in January 1914 that it would 'find its grave in some emporium which will provide the wives of young and advanced dons with suitable house decoration'. Generations later, the going rate for a plain upright Omega chair is well into the thousands, and the impulse for young wives to do it themselves is as strong as ever.

Art and Antiques 1984

The George Ortiz Collection

IT IS NOW THE CUSTOM OF CURATORS TO GIVE art exhibition titles that romanticise and obscure their subjects, coy, novellettish, pseudo-poetical. When the Arts Council gave us tree trunks and a live parrot in a masquerade of modern sculpture, they called it *Gravity and Grace*; at the Camden Arts Centre, newspaper clippings and boiled sweets belie the pomposity of *Symptoms of Interference, Conditions of Possibility*; and now, at the Royal Academy, we have *In Pursuit of the Absolute*, a pseudo-philosophical nonsense applied to the random acquisitions of a private collector over the past forty years or so.

There is nothing *absolute* about the collection of George Ortiz, nothing even encyclopedic, nothing remotely approaching the principles of scientific classification that should apply in museums, or that were brought by Ludwig von Koechel from his work as botanist and mineralogist and applied to Mozart's manuscripts – nor could there be in a collection of antiquities assembled in our lifetimes when the would-be collector has been the victim of market forces and constrained, we must demand, by strict archaeological disciplines and the heritage laws of ancient lands angered by centuries of plunder.

As his sumptuous catalogue too often reveals, Ortiz has a romantic view of the ancient past, and the scholarship of his enquiring mind is essentially that of the amateur whose sharp eye for quality is occasionally blurred by mania. My immediate reaction to his collection was the fierce arousal of the sin of envy, my mind dominated by it as powerfully as by lust or hunger, for many of these things are of extraordinary beauty, of museum quality, and of intriguing curiosity, and I suffer as much as any man (why is it that so few collections are formed by women?) the urge to possess those things that knot my stomach in response – but I saw nothing to justify the absurd assertion that Ortiz is in pursuit of any absolute, when he has merely bought what has been available to a man whose pocket is lined with power.

The collection ranges more or less coherently through things Egyptian, Sumerian, Anatolian, Greek, Hellenistic, Roman, and off into the wastes of central Asia, but then becomes incoherent and scrappy with a small gathering of ethnographical objects from Africa and the Pacific. It is with the weakness of this tail end that awe for the collection as a whole diminishes, and we begin to question the purpose of its exhibition, for far more marvellous things – relics, for example, of the Seven Wonders of the World – are to be seen in the British Museum, and the collections of the Louvre comprise a little more than just the *Mona Lisa* and the *Winged Victory of Samothrace*.

The exhibition is meticulously arranged and lit, and as most of the objects and glass cases are free-standing, they can be seen in the round. In the long view through the enfilade of rooms on the Academy's north face, the conjunctions are astonishing, a baroque Ghandaran head looming high above a life size marble lion from Attic Greece: from such an arrangement, the British Museum could well learn a lesson in display. Ortiz is a perfectionist in such matters, and his placing of one object with another is often witty, enlightening and utterly seductive, though it is by happy accident, no doubt, that he has set a terracotta bowl decorated with a painting of an elongated goat in line with Modigliani's drawing of an elongated lion in the neighbouring exhibition; the male nudes too, of Modigliani and of ancient Greece, each nourish our perceptions of the other.

With so much 'theatre' it may well seem churlish to challenge the connoisseurship of so distinguished a collector, but his eye wavers when assessing the quality of Roman sculptures, and his *Idealised Hero*, said to be Hellenistic and from Asia Minor, is unconvincing as anything other than a cooking piece. Ortiz is, I think, in error in accepting as Greek his small female idols in terracotta; of these, two are described as 'allegedly' from Thessaly, and the third is said to have been found in a well there, but these vague provenances may conceal an Anatolian origin, for the figures are very close indeed to others discovered at two Turkish sites, at Haçilar and, particularly, Catal Hüyük. For want of funds, the latter is now closed and the small excavated section refilled; the finds, dating from the 6th or 7th millennium BC, are remarkable – indeed amazing – and are the property of the Turkish state, so that the origins of any in private ownership must be concealed.

The most enviable sculpture in the collection is the marble head and fragmentary left shoulder of a Ghandaran prince, 'allegedly' found near Peshawar in Pakistan, and dating perhaps from 200 AD. It has all the baroque splendour and immediacy of the finest Hellenistic sculpture, the carving deep and realistic, the hair a rich riot of curls and top-knot, the face fleshy and sensual, the expression saturnine. This is sculpture to rival Bernini at work on 17th-century popes and kings, and as it is unique among Ghandaran survivals, which are usually in soft schist, I wonder if the sculptor came, perhaps, from the great workshops of Aphrodisias in Anatolia, even bringing the marble with him (Aphrodisians were expert in the transport of marble blocks from their local quarries); I wonder too, if this is more than a bust portrait, and speculate on the possibility that it is part of a standing figure of heroic scale, swathed in robes, armoured or even nude (Ortiz identifies him as Buddha, but this too is speculation). Whatever the case, as the hair was once leafed in gold and the eyes set with precious stones, it was a thing of overwhelming grandeur. If indeed it was found near Peshawar, and recently, should it not be in public possession there, demonstrating the confusion of cultural roots that are the ancient history of the Frontier Province?

The market in antiquities is utterly corrupt; from sites all over Italy various Mafiosi extort their price in finds; the Turks care little for the Byzantine heritage of Greeks, and the Greeks less for the heritage of Anatolia; wealthy Swiss and German dealers are active in illicit purchasing, and drive wretched peasants to pillage sites by night; auction houses provide innumerable smuggled finds with what seems something of a legal provenance. Thus are the archaeological records disturbed and destroyed, and our perceptions of past cultures distorted; thus is our scholarship forced into error. It should surprise none of us that page after page of the catalogue written by George Ortiz bears the legend 'Provenance: no indication,' or 'Allegedly . . .' The pursuit of the absolute must surely be the pursuit of truth.

Evening Standard 1994

Picasso Revisited

The Tate Gallery

GIOVANNI PAPINI, BORN IN THE SAME YEAR AS Picasso, 1881, is a forgotten man, but for one thing – he interviewed Picasso, and published the great man's confession that he was a fraud. 'I am only a public entertainer . . . exploiting as best I could the imbecility, the vanity and the cupidity of my contemporaries. Since Cubism, and even before, I have sought to satisfy an audience craving the new and scandalous with all the changing nonsenses that have come into my head – and the less they understood, the more they admired me. Mine is a bitter confession, but it has the merit of being sincere.'

Published in a plump paperback called *Il Libro Nero* (The Black Book) to celebrate Papini's seventieth birthday in 1951, this confession has from time to time been used to dismay those for whom Picasso can do no wrong. I doubt if many copies still exist, for the paper was of appalling post-war quality, and I doubt too if many who delight in the confession would do so if they had seen what company it keeps, for though interviews with Lorca, Dali, Aldous Huxley and Frank Lloyd Wright may arouse no suspicion, that Papini sat at the feet of Hitler and Molotov seems less than likely, as do his butterfly journeys from Mount Athos to the Antarctic and from Mozambique to Mexico, and that he discovered unpublished manuscripts by Goethe, Blake, Kierkegaard, Tolstoy and Kafka must be quite impossible. Besides, the introduction to *Il Libro Nero* makes it clear that the book and its central character, one Gog from Scotland, are mischievous inventions, often of light-hearted whimsy.

In 1951 Papini had a long-established reputation as a philosopher, devout Catholic and biographer of Christ, the small literary support that he had given the Futurists in 1913–14 more or less forgotten – a reputation that lent a veil of truth to the confession among those who did not know its context. It infuriated Picasso, whose friend Pierre Daix blamed it for the master's status as 'the most celebrated unsung hero' of the century (*unsung*? – Picasso?), and claimed that both Franco's Fascist police and 'the ideological services of Kruschev's Kremlin' lay behind its dissemination – a surely impossible combination of political agencies?

The confession has recently been denounced by Simon Wilson of the Tate Gallery, the holder of that extraordinary and much mocked position, The Curator of Interpretation – though I observe in passing that the denunciation might have been more accurate had he too read *Il Libro Nero*. What none of his ilk has cared to do is consider the offending confession, not as an insulting affront to Picasso, but as a criticism that reflected a reasonable response to work that seemed incomprehensible in 1951 (or whenever it was first composed), and seems so now. Cocteau's observation to Louis Aragon in 1956, both friends of Picasso, that he 'embodies that mixture of idolatry and iconoclastic rage that is so typical of the Spaniard and which spurs him onto ruthless creation and destructiveness', has never been questioned, and yet the accusations of rage and destructiveness are at least as damaging as Papini's charges, and just as close to the heart of many who are still puzzled by Picasso's work and reputation twenty years after his death. Both Papini and Cocteau express a truth that should not be dismissed with the mindless huff and puff of outrage.

Let us consider Picasso's Cubism. None should question the intellectual arguments that justify its various stages, but we have the right to ask whether or not it succeeds, and to express misgivings when the intentions change, are frustrated, and finally abandoned to the fundamentally frivolous business of mere decoration. Cubism in all its aspects, and in the hands of all its practitioners, proved a cul-de-sac, a thing of intellectual contrivance and aesthetic casuistry that by chance, because the traditional conventions survived in them, occasionally produced paintings that were magnificent failures and even beautiful, though most were as dry as theological argument in the Middle Ages. To painting that was austerely concerned with the permanent structure of things rather than their sensual surfaces, sculpture was of little help, for with such solid objects as the human head it was confused and, as Picasso himself told Roland Penrose, did not demonstrate its purpose with the smallest logic, and when he took to constructions – the random aggregation of bits and pieces of ordinary materials to see what chance could do for them – the intellectual argument was entirely undermined. If we ask the simple question 'Did Cubism work?' rather than 'Is Cubism an important field in the history of art?' – the answer must be that it did not.

It was, however, Picasso's only venture into intellectual argument, and recognising its failure, he returned briefly to the imagery of the Pink and Blue periods, and then embarked on the long erratic decline that was from time to time interrupted by such marvels of mastery as the Vollard Suite of etchings in the Thirties, the post-war sugar aquatints, and the grand patchwork of success and failure, contrivance and emotion, that we know as *Guernica*. That it was a decline was masked by violent changes of style and distorted imagery that had no true intellectual or emotional purpose, but merely challenged Papini's posited audience of admiring imbeciles. The critic Apollinaire was first to recognise that 'Surprise is the greatest source for what is new in art', and by 1925 Breton was able to observe of Picasso that he had carried the spirits of contradiction and *evasion* to their furthest points – *by 1925*, with nearly half a century of working life ahead.

The notion that Picasso's sculpture and painting are of equal importance in his work, each informing and clarifying the other, is incontrovertible and has been recognised since 1931, when his friend Brassai was commissioned to make an extensive photographic record of the neglected sculpture – and continued to do so for more than thirty years – but the sculpture nevertheless remained a more private activity than painting, rarely seen until the 1967 exhibition at the Tate Gallery. The reason for this privacy may be that sculpture in the round exposed weaknesses that the public could less easily perceive in the two dimensions of a painting, for paintings require a much greater intellectual effort of comprehension, and Picasso himself was unsure of the sculpture, remarking in 1931 that he never knew what might come of it.

In 1933 he made his *Woman with a Vase*, seven feet tall, a figure of stunted graceless ugliness that could well have been in Cocteau's mind when he described Picasso as 'some rustic squire who insults the Virgin Mary because she is not from his own village'. It is argued that Picasso's intended reference was to the female fertility goddesses of primeval times, but it bears scant resemblance to the Venus of Willendorf and her ilk in scale, proportion or symbolism, and is so indefensibly ugly in ways that they are not, that it can only be interpreted as an insult to all women by a phallocentric bore. Comparison with his *Man with Sheep* of ten years on demonstrates that Picasso could, when he wished, tellingly revise the classical traditions of sculpture by removing its surface beauties and revealing its emotional power – but then his jokes at the expense of men are rare, and when concocted from amusing bits of rubbish, as with the male figure of 1958, a thing of stumpy furniture legs and a crude painting stretcher, are more infantile than malicious.

Far more than an exhibition of his paintings, prints and drawings, one that is dominated by Picasso's sculpture reveals the underlying truth of Papini's 'confession' – that Picasso's genius was undermined by the 'new, strange and scandalous . . . games, puzzles, rebuses and arabesques' with which he reduced compliant critics to confusion, and amused himself at the expense of an imbecile audience. He does it still.

Evening Standard 1994

Late Picasso

The Tate Gallery

THE TATE GALLERY'S EXHIBITION OF THE LATE work of Picasso is not to be approached unprepared. A nodding acquaintance with the Barcelona of a century ago, a romp through the Pink and Blue periods, a skirmish with the *Demoiselles d'Avignon* as they lift the curtain on Cubism, awareness of the gallumping classical nudes of the Twenties, total recall of *Guernica*, and tolerance of the distortions, mannerisms and affronts that constitute the oeuvre that followed it, are simply not enough – the one essential, far more important than any of these, is John Richardson's essay in the catalogue. With this for *Baedeker*, the pilgrim may not enjoy his progress through the heaped breasts and buttocks, the intertwined deep-throating tongues, the exposed and fingered rimas, the penetrating penises, and general air of fevered sexuality and its puerile lavatorial expression, but he will understand it – and if my Pilgrim is masculine, this is not mere literary adherence to Bunyan, for underlying my response to the work of Picasso in his dotage is the thought that most of it must be deeply offensive to women.

Richardson tells eloquently and at length the tale of an old man grown impotent, but whose sexual appetite was not one jot diminished by the disability. In 1961, at the age of eighty, he took to himself as wife Jacqueline Roque, the woman forty-five years his junior who had been his mistress for the past decade. By her first husband and a difficult and damaging birth she had a daughter. Though no more children were possible, Picasso refused to let her have a hysterectomy because he 'did not want to make love to a eunuch'; when, in 1965, Picasso's prostate was removed, it was he who became the eunuch, and their roles developed into Jacqueline the childish, miserable, sickening masochist, and Picasso the sadist, with a lifetime of wanton womanising Spanish *machismo* to abet his destructive instincts. He portrayed Jacqueline more often than any other of his women, dismantling and reconstructing her, mocking her short neck, squat torso and stout legs, reducing her to a heap of female fatty parts, gashed by a rima and symbolic pubic hair. He sought to paint the smell of her armpits, and he did paint her emptying her bladder. At the end, he painted her into her coffin. Himself, Picasso reduces to voyeur, the gaze intent, and Richardson is convincing when he quotes another scholar's contention that the painter's native Andalusian society was phallocentric, with sexual activity a masculine monopoly, the plough furrowing the female earth – a primitive province where the eye of a man is recognised as an organ of sexual probing, and a gaze too intent is an ocular rape. Picasso portrays himself a rapist as well as a creator when he describes his palette as scrotum and his brush as penis. Like many another painter, he is amused by such sexual byways as the languors of the lesbian, and one of his most wittily cruel studies is of a creature who might be Alice's aged Ugly Duchess fingering her small root of pleasure with sharp enamelled nails.

Most of this work lends some weight to the argument of those feminist viragos who see the female painted nude, not as art, but as an image to stir the loins of men. I argue that at its best the art of a female nude far outweighs its potent pornographic imagery, that it is impossible to look at the women of Titian, Correggio and Rubens and see them primarily as exploitations, for they are first and foremost works of art in which the erotic element limps far behind; but I am defeated by Picasso, for his images have no conventional aesthetic beauty, nor the sensuality to stir any man's loins, yet they are manifestly sexual. The sexuality is the public display of private anguish, anger and revenge, and painting it is, as it were, the act of frantic and frequent intellectual masturbation. I am not convinced that art and genius are any part of this recipe, any more than I should be inclined to accept as great works of literature lewd limericks of rugby club standard penned by T.S. Eliot, were they now to be discovered in the wastelands of Kensington Court Place. This is the point of my suggesting that Richardson's catalogue essay be read before setting foot in the Tate, for to inspect these angry genital obsessions without knowing the circumstances of their conception, might cause us all to plague *The Times* with letters.

Understanding, sympathy and compassion for old Picasso's predicament do not make the pictures any better. The academic discipline of art history requires that we should know of them, but it does not demand that we must admire them – but admiring late Picasso has of late become a cottage industry for one American scholar renowned for his publications on pornography, and another so avuncular and benign that he is incapable of critical judgement. Richardson has, alas, joined this school, mocking his former mentor Douglas Cooper (no mean connoisseur of Picasso's work, even if he was Picasso's Falstaff) for describing as 'incoherent doodles done by a frenetic dotard in the anteroom of death' what Richardson now sees as 'a phenomenal finale to a phenomenal oeuvre', and 'a one-man apotheosis of post-Renaissance painting'.

The extended variations on themes first explored by Velazquez, Degas, Manet, Van Gogh, Rembrandt and Delacroix are, it seems, both the challenge of a man who though old, frail, shrunken and impotent was inspired by *amour-propre* to beat on their own terms the greatest painters of the Western world, and an aspect of Freud's psychic cannibalism, whereby the consumption of a rival endowed the consumer with the powers of the consumed – an interesting thought that for all his lifetime in Parisian society, Picasso's instincts were as primitive and barbarous as those of a Dyak from the forests of Borneo.

I don't believe a word of it. I see no point in romanticising an impoverished imagination and urging spurious greatness onto sad doodles far descended from the work of other men. The lie in all this nonsense resides in his whimsical development of that absurd picture by Ingres in which La Fornarina, Raphael's mythical mistress, sits on the great man's knee in front of her unfinished portrait. It is, like most of Ingres's paintings, de-natured and de-sexed, over-posed, literal, pop-eyed and ridiculous, but not content, Picasso had to add to it elements from an even sillier picture in which a slug-like Paolo slithers up Dante's demure and simpering Francesca da Rimini to plant a kiss upon her cheek, and from this unlikely cocktail he conjures a series of studio interiors in which a well-endowed and rampant Raphael conjugates with an enthusiastic Fornarina in the glum presence of the Pope. 'We must be like Ingres,' said Picasso a month before his death, and the current art historical thinking is that he admired the Frenchman's custom of repeating his pictures, distilling the anecdote and image until they approached perfection – that may work for Ingres (though I doubt it) but Picasso did not repeat the image, but varied it, each naughty thought the root of the next expression of lubricious humour. He gained no strength from eating Ingres.

No – the truth is that the silly old goat had long since run out of steam as a painter and been dependent on the stimulus of works of art already realised; it was not by any means a unique predicament – the obvious home-grown example is Augustus John, for whom self-cannibalism was a way of life for forty years, and a glance in the direction of Leonardo, Caravaggio and Rubens suggests many a respectable precedent. When Picasso ran out of steam as a sexual man, the only power left to him was painting, and art and sex conjoined to pup some of the saddest, most degraded, most humiliating, repetitive, tedious, uninspired, obsessive and crudely painted banalities that have ever masqueraded as art, with Picasso never knowing how to escape from the maze or dismount from the merry-go-round. A thousand years hence, historians will strive to reverse the chronology, finding it inconceivable that such adolescent graffiti could succeed the intellectual weight of Cubism and the emotional power of the Pink and Blue periods – turn it on its head and it works better backwards, for in his youth the brilliant Barcelona boy was never the nasty incompetent child that he became in his senility.

Tatler 1988

Pop Art

'I AM FOR AN ART THAT EMBROILS ITSELF WITH the everyday crap and still comes out on top . . . which is abandoned with great contempt, like a piece of shit . . . for art you can pick your nose with . . . I am for the art of ice-cream cones dropped on concrete. I am for the majestic art of dog-turds, rising like cathedrals.' Thus wrote Claes Oldenburg in 1967 when Pop Art was already past the zenith of its inventive energy, and all its grand old men (of whom he was the most eloquent, outrageous and purposeful) were settling into a complacent stage of polished classicism and market exploitation.

It seems a dark and pessimistic statement (though elsewhere in its considerable length the touch is lighter), but among the ice-cream lollipops made of synthetic fur, the realistic casts of baked potatoes and giant hamburgers, the huge extinguished match and tank-tracked lipstick, I know of no dog-turds, cast large or small, nothing that could cause dismay to Mary Whitehouse – indeed the presiding element is humour, and I am inclined to think that Pop Art was not solely the art of challenge and confrontation that historians would now have us believe, but the art of pantomime, legerdemain, fairground and freak show, to be enjoyed in Bank Holiday mood with candy-floss in hand and 'Kiss me Quick' emblazoned on one's T-shirt. Though the encyclopedic exhibition at the Royal Academy is presented as a scholarly and worthy examination of an art movement as fundamentally important for the history of art as were Cubism and Impressionism, Pop Art by its very nature undermines the high seriousness of the high art approach and demands to be treated with irreverence and ribaldry – how else can one respond to Jasper Johns's green penis lurking in its pigeon hole? I hope that the hallowed galleries of the Academy will this autumn echo the sounds of glee and laughter.

It is, of course, quite proper to consider Pop Art as an aspect of the post-war Renaissance in this country, as a social phenomenon, as a revival of Dada and Surrealism, or as an independent movement of at least thirty years' duration (longer by far than Impressionism, Expressionism and Cubism), for it is all these things; but for many visitors the exhibition will be much more a nostalgic indulgence, a return to the Swinging Sixties when youth was at the prow and pleasure at the helm. The Festival of Britain in 1951 neither marked nor made a change in British society and aesthetic attitudes; food remained rationed, boys continued to do two years' National Service, taxes were burdensome, and in a drab grey world the war that had ended in 1945 was still an ever-present memory. The change came quietly, almost unnoticed, and when social inequalities had been remedied by the Welfare State to the point at which Macmillan could, in 1957, astonish the British by telling them that they had 'never had it so good', the social debate turned, to some extent, to matters cultural – for the 1959 General Election the Labour Party published a manifesto promising a National Theatre and an increase in Arts Council funding, and by 1963 the

Conservative Government was promising an annual increase of 10%.

With an increasingly affluent and leisured society (across all social classes), factors that had never before influenced the arts came into play, and the debate shifted from the moribund fine arts for the few to the popular culture of the masses, and particularly to commercial television, which Richard Crossman in 1960 accused of doping the critical faculties that should have been stimulated by improved popular education. Commercial television reinforced the British love affair with America; the grey-haired grandees of the arts may have been anti-American cultural snobs, but the newly affluent classes far below them had inherited the myths of the GI Bride and the American cinema, and now had new idols in consumer goods that mimicked American design (even the Morris Minor was a scaled-down Chevrolet sedan) and in the singers of pop music. An art form that not only incorporated the perceived glamour of America but was an affront to all the horse and portrait painters of the Royal Academy (the only potentially popular art forum in Britain), was bound to appeal to a far wider audience than the traditional collector and those few who knew the latest Parisian developments: an art form that recognised almost no distinction between painting pictures and designing posters, and used the same vocabulary of sex and kitsch, that incorporated the pin-up girl scissored from the glossy magazine and the neon tube taken from the shop front, that showed no reverence for such revered symbols as the national flag or the sacred icons of old Renaissance masters, that elevated photographic images of Elvis Presley and James Dean to the heights of formal easel painting, that turned Coca-Cola bottles into sculpture and the strip cartoons of comics into the mural narratives of a newly pagan world – this was indeed the art for a generation that broke the old patterns of parental discipline, that had money to burn on briefly fashionable clothes and music, that knew nothing of good taste and propriety, and desperately needed new role models and the conviction that let them emulate without guilt.

Pop Art did not make the society to which it appealed, nor did the newly powerful young make Pop Art – they were mutually self-supporting and grew together. By chance, Pop Art developed simultaneously and without connection in both America and Britain in the Fifties – in the one as a revolution against the dominance of Abstract Expressionism, a nostalgia for the simple subject instead of wildly gestural sweeps of paint, and in the other as an intellectual attempt to bring the design of advertisements and manufactured goods into the realm of the artist and sculptor. Neither the Americans nor the British developed a tight theoretical programme for it, but Richard Hamilton, in 1957, proposed that Pop Art must be popular (in the sense of appealing to a mass audience), transient, expendable, cheap, mass produced, young in appeal, witty, sexy, gimmicky, glamorous and big business – the work of no British artist fitted the formula as perfectly as did that of Andy Warhol.

In Britain the powerhouse of Pop was the Royal College of Art, which has not since produced so famous a group of artists – Peter Phillips, Derek Boshier, Patrick Caulfield, Allen Jones, David Hockney (who always denies any association with Pop), Richard Smith, and, above all, Peter Blake, with, as tutors, Richard Hamilton and Eduardo Paolozzi (though they did not all coincide). The British public suddenly found itself confronted by the sexual fetish, the scrap-book page, the real instead of the painted object (singular, or accumulated in a cabinet of curiosities), the commonplace of the kitchen cupboard painted superhuman size, and canvases that were no longer rectangles, but any size, shape, or combination of shapes. The British press offered immediate support, British dealers opened their doors and set their persuasive tongues to wag, dissent was swept aside and the British Establishment surrendered – the sheer aggression of the young had won the day, and when American Pop invaded, it was irresistible.

Evening Standard 1991

Pornography and Art

I<small>T WAS WITH THE CONVICTION THAT IT WOULD</small> be yet another feminist rant that I read Clare Short's review of Madonna's now notorious slim volume, *Sex*, but I found myself largely in agreement. It is indeed wretchedly produced (my review copy disintegrated with the very first turning of pages), the photography scarcely professional (did her crew know nothing of lighting and camera angles?), the typography so erratic and over-printed as to be all but illegible (layout by an excited adolescent with Letraset?), and the content the stale repertoire of the commercial pornographer; all these faults might be forgiven were the book a plea for liberalism, for a consideration of the function of and need for pornography, or a celebration of Madonna's own response to a sexual odyssey, but it is none of these – it is merely the exploitation of her disco audience and its expansion, briefly, into the world of jaded prurience.

One sentence of Clare Short's lucid diatribe, however, raises a second thought, for within it lies a universal condemnation, if not of women, certainly of men; in accusing Madonna of understanding 'nothing of the beauty of sex and eroticism' she damns all sexual activity and interest that is not within that surprisingly broad (but not broad enough) description. No man has the right to speak for women, whose sexuality, I suspect, is infinitely less consistent than that of men, and concerned with procreation in ways that no man can understand; the response of women to pornography is alto-gether less alacritous (if they respond at all), though it is possible that women are not entirely honest in this matter. No woman has the right to speak for men. The sexual undercurrents that bedevil a man's boyhood remain just as constant and at least as near the surface of his conscious mind in adult life, when they are as likely as ever to be triggered into lively speculation in the Underground, the street, and even in the National Gallery. Most men are in some

measure constantly aware of their sexuality and constantly respon-
sive to the peculiar stimuli that arouse them – and the concern does
not diminish with age. Women must recognise that for men the
mechanics of congress have little to do with procreation and that
sexual acts range from loving tenderness to fierce aggression and the
catharsis of almost lavatorial purging; in this last particular, in which
masturbation plays an essential part, pornography comes into its
own.

Pornography is a subject that conjures images and language that
many find offensive: by erotica we may be amused, albeit with a
frisson of distaste, and at obscenity we are compelled to shudder, but
pornography reaches from one to the other and carries sub-texts
and subliminal messages that the innocent do not recognise, that the
clean-living (for want of a better description) do not care to
acknowledge, and that the worldly, depending on their degree
of exposure and experience, will easily comprehend and even enjoy
at many subtly different levels. It is impossible to reach a definition
on which all must agree, and we are left with the paraphrase
'pornography is in the eye of the beholder' – but if that is true, then
the burden lies not with the pornographer but with those who, on
seeing his work, respond to it: taking an extreme example, a pre-
pubescent child is unlikely to receive any stimulus to curiosity or
activity when confronted by a photograph of legs encased in black
leather jeans, but to those who bought Madonna's book this image
is expected to be an immediate trigger; mere nudity of the kind
illustrating many a daily newspaper, on the other hand, is often of
overwhelming interest to that same child when sexual curiosity and
gender differences concern him, and he is learning the mysterious
businesses of his body. The sexual fetish has, perhaps, to be learned,
is not necessarily universal (are leather and chains of much appeal
outside western society?), and may be transitory (the lumberjack
look for homosexuals lasted less than a decade).

The distinctions between erotica and pornography are too subtle,
and their emergence from the fertility rites and symbols of man's
unwritten past too long a history to be dealt with here; it is enough

to say that in the Mediterranean basin the erect phallus was scratched and scribbled on walls as soon as man learned to hold a tool, and that the ancient gods of the Mediterranean civilisations from which our own descends, crossed all our present sexual barriers, and employed symbolism that was robust and vigorous. Even ancient Jewry, blamed for many of the proscriptive attitudes adopted by all branches of the Christian church as heirs to the loud condemnations uttered by St Paul (there is no evidence in the New Testament that Christ himself took so narrow and uncharitable a view of man's sexual failings), had heroes, some of whose acts were hardly edifying – Samson the adulterer was amused by bondage, when Saul bargained with David for the hand of his daughter he demanded a dowry of one hundred foreskins (and was given two hundred for good measure) – the Song of Solomon is open to far reaching interpretations, and the Talmud maintains that girls who have been sodomised, even by ten different men, are still technically virgins. Further afield, in Arabia, Persia, India and the far east, there are literary and visual records of sexual activities that are accepted as art, but which, if translated into modern western terms, would at once be condemned as pornography, child abuse and worse.

We forget at our peril that the gods and goddesses of the Greeks and Romans were as much occupied with love as with affairs of war and earthly politics – with loves indeed that were adulterous, homosexual, lesbian, and occasionally bestial. In the written past of Greece and Rome, surviving literature is as much concerned with rampant sexual activity as with the tedious plod of history, and in the visual arts the erotic element was frank and ubiquitous; the lewd, dissolute and suggestive performances of which there is a hint even in Aristotle's *Poetics*, and an example in the work of Herodas of Miletus, where two women discuss the particularly fine leather dildos made by the local cobbler – '. . . the handicraft of Athena herself . . . smooth as a dream, the lacings of wool instead of leather thongs . . . men cannot make theirs so erect . . .' – established a vein of phallic humour that descended into Byzantine bawdy, medieval carnival, the Commedia dell'Arte, and on into the present day where they survive in the innuendo of the stand-up comic with, if I may make another pun, the homosexual as his butt. In Greek vase and amulet of the tumescent penis, in exquisite mural in the Roman bedroom and vulgar graffiti in the neighbourhoods of brothels the visual jokes of sodomy and priapism abound, to be echoed in the painted corridors of the Uffizi and the Lysistrata suite of Aubrey Beardsley, and to be collected with such relish by the sculptor Thorwaldsen and other 19th-century cognoscenti. In the Renaissance, the greatest painters concerned themselves with the sexual ecstasies of women seduced by showers of gold, clammy swans and clammier clouds, legs apart, heads thrown back, eyes closed in climax, and every man proclaimed his strutting, rutting sexual potency with the ever erect codpiece. For the courtiers of Louis XV Boucher painted the upturned bottom of little Louise O'Murphy, an invitation to them all. These paintings, and the pretty boys of Parmigianino and Caravaggio, we now see as remote masterpieces, and no longer perceive the sexuality that informed them, yet they demonstrate that art and pornography have throughout the development of our culture been intertwined.

Pornography at its best *is* art; at its worst it is Madonna's book – a checklist of fetishes illustrated with the pose but not the passion. It is the heartfelt passion of such artists as Egon Schiele and Jean Cocteau that elevates their imagery into realms far beyond the imagination and achievement of the commercial pornographer and brings it close to the religious ecstasy of saints – witness the writhing sexual attitudes in many an ecclesiastical altarpiece and sculpture, of which Bernini's *Blessed Ludovica Albertoni*, *Truth Unveiled* and *Ecstasy of Saint Teresa* (a Cupid and Psyche with all the phallic symbolism of the piercing arrow) are the most remarkable examples. The argument that the best pornography (in an aesthetic sense) is that produced by an artist for himself without losing his integrity as an artist, is the best defence for Robert Mapplethorpe's photographs of the extremes of bondage and penetration achieved by homosexuals; cool judgement of their composition, lighting, texture and all other technicalities of the photographer's skill must concede that they are masterpieces of their genre. For me the problem is that I cannot accept that photography is art in the same sense as painting – but that is altogether another matter, and I observe only that I have seen painted and drawn imagery of the same ilk that, though far from Michelangelo in achievement, is infinitely more disturbing, infinitely more likely to clench the muscles of the stomach and the bowel than any photograph: in this *Paragone* one might argue that bad art is better than good photography.

To return to the main issue: ours is a hypocritical society. We have had our fill of censorship and must not forget those great battles of the Sixties – Lady Chatterly, Fanny Hill, Aubrey Beardsley and Oz among them – that led to what intellectual freedom we now enjoy when sex is the subject of art and literature. The option for those ready to find offence is to walk away from it; the television set is easily extinguished, the book returned unread, the film and exhibition eschewed, and no one should tell the rest of us what we may and may not see, no one should remove our right to make our own judgements in these or any other matters.

Feminists demand the removal of the naked girl from the pages of the *Daily Speculum* and would have Madonna and her ilk burned at the stake, for these, they argue, reduce women to the level of sex objects – yet most women spend their lives *striving* to be sex objects, painting their faces, prinking their hair, pouting their lips and boosting the prominence of larger parts in such ways as to make them an inescapably obvious invitation to men. Moreover they encourage their small daughters in such mimicry as invites the danger of an adult response. The hypocrisy of men is all too often demonstrated in the House of Commons, where it seems that hardly a member was not sired by Outrage out of Mrs Grundy, and not one of them has ever with curiosity fingered the pages of a pornographic magazine, fumbled in the crutch of his schoolboy peers, indulged in a sexual fantasy far beyond the marriage bed, or pursued sexual pleasures that have nothing to do with procreation.

From the influence of repressive churches we have inherited unnaturally narrow views of sex and sexuality, and still adopt moral stances at variance with common sense, history and practice. We persistently underrate the sexuality of children, and in perpetuating the myth of innocence forget our own pre-pubertal prurience and the damage done by the failure to give us proper, no-nonsense, functional sex education at an early age. Many offences against minors might not occur if minors are made wary with real knowledge; the effect of many such offences lies less in the offence than in the hysteria of parents, police and court room – we should remember that the average age now of Bangladeshi women at their first childbirth is fourteen, just as it was in medieval England, and that offence is a matter of time, place and custom. We condemn the prostitute and will not acknowledge that her resource has saved many a marriage and the sanity of many an unmarriageable man – as has pornography. We damn the pornographer too readily without recognising that his work is as old as art and often part of its purpose, and that its crudest forms are much more a stimulus to quick release than an encouragement to mimicry and a specious excuse for the rapist caught in the act.

Too many of my generation were too damaged by repression ever to accept without misgiving the liberality that followed from the Sixties, and we should no longer lay down the law on sexual matters – these must now be the concern of younger generations who have the right to be free of the prohibitions and hypocrisy of the past, free of pretence, inhibition and deceit.

Arts Review 1992

Ready-Mades and Multiples

THE CATALOGUE OF *ART UNLIMITED*, THE ARTS Council's collection of curious objects known as multiples and ready-mades, is itself an example of the genre, a thing seeming to deny or obstruct its function. Its pages are not bound, but screwed together, tight shut, and in its virgin state, shrink-wrapped in transparent plastic, the two handsome brass screws are set in diagonal corners; to benefit from its text the would-be reader must first note (though only with a magnifying glass is this possible) the rubric printed on the cover, and obey it – 'Remove screw from top right corner . . . place in left hole . . . open book . . . reverse process after use.' From now on, I suppose, we must carry a tool-kit to Arts Council exhibitions.

The instructions followed, the impractical nature of screws as a form of binding is immediately apparent, for the deeply guttered pages will not, indeed cannot, so compressed are they, stay open, and must be held apart by force – a two-handed or thumb-crushing exercise – and then one is rewarded with too many pages printed on paper livid pink and painful to the eye. And the instructions followed, one senses that irreparable damage has been done to the catalogue as an art object with the breeching of its plastic wrapper and the loss of mystery as pages turn, for to be a true example of the Neo-Dada revival that has intermittently amused the sceptic with such things for the past thirty years or so, the catalogue should at the very least have blank pages, and at best be quite impossible to use.

But it is a book, and writ large on an introductory page is Marcel Duchamp's Dada exhortation 'Wipe out the idea of the original, which exists neither in music, nor in poetry'. Duchamp, one of the iconoclastic movement's founding fathers, is now regarded as an oracle, if not the ancient god of Goldsmiths' College, his words as worthy as scriptural revelation and not to be questioned – but he was wrong, for paintings depend on a unique substantial presence for their aesthetic purpose and effect, and do not require, as do the arts of music and the word, the intermediary skills of a performer.

It is seventy years since Duchamp confused the public by exhibiting as art the banal objects that he dubbed 'Ready-Mades', signing them and giving them titles sometimes wholly alien to their simple purposes, as with coathooks called *The Trap* and a bottle-rack called *The Hedgehog*, sometimes laterally related to their use, as with a snow shovel exhibited as *In advance of a broken*

Arm and the famous urinal known as *Fountain*. None of these was a multiple, and few, if any, of the original objects have survived, but this has not mattered and identical objects are now exhibited as genuine Duchamps.

The simple definition of a multiple proposed by the Arts Council is that it is one of innumerable identical art objects mass-produced by an artist, but with the introduction of objects that are *not* manufactured by artists, the exhibition blurs this simple notion. The shoulder length plastic glove, for example, used by veterinary surgeons for uterine investigations, is not work made by an artist but can be had for pence from any veterinary supplier – and in this particular case was bought from a 'Supastore Boutique' – but with an artist's blessing (the age of miracles is not yet over), what was originally intended to play its small part in righting a misplaced foetus may be hung upon the wall as art, given a label, a date, a provenance and a title ('Poor Cow'), and then accorded the veneration more properly given to paintings by Soutine and Thomas Sidney Cooper.

The business of the multiple and the ready-made seems to be a conflation of the *objet trouvé* (the stick or stone formed by nature into the semblance of sculpture), with the recognition of (perhaps) good design, and the opportunity to make a visual pun. But why should this be the privileged preserve of artists? Do we not all have the right to recognise some quality that lifts the common object above banality? Am I alone in buying one French cheese in preference to another because the design of the fragile wooden box and the typeface that advertises its contents have style and function that appeal to me? I do not smoke, but I collect cigar boxes – on the poorer ones I paint, but the finer designs give me pleasure in their colour, texture, function and respect for the material. I buy a particular brand of tea only because it is packed in stout wooden boxes gaily stencilled with a lion among the lettering. All these surely qualify as multiples and ready-mades, lacking only the endorsement of an artist and his title. Well – a fig for all these arrogant artists.

If anything is to be learned from this exhibition of objects bought by the Arts Council and commissioned in the Nineties (some of them specially for this occasion and for immediate sale from it), it is that good industrial design is the most accessible of art forms – and as an aside I must observe that we are disgracefully denied it by the makers of everything from motor cars to tin openers. The rest of it we know from long and wearying exposure to its ilk – Damien Hirst contributes a ping-pong ball in a tall glass of water, with a sheet of instructions on altering the levels from time to time, Rachel Whiteread offers a pair of old brass door handles mated on a stock, and Mark Wallinger a toy jockey on a toy horse. Modest interventions that destroy function offer momentary amusement, but the humour of a hinged coathanger that cannot be used, of spectacles with arms attached in reverse, and of the chess set in which all men are white, must soon wear very thin indeed. Inconsequential conjunctions occasionally make etiolated references to the original Dada jokes and nonsenses of long ago, but an aluminium mug pierced to take a shoelace binding, a birdcage containing a tousled fur, the knuckleduster masquerading as a pipe-rack, and Anya Gallaccio's paint tin that contains the chocolate with which she smears the walls of a gallery as art, have not a jot or tittle of the power of outrage that made Meret Oppenheim's fur-lined tea-cup memorable.

None of these things has even the slightest aesthetic virtue, and the exhibition is a bleak array. Far more enjoyment is to be had in shops that make some attempt to educate and amuse their customers, teasing them a little, subtly educating – the Conran Shop, for example, and even British Home Stores; far more enjoyment is to be had among the parts of motor cars, and few manufactured things are more beautiful than a camshaft. Look about you – you do not need a bunch of fraudsters posing as the elite of the Arts Council's chosen artists to tell you what is fine among the ready-mades and multiples – you have only to open your eyes in Sainsbury's or Boots and make decisions for yourselves.

Evening Standard 1995

Gerhard Richter

The Tate Gallery

GERHARD RICHTER WAS BORN IN DRESDEN IN 1932, and, like many German artists of his generation, remained virtually unknown in this country until the Royal Academy mounted its now notorious exhibition *A New Spirit in Painting* in 1981. There had been a one-man show of his abstract paintings two years before at the Whitechapel Gallery, but I do not recall that it caused much of a stir, and it was in critical terms very much second fiddle to the contemporary exhibition of Hamish Fulton and his funny walks in the upper gallery; I mention it only as an historical fact and because the Director at the time was Nicholas Serota – Serota was also one of the three presiding geniuses of *New Spirit*, and is now Director of the Tate Gallery, where the latest, largest, and most completely retrospective Richter exhibition is on view. Add that between *New Spirit* and now, Richter's work has again been exhibited at the Royal Academy (in its monumental survey of twentieth-century German art), in a one-man show at the Institute of Contemporary Arts, and several times on the premises of that celebrated adventurer in the avant-garde of art, the dealer Anthony d'Offay, and we begin to realise that Richter has for more than a decade had powerful allies here, and that for one German painter at least, London is no remote provincial backwater. The cynic might suggest that Richter has indeed been the beneficiary of a remarkably skilled promotion job.

His work has been, and still is, photographic, abstract, expressionist, plain colour field, textured colour field, mixed colour field homage to old masters, and drearily representational; there has been no orderly shift from each of these to the next, but constant overlap and retrospection, and I have heard it said that in commercial terms he has been extraordinarily successful simply because any museum wishing to own work representative of any particular year has felt compelled to buy at least three pictures in three different styles. My inclination when confronted by such a variety is to base my critical opinion on those works that conform most closely to the long western European traditions, for if he paints a conventional still life of candles flaming, or a landscape that in general terms hints at German Romanticism, then it is by the standards of seventeenth-century Dutchmen and Caspar David Friedrich that he may be tested. It is too easy to re-hash on monumental scale a humdrum press photograph chosen at random, too easy to paint a canvas grey, too easy to smudge and smear and let fickle choice dictate whether the accidents happily resemble some bright revision of the lilyponds that Monet painted when he was all but blind, or are so bogged in smirched confusion that they must be scrapped – students by the thousand take these risks – and only the professional presentation of an art dealer (frames, catalogue, private view and outrageous price) tells the wondering spectator that he is looking at the work of an esteemed old master and not the desperate daubs of callow youth.

Using the landscape test, one is compelled to see that Richter is no better than the feeblest contributors to the Royal Academy each summer; the compositions are no more accomplished than those of last minute holiday photographs taken to use the last frames on the reel; they lack any substantial subject, and if they are not kept close to photographic precision they have neither content nor descriptive detail; mystery and interest reside only in the blurred focus borrowed from poor photography. If in what is recognisable to us all Richter makes such a poor showing, why should we assume that his work is overwhelmingly more significant in its abstract formulae? Certainly the red abstracts painted earlier this year are superficially impressive, but then red is a resonant colour to which we all respond like Pavlov dogs – not for nothing is it predominant in military uniforms and Enzo Ferrari's motor cars, and when flecked with yellow it takes on aspects of sunset, cataclysm and hellfire – should we necessarily be seduced by it and think it good? (I have always assumed that the Serpent's apple was red, and that Eve's response to it was thus instinctive and irrational – had it been green, she would probably not have fallen for it.)

There is something inherently seductive about smeared paint, repellent but seductive, and psychoanalysts concerned with the infantile response to faeces might well make useful comments on Richter's now favourite technique. As for the images among the smears, encouraged, as we all have been, to perceive as miraculous Monet's waterlilies (even in their most muddied variants, the dross of American private collections and the auction rooms), it is inevitable that some will wax ecstatic with wonderment at abstract drips and smears of highly coloured paint accidentally fallen into an arrangement of autumn creepers in the hanging gardens of some watery Babylon; I realise that the picture presented to the Tate in 1988 by the Patrons of New Art evokes the picnic grounds of Glyndebourne, and that it is in its slick way quite pretty, but can even Nicholas Serota argue that it is a great painting fit for a great national gallery? – I have the response that were it to hang in an Indian restaurant it would be dismissed as an execrable distraction from the vindaloo, if not indeed thought painted with some of its constituents.

I can see no point in pictures based on photographs, whether these were taken by Richter himself or culled from the daily press; I see no point in out-of-focus lions and tigers, other than as questions in an intelligence test; I see no point in vast grey canvases, whatever the texture of their painted surfaces; I see no point in re-hashing a great work by Titian in such abstract terms as to resemble the violent and bloody slaughter of a chicken (though one could interpret it as a resentful response by the Blessed Virgin to the angel Gabriel's annunciation); I see no point in painting a silvery moonlit seapiece with the verisimilitude of old Montague Dawson and omitting the svelte clipper under full sail. I recognise the ingenuity of it all, and the business of anything you can do I can do too, but apart from thinking that the recent abstracts might reproduce quite well as endpapers for expensive books, I see little virtue in any of it. The work is neutral, uninvolved, indecisive, only partially under control, and as Richter himself has said, has 'no style, no composition, no judgement'. It demonstrates the dangers of skill in the hands of those who have neither talent nor emotional force and fervour.

Evening Standard 1991

Mark Rothko

The Tate Gallery

MARK ROTHKO IS REGARDED NOT ONLY AS A grand old man of American twentieth-century painting, but as one of the world's great old masters. The Director of the Tate Gallery suggests a kinship with Turner, and a learned American professor ties him to the great German Romantic painter of mists and mysteries, Caspar David Friedrich, and proposes a new category in art, 'The Abstract Sublime'. Another American, one Robert Goldwater, offers the perfect poetic nonsense: 'the apparent end lies close to the apparent beginning – so close in fact, or in apparent fact, that they are almost indistinguishable'.

Dear old Roger Fry, the father of foolish criticism, must take the blame for all this rubbish. It was his notion that one should stand in front of a picture with a mind emptied of all fore-knowledge, and wait for it to happen – it, in this case (since the pictures are hypnotically boring), is inevitably either nothing or a heady mixture of intellectual and emotional responses self-induced. Having invested fifteen minutes in contemplation one must save face with a boiling, bubbling, gaseous eruption of ideas that have no more value than flatulent emissions not commonly identified as intelligent communication. Looking at pictures under the influence of Roger Fry has the nature of religious experience – much is a matter of pretence in the hope that conviction will follow observance.

Mark Rothko's paintings are the icons of our time: we stand in their presence, awed and undone (if not unhinged) by the expectation of religious experience, and in their coloured wastes perceive cosmic narratives to match *The Last Judgement* of Michelangelo, hallucinating with responses self-induced. His friends and contemporaries spoke of him as an Old Testament prophet, distant, dignified, removed, of 'Rothko the rabbi'; he spoke of himself as a prophetic visionary – 'The struggle is beyond painting, not with painting' – and for days on end, staring in silence, he contemplated the unfinished fields of colour. 'The myth is dead,' he once proclaimed as an argument in favour of abstraction, and embarked on a search for a stylistic territory from which all others could be excluded; he found self-worship and a territory so limited by release from representation that he abandoned it in suicide, his last colour field blood red as he exsanguinated from slashed wrists.

Suicide not only raises the price of a painter's pictures, it silences his critics. Clement Greenberg thought Rothko's ideas on art the banal commonplaces of art-jargon, Clyfford Still thought his pictures suffocating examples of 'bloodless febrility', Ad Reinhardt ridiculed him, Barnett Newman rejected him after years of tolerant friendship, and time and again his peers described him as combative, bitter, deprived, adversarial, contentious and festering with resentment and indignation as they watched him affront the meek with deliberate vulgarity, threaten with legal suits, slash his pictures in a rage or thump his fist through the window of an art gallery. The consolation that he sought in alcohol, chain-smoking and gluttony as he struggled to find an identity, both social and aesthetic, was not a pretty sight. Death, however, silenced contrary voices.

Marcus Rothkowitz was born in 1903, in Dvinsk, a Russian town midway between Leningrad and Warsaw that had been Polish, Lithuanian and Latvian; it was within the Pale, half its citizens Jewish, and when at the age of ten Rothko emigrated to Portland, Oregon, he took with him folk memories of Cossack murder and mass graves. With difficulty he learned English, and low grades, anti-Semitism and self-pity drove him from his place at Yale to New York, where he became a painter almost by whim. He learned a little from Max Weber, Arshile Gorky and Milton Avery, but was essentially self-taught and scarcely competent. In

1935, with other now forgotten painters, he formed *The Ten*, first-generation Jewish artists bonded against the *goyim* of the old establishment in a bitter expression of social hostility, but in 1940 he changed his name to Mark Rothko as a rejection of his Jewish roots. He grew in vanity, pairing himself with Rembrandt; he grew a little more and paired Rembrandt with himself. By 1950, having worked his way through borrowings from Berlin and Paris, ill-judged experiments in Surrealism and natural forms, he arrived at the anchored fields of colour for which he is now famous. For ten years he was sustained by jolly permutations of yellow, blue, vermilion and a light-hearted palette, but then they were succeeded by darker and less scrutable contrasts that expressed the neurotic depression and alcoholic misery that had descended on his private life. Rothko thought these last to be expressions of tragedy and ecstasy, of the dark hours before dawn in which he painted them, and he wished his audience to weep with him. Yet all that can in fact be seen in the huge canvases is a field of drab, light-absorbent colour, with some tonal variation that suggests a silhouette of sorts, or a contrasting border. In the life they are great bores, these fields of flat maroon and purple, seen in the flat, reduced light of the Tate. Admittedly Rothko, who worked under high-intensity lighting that could have served a theatre, preferred a low level when his pictures were on view, the tonality and contrasts completely changed, but if ever pictures were desperate for the fluctuating intensity of strong natural light to take advantage of the increasing transparency (with age) of the upper layers of paint, these are they.

Rothko is that rare thing, a painter whose work is flattered by reproduction; on the small scale of the catalogue page, the paintings take on a brilliance and translucence wholly lacking in the realities that he resolutely refused to varnish. Here they assume vague architectural forms, resemble landscapes with the black skies of summer storms, the flare of blazing sunset, the dawn cloud – but on the gallery walls the most mature are no more than sombre backgrounds for the passing crowd. It was a small achievement, this graduation from mimicry into simple fields of colour. Any painter worth his salt knows that colour in isolation is not the same when it has neighbours, and that yellow on a white ground is radically changed when super-imposed on blue. As Rothko moved into abstraction, the common practice of all painters became an end in itself, and he painted pictures of a technical trick, big and bold, gaining intimidating authority from sheer size – the poor public cower before their propaganda, not understanding, but convinced that they must be in the presence of something significant if it has to be so large.

Rothko petulantly observed, 'I'm not interested in the relationship of colour, or form, or anything else.' When he denounced Pop Art as the work of charlatans and opportunists, it never occurred to him that he might seem one himself in uttering in the context of his own work such scraps of wisdom as, 'Art is an adventure into an unknown world', and, 'There is no such thing as a good painting about nothing' – particularly now that we know his technique to have been so unstable that few of his pictures still reflect his intentions, and that in the late Sixties he hired an assistant to do much of the non-contemplative business of putting pigment on canvas. When Rothko committed suicide he was the victim of a formula that even he had at last been compelled to recognise as sterile. He could let go with this last act of honesty, but dealers, auctioneers, critics and curators have invested too much in the futile aesthetic fiction that surrounded him, and dare not recognise the truth.

Evening Standard 1987

Ruskin and the English Watercolour

FOR MORE THAN TWO CENTURIES THE WAYS IN which we respond to works of art have been controlled and directed by only three critics. Of these the first was Johann Joachim

Winckelmann, an 18th-century Prussian homosexual whose drooling over the marble testicles and buttocks of headless antique sculpture still conditions the correct response for swooning visitors to Bloomsbury. The last was Roger Fry, who invented Post-Impressionism and preached that we should stand empty-headed in front of works of art and hope for 'pure aesthetic sensation' bordering on ecstasy, on which lunatic passivity most modern art depends. The most famous, most prolific, and still most widely influential of the three, was John Ruskin, who bestrode the reign of Queen Victoria and proclaimed ideas that went far beyond the fields of art and architecture.

Ruskin was Turner's executor, a defender of the Pre-Raphaelites, an abuser of Whistler and all modern painting – 'Cut out all those dab and dash people . . . I felt as if my coat must be all splashes' – and no mean painter of watercolours. He wrote innumerable books, pamphlets and articles, and an unrelenting flood have been written on him. It is said that his ghost inhabits the form of Peter Fuller, founder and editor of the eximious magazine that pays him homage with its title, *Modern Painters*, first used by Ruskin in 1845. The art market pays another kind of homage – £45,200 was bid at Christie's last month for a watercolour blemished by a bad attack of pox. Under the influence of Roger Fry, Ruskin's influence waned, and in 1964 Lord Clark of Civilisation opined that three-quarters of his written work was so unreadable as to reduce the intelligent reader to hysterical despair; Ruskin, Clark maintained, was a popular moralist, a thumping preacher, a Bible Christian, embarrassing, incredible, dogmatic and rhetorical. The 39 stout volumes of his collected works are a barrier to the exploration of his rambling mind, and Henry James described even his popular pamphlets as 'aids to depression'.

Ruskin was born in 1819, when it was still possible for a rich and educated man to have a passing awareness of the sum of human knowledge, to be both artist and scientist, thinker and worker. This thundering aesthete opened a tea-shop in St Marylebone, and himself swept the streets of St Giles. He spoke against cruelty to animals and for the nationalisation of the railways (in 1868). He concerned himself deeply and extravagantly with the education of the working classes, and was a benign influence on the early fathers of the Labour Party, with a political philosophy of which its present leaders would do well to be mindful.

We tend to mistrust men of left-wing principle who preach from a comfortable base of privilege and wealth, and Ruskin had both in abundance. He was essentially an aesthete, but he loathed social injustice, the urban sprawl, and the industrial destruction of the countryside, and if much of what he said was contradictory and silly, much was profoundly sensible and as relevant today as it was a century ago. The difficulty in taking him seriously now lies in his private life, and some would describe him as mad, bad, and (if you were a little girl) dangerous to know. He was a mawkish paedophile yearning for the pre-pubertal girls whom he addressed as Dear Bird, Dear Pet or Darlint (sic) with sickening sentiment (he also greeted his gardener as Darling) and his marriage broke down on the first night when he discovered that his young bride had as much pubic hair as he. He also had long periods of lunacy, delusions, hallucinations and psychotic episodes which he himself described in the *British Medical Journal*, published exactly a week after his death in January 1900.

Ruskin's madness may be attributable to sexual frustration, but it may have been congenital, for his grandfather was mad enough to cut his throat and his parents were first cousins – they were also domineering and sadistic. There is clear and constant evidence of his sexual ambiguity, of a fear of castration, of willingness to wear women's clothes, of playing with little girls, of his confusion of the imagery of the serpent and the toothed vagina that might snap shut upon his phallus. During the celebrated libel trial that followed his assertion that Whistler had flung 'a pot of paint in the public's face' (itself a sexual image) Ruskin had an hallucination in which a black cat (tom or queen not specified) ordered him to perform sexual acts before a mirror. He feared the covert homosexual nature of Michelangelo's nudes, yet was as much dismayed by the sensuality of Titian's women. There is even a hint of necrophilia, provided that the corpse be young and female.

Many will argue that these private facts and suppositions are irrelevant in any assessment of Ruskin as an artist and critic; not so; they are closely interwoven. He was a bully who preferred feeble professional painters submissive to instruction from an amateur. His affections for Kate Greenaway and the ghastly Helen Allingham were founded on their dainty pre-pubertal subjects – 'how very very wonderful it is that you can draw exactly the creatures that I like so much', or 'she's just a month or six weeks too young for me'. He thought Greenaway greater than Raphael, Bird's Nest Hunt the equal of Tintoretto and 'the best painter of still life that ever existed', J.D. Harding 'indisputably . . . the most accomplished landscape artist'; Constable he ignored, and Turner he thought owed his worst imbecilities to the influence of Claude. In turn, Millais thought Ruskin's 'eye only fit to judge the portraits of insects'.

The Ruskin exhibition at the Bankside Gallery is an amusing, scholarly, and no holds barred account of the critic, the artist, the bully and the hypocritical paedophile who saw to it that all Turner's pornographic drawings were destroyed. Few will see it without wanting to know more about this flawed 'Luther of the arts' whose moral rectitude was so disturbed by schoolgirls, whose social experiments were far-sighted but abortive, and whose aesthetic judgements were as much affected by the stirring of his loins as of his intellect. Thirty-nine volumes of collected works await the curious.

Evening Standard 1989

Robert Ryman

The Tate Gallery

WHITE, MORE THAN ANY OTHER, IS THE COL-
our of familiar experience. Commonplace, it is the colour of
bedclothes and towels, tablecloths and napkins, of tissue paper
and paper tissues, shirts and underwear. It is the colour of serene
terraces in Kensington and the invading middle classes in Stoke
Newington, of rough plaster in Italian restaurants and the smooth
plaster on the broken limb. It is shaving soap on the crumpled
morning face, cheap bread sliced dead lying on the breakfast plate,
and last night's toothpaste droppings drying in the washbasin. As the
linen of St Veronica's Sudarium, the breech-clout of Christ
crucified and the stuff of Gethsemane grave-cloths, it has deep
significance for those steeped in the Christian tradition; and to the
Muslim it signifies purity, simplicity, innocence and candour.
Sublime as the colour of clouds and distant mountain peaks, it is
the symbol of spiritual aspiration.

Absorbing the craft of painting, the student learns that white (like
black) is a creature of many colours and textures; the theory in my
day was that the three primary colours (red, yellow and blue) if
properly mated should produce it (Newton's notion, I vaguely
recall) but, lacking the essential element of alchemy, mixed mud
was always the only consequence. Since Roman times white has
been made from lead; poisonous, but of great covering power, it
used to be called Flake White, or Krems White after the Austrian
town where it was manufactured from local mines (and Vienna
White for those whose geography was weak) – but was also made
with lead mined right across Europe from Cornwall to Romania.
Zinc White retains its brightness, Titanium White turns yellowish,
and Permanent White belies its name and is a poor thin material. To
any of these may be added marble dust, chalk or fine sand to give
them greater substance, and their response to brush or knife will
vary greatly according to the oil or turpentine with which they are

mixed or thinned. In their present manufactured states they are not
of the same colour, nor do they go off key at the same rate; they are
not of the same opacity or translucency, they blend differently with
the touch of other colours, and respond differently to the same
neighbours, whether these are beneath or next to them. Acrylic
whites are not the same as oil whites, and early acrylics (they date
back to the Thirties) were inconstant and inclined to yellow.

This simple introduction to the complexities of white paint may
be of use to those who find little else to look at in the pretentious
paintings of Robert Ryman, an owlish American celebrity of
something over sixty years who began life as a jazz saxophonist.
He has progressively eliminated from his canvases almost all trace of
other colours and their influences, and his assembled works demand
of the viewer either the wrapt contemplation of the emptied mind,
or an overwhelming interest in the substance of paint and the act of
applying it to canvas or an alternative support.

Ryman, it seems, thinks that representation is a lie, that paint
itself is the only truth for a painter, and that it is enough for him to
take the materials of painting and in their substance record the
sweeping gesture of his arm, the pressure of his hand and wrist, and
the size and character of the brush. This is, no doubt, abstract art, for
it has no subject, but it is not the extreme abstraction of the painting
from which all evidence of human activity has been removed – in a
sense, Ryman's paintings are pictures of himself at work, but with
himself eliminated so that only the work becomes the subject of the
self-portraiture.

All sorts of claims are made for Ryman – from the absurdity of
'making paint look as good on a painting as it did in the tube' to
'Ryman is undoubtedly one of the great painters of light'. The
Curator of Interpretation at the Tate Gallery (a ludicrous appoint-
ment, newly invented) and others of his ilk liken the man to
Cézanne and Morandi, Picasso and Chardin, Mondrian and Oudry
– at which point I feel inclined to throw in Vermeer and Velazquez,
Zurbaran and Pasmore, Saenredam and Fabritius, and why not
Titian too, who knew more than any man how to manipulate paint

on canvas, and Michelangelo, who in the Sistine Ceiling outwitted all his contemporaries in the exploitation of the whiteness of white plaster. Not one of these Curators of Comprehension recalled Malevich, the Russian Suprematist who well before 1920 had done away with the subject and painted white on white (and black on black); he was the only real forerunner of Ryman in this and in the matter of painting square pictures that could not tap into the spectator's landscape expectations of the rectangle, and as Malevich is not exactly unfamiliar to American audiences, it is difficult to believe that Ryman (who worked as a guard in the Museum of Modern Art, New York, for the seven years 1953–1960) was and is ignorant of so significant a predecessor.

Tacking Ryman to the tail of European painting and its ancestral traditions is pointless, for his work is at best a student exercise in materials and technique, and at worst an empty gesture inflated by the flatulent responses of critics and Curators of Perception. Nothing seen in these white paintings is new – look at the list of antecedents and the whiteness and the substance and the handling variations are all there, but employed to some purpose and not just for the manufacture of a material icon. In the beginning there may have been a certain honest naivety (think of Ryman as the Alfred Wallis of Manhattan and the huge size of his childish signature and date becomes excusable), but long ago he was corrupted to vanity by the praise of dealers, critics and Curators of Enlightenment who claim that he has expanded abstract art to its furthest limits (a manifest absurdity), that his work is an icon on which contemplation must be focused, that his resolute pursuit of white provides starting-points rather than endings, and that it is life-affirming and surface-activating. Stripping away all the meaning-evasions of the contemporary Curator of Exegesis, we can see Ryman's work for what it is, the scales of the jazz saxophonist, without the melody or harmony – in his own words he 'wanted to paint the paint', a paltry ambition, easily achieved. I shall continue to enjoy at least as much aesthetic benefit from the white on white of toothpaste in the washbasin.

Evening Standard 1993

Saatchi: Young British Artists IV

T HE FOURTH IN THE SAATCHI COLLECTION'S
series of exhibitions devoted to *Young British Artists* is unremarkable
but for the paintings of Brad Lochore. At thirty-five he is no longer
young by Italian Renaissance standards (Raphael was dead at thirty-
seven), nor by those standards is his work a serious contribution to
the history of western civilisation – but that is not a claim that can be
made of any artist working now, no matter what his medium. His
pictures are images of shadows dissolving in diffused light; they are
beautiful, evoking an experience that is, though perhaps unnoticed,
common to us all, but by their separation from their surroundings
and immediate cause, the shadows take on an abstract cast
suggesting the intervals of music and mathematics, implying a
space contained by irregular angles and geometry.

Lochore, for all his dependence on computer-generated simula-
tions rather than the observed realities of light, its fall and its reflection,
that served Caravaggio and Rembrandt well enough, belongs to the
tradition of painters who were in thrall to its mysterious qualities, and
paints it with consummate subtlety. It can be argued that windows
have long been the commonplace of painting, the frame within the
frame, the proscenium that controls the drama within and the
landscape without, the perfect excuse for the Romantic portrait
contre-jour, the face in shadow, light flooding through the tousled
curls, and for that scrutiny of plaster on the kitchen wall that gave
Vermeer such pleasure; in all these there is a structural logic, a sense of
planes vertical and horizontal containing the picture space, even of
the peep-show, but from Lochore's paintings these anchors have
been eliminated and we see nothing that is real – there are no
windows, no shafts of light, no objects to play the part of Rembrandt's
tattered books or Vermeer's pots and tie us to perceived reality, and in
the swing and sway of space untethered nothing tells us whether we
see his shadows fall on floor or wall or ceiling.

These large paintings look well in the Gallery, a converted factory with white paint everywhere, even on the floor, industrial architecture seeming the source for paintings of industrial scale, paintings urging us to lift our eyes and look about us at the building, each informing the eye about the other. From a distance the images are sharp, but close to they blur and in losing definition imply the scatter of reflected light that softens edges. Sarah Kent, writer of what passes for a catalogue, tells us that Lochore's paintings have a uniform sheen and deny 'the physicality of paint on canvas'; this is not so – that they are painted to conform with slides projected on the canvases may cause a mild misgiving, but that they are indeed painted with a response to the material of paint and are even painterly, cannot and should not be denied; one is compelled to wonder if Miss Kent, misleading, has looked at transparencies rather than the pictures.

His shadows, beautiful though they are, may prove a trap for Lochore, for danger is inherent in exquisite achievement, and to continue into dull repetition with variations on the semi-abstract theme may well discredit the Saatchi pictures, works of fulfilment, not of promise.

Of the other contributors to this exhibition, little should be said – though Miss Kent says quite a lot, her text alternately subsiding into breathless intellectual masturbation, and leaning on her card index of useful quotations culled from cod philosophers. Marcus Harvey is a crude painter of crude sexual images derived from crude pornography, his headless and limbless icons of the anus and vagina embellished with scant knickers and the hint of chains, illuminated with such titles as *My Arse is Yours*, *Golden Showers*, and *Half Way Up*. Harvey's obsession may be of interest to Harvey and to those who share it at the schoolboy level of the locker room, but for a man of thirty-three with pretensions as a painter, it suggests only sexual arrest in adolescence, his paintings a desperate therapy that should be private.

A graduate of Goldsmiths', Harvey constructs his unconvincing style from the appalling teachers there, Basil Beattie the source of his rough-handled paint (literally so, for it is smeared onto the canvas with his fingers), Michael Craig-Martin the source of the inert black lines imposed on the chaotic confusions of pink and blue, yellow and red, to construct the outline images. Miss Kent thinks these gorgeous, sensuous, succulent, elegant, beautiful and juicy (twice) as well as erotic, seeming not to recognise any distinction between erotica and pornography, and claims that in their deft control Harvey revitalises the exhausted genres of painterly painting and the female nude; the painterliness is, however, no more than wallowing in the mess of de Kooning at several removes, and to link these obscenities of labia and pubic hair with the nudes of Rembrandt and Velasquez is to promote an obscene travesty of the traditions of western art and its concern with nudity.

Harvey may, obsession purged, borrowed mannerisms abandoned, develop into something of a painter, but for the contributors to this exhibition working in three dimensions (the term sculptor scarcely applies) there is little hope. Gavin Turk has perhaps a little wit and mischief with visual puns and an ability to parody – blobs of chewing gum seeming to float in a glass tank lampoon the work of Damien Hirst, a print of his right hand presented in a fake Spanish baroque frame is a pastiche of reliquary art (a variant of the thaumaturgical arm of St Epimachus), and a life-size waxwork of himself as Sid Vicious is a multiple pun on pop art, pop music, pop star and pop gun, with references to Elvis and Warhol, and the glass case another nod to Hirst – all clever whimsy, utterly ephemeral.

Marcus Taylor makes boxes in sanded perspex that resemble refrigerators, the now stale business of machines and furniture that cannot function, and John Frankland shrink-wraps in skins of glistering gold and silver plastic such banal things as garden sheds and hotel vestibules, tiresome ingenuities that may have some application in the world of window dressing. For their promotion as art we have the cant and casuistry of such critics as Miss Kent to thank.

Evening Standard 1995

Julian Schnabel

W ITH THE FIRST GLIMMER OF CIVILISATION
man began to paint. He has used pigments taken from the earth and
distilled from plants; he has drawn with the soot from oil lamps and
still makes use of charred sticks; he has suspended colour in the yoke
of eggs, the oil of sturgeon's roe, in honey and in wax. He has
worked on the living rock, on cut stone, on mud brick, on plaster,
timber, cloth and paper, but not until the summer of 1978 did it
occur to any man that the shards of broken crockery could provide
a suitable support for the painted image. That man was Julian
Schnabel.

Superbrat and *Wunderkind* of the American art market, Schnabel
had until then been a painter remarkable only for the anonymity of
his work. In their large scale, the techniques of graffiti jostling with
bucket and slosh, the crowded absence of composition, and the
excessive loading with contrary clichés, images and hieroglyphs, the
finished pictures paralysed interpretation and obstructed all attempts
that the weary spectator might make to understand. In this,
Schnabel was tilling the ground common to a generation of art
students all over Europe and America for whom the blundering
expression of the empty was the prime concern, and who had been
encouraged by indulgent and incompetent teachers to discard all
those academic disciplines of painting and drawing that have
throughout the history of art armed the true revolutionary. There
are critics who see the young Schnabel as an eclectic, but his
eclecticism was that of a Hoover without a bag – he sucked up other
men's ideas and regurgitated them in noisy and attention-seeking
confusion; yet, like all clever thieves, he became a man of property,
of Bentleys and swimming pools, of Cadillacs and tennis courts, and
of homes worthy of publication in the glossy pages of *House and
Garden*. For this, the miracle-working agent was the cracked cup,
and even that he stole from the Barcelona architect, Antonio Gaudi,

whose bravura use of shattered faience in the Parc Güell sent this American Autolycus scampering back to New York to raid the crockery store of the Salvation Army.

Schnabel's crockery is not in smithereens, but merely broken; jugs, cups and vases are proud and prominent among the plates and saucers bonded onto timber, and when the thick dull paint (Schnabel has no natural sense of the emotional resonance of colour) is smeared across the lot, they enliven it with a surface flicker of light and shadow that is ready-made and random. The immediate effect is of instant Cubism, as though the intellectual efforts of Braque and Picasso could be surpassed with an easy sweep; in passing, the surfaces are akin to those slatted advertisements that, caught in mid-turn, seem to promote the images of both PanAm and Peugeot, or to the distortions of those fore-edge paintings that are the delight of bibliophiles; applied to portraiture, the technique lends strength to the notion that the sitter's eyes follow the ambulant spectator. No second thoughts develop from these first impressions, for Schnabel's roughshod art is not concerned with subtlety, but with obliterating impact – he is a bruising Rambo, and his pictures are both battlefield and weapon.

It was not always so, for this bellowing bombast grew from a classic case of the split ego, the unconscious defence mechanism of the man who has no central self and must have an external self to take the blame for failure. Schnabel, born in Brooklyn in 1951, had as a small boy some talent for caricature, but was a solitary child who spent his spare time tented under the kitchen table working with his crayons, forced to invent for friendship a *Doppelgänger* whom he called Jack the Bellboy – of whom he says in his precocious autobiography, 'I have continued to let him make my drawings, paintings and sculpture even since.' When Jack and Julian were both fifteen, the Schnabel family decamped for Brownsville, where the boys' long hair, bell bottom trousers and guitars were not well received by hearty Texan teenagers; now too big to fit under the kitchen table, they isolated themselves elsewhere and painted as a solitary pastime.

Schnabel does not make it clear whether it was he or Jack who graduated from the Brownsville High School in 1969 and went to Houston University to study art, but it was apparently only himself who, in 1973, came to New York on a Whitney Museum study programme. He drove a cab, sold sunglasses and worked for a man named Ruskin (which should please Peter Fuller) whose bar was popular with artists; it was there that Schnabel met Sigmar Polke and other contemporary German painters preaching the gospel of Joseph Beuys, as well as the American denizens of SoHo, and made his 'first entry into Parnassus'. Parnassus did not recognise him, and after completing only six pictures, on one of which he dismayed even himself by writing *Nuns are Nuts*, he returned to Texas and 'became Jack the Bellboy'.

Few of Jack's paintings survive – they disappeared, or were repainted by Julian, and one was thrown away with the garbage by a woman who leased his studio space in Houston. The autobiographical painting of Jack as *The Bellboy in Hell* – a blank white face surrounded by three television screens and some forty marks that resemble both cockroaches and the seven-day scratches of a prisoner without a calendar – was rejected by the jury of a competitive show in Fort Worth, but had the virtue of breaking the bounds for him, for with it he realised that a painting could be an object and need not conform to the standard pattern of a rigid canvas in a rigid frame.

If distinguishing Jack from Julian is tedious, and more work for the analyst than pleasure for the patron, it pales beside the labyrinthine complexities of aesthetic argument over the last decade, which has spawned a cottage industry of ekphrastic articles on Schnabel in the impenetrable art jargon of Post-Modernism, Neo-Expressionism and Deconstruction. The sudden presence of his pictures on the walls of influential art dealers and respected museums has had a hallowing effect, and the tranquillised art critic has been compelled to emit a fog of language to conceal the crack of doubt in his perceptions – consider 'the juxtaposition of materials and images is made in the hope of the transcendence of their facticity' and contrast it with those critics who argue that Schnabel 're-directs our attention to the world outside art . . . thingy in the extreme': can they have it both ways and both be his apologists? The least confused writers are Schnabel himself and those who abuse him under such titles as *The Golden Age of Junk Art, Smashing Time, Schnabel Breaks Free, Schnabel le Bulldozer*, and *Le Blitzkrieg Schnabel*, dubbing him an opportunist charlatan, or who, like William Feaver, accuse him of painting visual gibberish with nothing to sustain it when the ballyhoo of marketing dies down.

The marketing is all. In 1977, Schnabel, again cooking in one of Ruskin's New York cafés, was once more climbing the foothills of Parnassus. He served schnitzels to Carl André (he of the Tate Gallery's bricks), Nick Serota, and Mary Boone, a budding dealer who promised him an exhibition. She delayed it when a Düsseldorf dealer gave him a show in the summer of 1978 but sold nothing and secured no reviews. She expressed enthusiasm for the first two plate paintings that in the autumn broke away from that pattern of failure, and sold one of them to the Saatchis, who were to buy many more. At that, Leo Castelli, the most powerful entrepreneur of the arts in America, moved in on Boone and they shared a Schnabel show in 1981 – the *annus mirabilis* in which a one man exhibition was sent on tour to public galleries in Switzerland and Germany, and the Royal Academy presented him to the British public as a New Spirit in Painting.

In only four years Schnabel had realised the rags to riches dream of all penurious Americans, and with the smooth co-ordination of a market strategy that could as well have sold Coke or Volkswagens, moved on to unprecedented wealth and the popularity of the footballer, the pop star or the *Playgirl* centrefold. Schnabel became Schnabel, and no more was heard of Jack the Bellboy. With the itinerant retrospective his mentors exploited the anodyne effects of a benign museum system whose compliant curators would quite certainly fail to recognise the absurdity of so prematurely honouring a mushroom painter. With a large and lavish book that passed for autobiography and aphorism, Schnabel graced the coffee tables of the rich with propaganda that promoted him as peer to Van Gogh, Goya and El Greco. With the image of the puissant phallus, with paint that resembles excrement (the first medium of many an infant), with such titles as *Circumnavigating the Sea of Shit* and *A Motherfucker*, and with the declaration that he needed to make his paintings horrible, he declared war on good taste and challenged a punch-drunk art market to be liberal in its response: it was, yet all that had been demonstrated was Schnabel's pictorial and aesthetic bankruptcy. With 'I can go where I want, eat whatever I like, make a pig of myself – and will continue to do so as long as I've got the money', he gave abrasive expression not only to his own prime concerns but to the American *amour-propre* of the Reagan years, and, like Reagan, became the larger than life hero.

As vanity fattened on success, and success on vanity, Schnabel himself saw that he was heroic. The more heroic he became, the larger grew his pictures. His psychotic disability went into reverse, and the personality that had once timorously depended on its *Doppelgänger* now became so inflated with manic belief in its genius that Schnabel could impertinently claim his broken plates to be an evocation of the horrors of *Kristallnacht* half a century ago in Nazi Germany – his editors let him spell the word as though it were the Christian name of Mrs Carrington. Manic egomania has forced him out of his studio, and only his tennis court can now provide him with the necessary working space; no canvas is woven large enough, and he has taken to the tarpaulin, preferably second-hand and battered by abuse in the marks of which he finds images emerging from an 'incredible deep space'; ravaging weather adds more stains, more images for him to decipher. Now a Renaissance master, he needs assistants, strong, bare-chested all-American males to handle his overwhelming materials and smash his crockery, one of whom must fly demented from patron to patron gluing back the shards that all too often break their bondage.

Schnabel provides exactly what his nervous American patrons deserve. Economically successful, educationally ignorant, culturally insecure, they advertise their social arrival by becoming collectors of art. They know nothing of the past and are convinced only of the myths of self-expression and of the artist as the wayward hero whom the indulgent middlebrow must support. Their predecessors all bought the same English family portraits and the same French Impressionist landscapes, but as these are no longer available in quantity or quality for any but the very rich, the present generation of social aspirants, governed by the same herd instinct, must patronise the present generation of artists, their touchingly naive belief in genius confirmed and comforted by major dealers who assure them that their investment is secure and never to be vitiated by the whims of fashion; a painting by Schnabel, immediately recognisable, speaking money, social status and cultural awareness, is the perfect match for the aspirations of the collector with the latest Cadillac.

None should be surprised that Reagan's America, symbolised as it is by the adolescent humours of Sylvester Stallone, has spawned the Schnabel phenomenon, of which the machismo has offended only a band of four anonymous feminist critics rejoicing in the pseudonym *The Holy Ghost Writers*. His apologists, including Nicholas Serota, require that we ignore the sounds of ranting self-promotion and of dollars in the cash register, and look beyond Schnabel's deliberate inflation by a hyper-capitalist culture in which connoisseurship is governed by profit, tax exploitation, investment promise and social climbing, to see him only as a Romantic painter concerned with the great Romantic themes of melancholy, heroism and divine afflatus, as though he were attempting another Napoleonic conquest – would that he were indeed Sadak searching for the Waters of Oblivion.

Those who thought that they could perhaps see something more than empty bombast in the huge plate paintings and the acres of tarpaulin, of which Schnabel said, 'I think it's a mistake for me to eulogise over my own work, though I don't know of any paintings that are better', must be disappointed by the degeneration of his latest offerings – the cheap realism of New York Society portraits and the infantile vulgarity of the much repeated message *La Banana e' Buona* supported by a graffiti penis in mid ejaculation. A new word is abroad in New York – the man who buys junk art is said to have been *schnabled*; in old colloquial German, *Schnabel* was a vulgar word for *mouth*.

Sunday Times Magazine 1988

Nicholas Serota

THE TATE GALLERY IS A VICTIM OF HISTORY, OF the time-warps that bedevil museums in this country, of changing status, and of conflicting demands that it has never satisfied; it has always been, and is still, an anachronism. Opened in 1897, it was intended to serve only one purpose – to be the national collection of modern British art. In 1890, Sir Henry Tate had offered the National Gallery his modest collection of three bronzes and sixty-seven paintings by the ilk of Lady Butler and Briton Rivière (lifted a little by Millais's *Ophelia* and three marvellous Orchardsons), and been refused, but his subsequent offer to build a separate gallery was, after some demur, accepted by the Government, and in 1897 the Prince of Wales cut the pink ribbon and opened the door.

It was not, however, the independent gallery for which Tate had hoped, but was instead an adjunct of the National Gallery devoted to modern British art, and thus became a bastion of the exhausted and etiolated traditions fostered by the Royal Academy, its primary collection, Tate's, larded with the works of Dendy Sadler and the execrable Benjamin Williams Leader, the titles ranging from *Little Dormouse* and *Hush!* to *Cupid's Spell* and *A Country Cricket Match, Sussex*. Not until 1915 was it recommended that the purposes of the Tate Gallery should be revised, and, shortly after, it became the national collection of British art of all periods, and the national collection of modern foreign paintings; in 1937 it became the national collection of modern foreign sculpture.

These changes came far too late to let Tate's building serve its new purpose as a National Gallery of historic British Art. The National Gallery itself had its fair measure of British paintings, important and unimportant (a comparison between the catalogues of 1946 and 1986 demonstrates the extraordinary reduction of the holding), for in the 1820s, when Sir George Beaumont and his friends recognised the urgent need to found a National Gallery, British art of the past was deemed to be part of the mainstream of European art. As British art of the then present was not in general thought to be part of the National Gallery's purpose (the Turner Bequest of 1856 was something of an embarrassment), it was inevitable that with the foundation of the Victoria and Albert Museum (progressively from 1852 to 1857) John Sheepshanks should, in 1857, offer it his substantial collection of then modern and contemporary British paintings, with the intention of establishing a National Gallery of British Art to develop in parallel with the National Gallery in Trafalgar Square – his 531 paintings and drawings almost, at a stroke, equalled the holdings of the National Gallery, then only 560 paintings. Sheepshanks succeeded in providing a focus for other gifts of paintings (including the residue of Constable's workshop in 1888) that, though they make the V&A's holding of British art an unbroken thread over virtually the whole of the 18th and 19th centuries, alas divided the purposes of the Museum – a contrary pull that was not resolved with the founding of the Tate Gallery, and is still not resolved. The National Portrait Gallery, established in 1856, provided yet another home for major and minor British paintings. The British Museum, of course, ever since its foundation in 1753, has collected British prints and drawings in its Print Room.

It must be argued that the Tate Gallery was, at the revision of its purposes in 1915, either superfluous, in that historic British art was already adequately collected by four other London institutions, or a failure, in that it did not draw from these same institutions (excepting, for particular reasons, the National Portrait Gallery), works of art that were irrelevant to their larger purposes (it is still the case that the Print Rooms of the V&A and the British Museum compete with and overlap not only each other, but the Tate Gallery, with the wasteful extravagance of unnecessary duplication at public expense). In the field of European art the Tate Gallery was certainly a failure, and without the energy and gift of Samuel Courtauld, hardly a single major Impressionist or Post-Impressionist painting would ever have graced its walls, though in these fields it was bedevilled by the curious arrangement with the National Gallery that whenever a painting reached the age of fifty it became an Old Master eligible for removal to Trafalgar Square. Without a purchase grant, acquisitions between the wars were made by gift, through the Contemporary Art Society, or by means of the Clark Fund of less than £600 per annum; no doubt it suited the Gallery in Fry-ridden, xenophobic, isolationist Britain, to become all but synonymous with resistance to the continental avant-garde, even in its feeblest forms, but its collections now suffer gravely from past failure to recognise, if not the importance of, at least the interest inherent in Cubism, Futurism, Expressionism, Constructivism, Dada and Surrealism – no work by Salvador Dali entered the collection until 1968.

In international terms the Tate Gallery's holding of major works of art from Impressionism to Surrealism ranks lower than many a minor museum in provincial Germany – it lacks, for example, worthy paintings by such popular and prolific artists as Degas, Renoir and Van Gogh. Sir John Rothenstein roused the Gallery from torpor when he became Director in 1938, but was never given sufficient money to close the gaps in the collection – the Government first gave him an annual purchase grant in 1946, of £2,000 (a derisory sum even then). At the end of his administration, torpor returned, and under Norman Reid and Alan Bowness the Gallery was remarkable only for frightful Sixties-style interventions in the building, and such random sentimental acquisitions as the outrageously expensive cabinet pictures by Picasso and de Chirico that had belonged to Herbert Read, and, of course, Carl Andre's bricks, the subject of much indignant and scurrilous comment by a popular press wholly ignorant of the Gallery's duty to build and maintain a national collection of modern foreign sculpture.

Twenty years have passed since the bricks, *Equivalent VIII*, were bought; they not only became an engaging episode in the Gallery's mythology, but marked a radical change in the public perception of the Gallery's purpose, adding to its functions the new duty to be the nation's gallery of contemporary art. More than any other work, the bricks established for the British that art may be made of or on any material, may introduce any technical medium or trickery, and may so cross, extend and confuse the conventional distinctions of and between painting, sculpture, photography, theatre, cinema and the *objet trouvé*, that the historically accepted meanings and purposes of art may be altogether abandoned.

This change of mood and interpretation has long been reinforced by the exhibitions of the Arts Council and the British Council, by such influential dealers as Nicholas Logsdail, Leslie Waddington and Anthony d'Offay, by the Kassel Documenta and the Venice Biennale, and by exhibitions at the Whitechapel Gallery and even the Royal Academy. No exhibition (other than, perhaps, *Picasso and Matisse* at the V&A in 1945) has caused more outrage and protest than *A New Spirit in Painting* at the Royal Academy in 1981; that eleven years on it now seems remarkably tame and uncontroversial, is a measure both of the then British ignorance of the international avant-garde (for want of a better term) and its current awareness – an awareness for which one of its two British organisers, Nicholas Serota, is primarily responsible through his programme of exhibitions as Director of the Whitechapel Gallery. It can be argued that for at least two decades, in addition to internal curatorial pressures, the Tate Gallery has been under constant external pressure to establish and maintain a position as the national gallery of contemporary art, partly from long and self-serving cliques within the Arts and British Councils, partly from self-serving dealers, partly from the unwarrantedly famous artists whom those dealers support, partly from Friends and Patrons, and partly from its own Trustees: all these small groups are financially, politically and professionally powerful, and most are cross-pollinated in symbiosis.

When Nicholas Serota became Director of the Tate Gallery in

1988 we knew that it would be subject to rapid and radical change. Though a post-graduate student at the Courtauld Institute, his appointment had nothing to do with the elite Courtauld Mafia in which so many believe, but was in most sane minds the logical consequence of his twelve years' work as Director of the White-chapel Gallery. It is not, however, without significance that his first professional post was as a Regional Art Officer and Exhibition Organiser with the Arts Council (1970-73), that since 1976 he has been a member of the Fine Arts Advisory Committee of the British Council, and that for the years 1983-87 he was a Trustee of the Public Art Development Trust – all remarkable opportunities for patronage at the time, and for continuing influence since; the years 1973-76 were spent as Director of the Museum of Modern Art in Oxford.

At Whitechapel, as well as paying necessary lip service to local needs with the transitory dross of amateur, ethnic and popular events (I have in mind particularly the *Whitechapel Open*) forced on any curator who has as paymaster a local authority (of any political complexion), Serota mounted a series of exhibitions of contemporary British, European and American artists that some might describe as inspired – Richter, Lüpertz, Merz, Baselitz, Marden, Kiefer, Kounellis, Guston, McLean, Morley, Hodgkin, Kirkeby, Schnabel and Twombly (all painters chosen for *A New Spirit*), and Long, André, Webb, Fulton, Cragg, Gormley, Gilbert and George (local amateurs, perhaps), Flanagan, Clemente, Smith, Nauman and Deacon – a series that not only declared Serota's interests and established his national position in the politics of art, but brought the gallery itself a new level of international esteem, just as the Royal Academy had willy-nilly profited as Norman Rosenthal's instrument of personal aggrandise-ment (Rosenthal was Serota's rival for appointment to the Tate).

Since 1988 Serota's most obvious physical changes to the Tate Gallery have been his stripping it of wretched architectural inter-ventions, thereby (among other things) restoring the bogus gran-deur of barrel vault and domed rotunda that form the long axis through the heart of the building. His most obvious intellectual changes have been the annual re-hangings. The first of these was greeted with pleasure and delight, but in the second, much less careful, startling change no longer blinded enthusiasts to the sad inadequacy of its claim to be 'a simple chronological path through the Collection', and the intellectual leaps required of the visitor as he moved from the historic British Collection to contemporary art induced unease; the fashionable wide-spaced hanging demanded a response not short of genuflection and reduced the number of works on view to six hundred or so, and identification labels were so far and so confusingly removed as to leave most visitors in ignorance; those who complained that masterpieces long resident in the galleries had been displaced by wretched rubbish and the second rate for the sake of bringing forward 'in turn, different aspects of the chronological sequence' were put down as domiciled in Tunbridge Wells. With the third annual hang, the novelty worn very thin, critical response was largely hostile, at last recognising the sense of insecurity that constant change had brought to the Gallery, the re-hanging now a disruption throughout the year, with rooms closed and the chronological paths diverted as elements in each new display proved to have a duration of not even half the promised year, and the number of works on view occasionally dropped to some four hundred and fifty.

In *Who's Who* Serota lists his recreation as 'hanging pictures'; in the Tate Gallery his private hobby has become his public political manoeuvre to demonstrate that it has vast resources but nowhere to put them on view – an argument undone by the wastefully sparse distribution of pictures on the walls (a small Magritte is separated from a small Dali by fifteen feet of blank wall), the dismal quality of much that has been briefly resurrected (particularly of late 19th-century British pictures of the ilk of Farquharson and North), the pious extravagance of Minimalism, and the prodigal use of a whole gallery for the installation of a single work, of which Rebecca Horn's *Ballet of the Woodpeckers* (an absurdity within the immediate intellectual grasp of any who can comprehend a cuckoo clock) is an example. From such a manoeuvre we all suffer, for in turning the

Tate into a constantly changing exhibition hall, though he may the more amuse those who live in London, Serota neglects a duty to the nation as a whole and to the international visitor, for these have reason to expect the Gallery's masterpieces to be permanently on view. Those from abroad who visit the Gallery now must not only have the most erratic impression of the history of British art (a whole room given to Gainsborough, but Reynolds reduced to one portrait, and that keeping rum company with Clarkson Stanfield, a range of Hogarths but no Stubbs), but believe that the National Gallery of Modern Foreign Painting is virtually devoid of representative Impressionists, Expressionists and most of this century's serious intellectual and aesthetic developments. His imposed pattern of fast change makes casualties of his best hanging; the Mondrians have never looked lovelier than in the second hang, seen in the little octagon with the Anrep mosaics, enchanting through an enfilade of rooms; these were replaced by the current witty hanging of William Roberts, but this comes down in May, destroying the telling balance with Fernand Léger in the pendent octagon. Add to the constantly changing stock from the permanent collection the disruption of temporary exhibitions in the Duveen Galleries by sculptors whose work, as in the case of Richard Long, is almost too well known and too frequently exhibited, and the management of the Gallery seems as giddy as a merry-go-round. Serota, in continuing the exhibition habits acquired as an Arts Council minion and long nurtured in Whitechapel, succeeds only in suggesting that the Tate's holdings are so weak and uneven as to put in doubt its standing as an international gallery, yet the sponsors of the annual re-hanging, British Petroleum, have announced that their support is to be extended for two more years (a decision made in advance of any critical response to this year's hang).

Perhaps in part this constant retrieval of forgotten works is a substitute for acquisition, for it is certain sure that the current annual purchase grant does not permit Serota to have a coherent acquisitions policy – he can do no more than fill an occasional small gap in the collections of the past, or point, as with Horn's *Woodpeckers*, to the immediate present. He is, in a sense, the victim of those with generous instincts, and must take what they give him (the recent Saatchi gift, for example), compromising on quality and interest if by so doing meagre funds can be applied elsewhere. In the open market he must buy what he can afford, when he can afford it, and not what he deems best – his penury defeats his duty as a curator and ensures that artists are represented by work that is neither their best nor of true museum quality. In this area Serota's work is thankless, for one worthy 18th-century British masterpiece or great Bacon triptych may easily absorb all (and more) of an annual grant that would scarcely buy a straw hat by Renoir or a single sunflower from a bunch by Van Gogh, and no major painting could be imported from abroad; he is, moreover, frustrated by a 'Heritage' attitude that foreign works of art are only of interest if they have long been in this country – which means that the Tate is unlikely ever to acquire a major Matisse or Beckmann, indeed it will never have a significant holding of pre-war German art, for it will never be rich enough to go marketing abroad where it cannot call for the help of the NACF, the CAS, or the Heritage Fund.

Corporate sponsors, even at £25,000 a year, can hardly add real purchasing power to the paltry £1,800,000 annual purchase grant; nor can restaurants and bookstalls – generating income, these are now, it seems, fundamental to the well-being of all galleries, and if the sale of souvenirs and postcards takes the hanging space of pictures, so be it, for this is now the way of things and we should not complain. One thing, however, we should not tolerate in these small halls of Mammon – the sale of undistinguished coloured reproductions as limited edition prints, each bearing 'a certificate from the Tate Gallery', six for the 'special Connoisseurs' price of £395'. The Gallery is disgraced by such deceptive language, and no profit, however handsome, justifies lending its name to such a scurvy enterprise.

Serota's is an impossible task – but it was impossible even in Rothenstein's day and is worse now only in degree and in the Gallery's having to serve an extra purpose. The solution is, and has long been, obvious: the Tate Gallery should be divided into its constituent parts (though the divisions could never be precise), leaving the Turners and British art in Millbank, sending the ilk of Van Gogh, Degas, Matisse, Corinth, Munch and Kirchner to Trafalgar Square (where Neil MacGregor, in accepting the Berggruen loan, appears to have changed his mind about using c.1900 as the *terminus ante quem* of the collection) and opening an entirely new gallery (the Smithfield Market building would be perfect) for art of the kind that Serota clearly understands better than the rest of us, and for which, in half a century, our children may perhaps be grateful.

Modern Painters 1992

The Serpentine Gallery

TWENTY-FIVE YEARS AGO, IN 1970, THE gloomy and disagreeable café in Kensington Gardens that had long been notorious for stewed tea and, but for the meanest scrape of margarine, the driest, dustiest scones in Christendom, was converted into a showplace for the visual arts. To celebrate this silver jubilee, the Serpentine Gallery now offers us an exhibition that pretends to be a potted history of British sculpture since the Festival of Britain in 1951, but the contributors are only sculptors who have exhibited there – with the exception of the noble Henry Moore, a narrow choice made entirely from passengers on the bandwaggon of contemporary art who have abandoned the disciplines and traditions of ancestral sculpture, and demand that we accept and revere them for their anarchical excursions with the rag and bone man, many of them riding on his donkey.

Most of the work exhibited seems wearyingly familiar, the artists doggedly conforming to the diktat that they must constantly break boundaries – 'innovate,' as current jargon jabber has it. Innovation only for innovation's sake, however, makes miserably meagre art, and it matters not a jot how loud the critics and curators sing 'Wider still and wider, shall thy bounds be spread', if only the work of their favourites is shown and the aesthetic consequences are utterly negligible. Mona Hatoum, one of only eleven artists in the whole wide world who will see us into the next century, if the Tate Gallery is to be believed, is here with a contraption that resembles a shopping trolley adapted to slice ostrich eggs for gigantic sand-wiches. Rachel Whiteread is here with yet more hidden spaces converted into yet more solid blocks of resin, untitled, but presumably casts of the space beneath the kichen stool. Jane and Louise Wilson are here with the scribbled *Note* that made them famous in 1992 – 'I am the person who smashed your door. I was not well . . .' – this time incorporated in a photograph of kitchen squalor bathed in light of Mephistophelean red and green (and when did bad photography become great sculpture?). Damien Hirst shows us his sheep in formaldehyde again, with the lid screwed down against the resurrection men.

Nothing here lifts the spirit or convinces us that the makers of these aberrations are the heirs of Michelangelo and Rodin. The names are often famous, but Paolozzi with a frog that has the likeness of Leggo pieces pressed into a baked potato, Ian Hamilton Finlay with a neon sign, Caro with a contraption of old iron that has collapsed under its own weight, and Richard Deacon with another that resembles less the primitive water-raising machine that the Egyptians call *shaduf* (Deacon names his sculpture *Troubled Water*) than a metronome with drums, give us meagre things indeed. Even lower down the scale we have bits of bent wire, litter fragments, a video with maddening music (the switch is at floor level by the window and can be flipped up with the toe), paper smirched with stains and drips and squiggles (sculpture?), and sheets of silver plastic framed in flashing lights and accompanied by tick-tock percussive noises that infuriate the dogs – and to these we must apply the concept and theory at which some art critics are so adept that their justifications are far more ingenious, important and fundamental (in the antique sense of fundament as anus) than the artists' art.

What passes for a catalogue is the wisdom of Miss Sarah Kent – a history of the Gallery, signed by Sarah Kent, an outline of the renovation scheme, signed by Sarah Kent, and a thumbnail (cruelly long) sketch of British sculpture, signed by Sarah Kent – all too much like the last chapter of *The Wind in the Willows* with its Speech by Toad, Address by Toad, and Song by Toad. This is another uncomfortable subject – the question of the art critic who plays the hybrid role of commercial promoter as well as consumer guide too closely bound to the subject by blind enthusiasm and substantial fee ever to be dispassionate in criticism – and one is reminded of the cynical curator who said 'Don't read the rubbish, measure it'.

The Serpentine Gallery has in its twenty-five years mounted a few exhibitions that were retrospective, even contemplative, considerations of artists well-established or even dead (as with Ivon Hitchens), but they have been far between, and its present policy is almost wholly of support to the extremists of contemporary art; in this, its offerings are indistinguishable from much that is to be seen in the the Camden Arts Centre and the Whitechapel, Hayward and Tate Galleries, its adherence to the Serota Tendency devout and unquestioning. It has become another instrument of the very small group of people whose cords of power are so closely interwoven that they have virtually absolute control over the public exhibition spaces in London, and, perhaps even more important, over sources of private as well as public patronage. The lenders to the exhibition too are few and close-knit with these cords – the Arts and British Councils, Saatchi, and the commercial galleries in this small field – Jopling, Reynolds, Lisson, Schubert and Juda, for example – are mighty prominent. The point must be made that the number of artists to the fore, their promoters and apologists, is very small indeed, yet their share of public funds, well-managed limelight, and press interest, is enormous and virtually exclusive. As Sarah Kent has said of figurative art – 'it is irrelevant'.

As a celebration of the Serpentine's purposes this exhibition tells a deplorable truth – that though British sculpture is at a low ebb, intellectually insubstantial and aesthetically arid, the Trustees and Curators of the Gallery are happy to support it.

Not one exhibiting artist is capable of dealing with the vacant plinth in Trafalgar Square – suddenly a matter of interest and speculation – though Caro might tumble a few iron girders there and call them Mrs Thatcher. Surely we are sick of the so-called great and good, of politicians who lie, dissemble and are pusillanimous? Were Churchill not already up and standing, it would now be difficult to support the statue of a man who surrendered the whole of Eastern Europe to Russian domination, the Iron Curtain of his making, his feet indeed of clay: should one wish for Wilson, Eden, Douglas-Home, Major? – the notion is utterly risible. One proposal is worthwhile: most men of my generation were National Service-men, and with the minimum of preparation many, mere boys, were sent to die in futile skirmishes in Korea, Cyprus, Aden, Malaya and elsewhere, with nothing of the ballyhoo and braggadocio given to the Falklands War. To these there is no War Memorial. Let there be one now, a monument of beauty and pathos – if any man can make one.

Evening Standard 1995

Cindy Sherman

CINDY SHERMAN IS YET ANOTHER PHOTOGRA-pher whose work is classified as art by the panjandrums who decide such matters, and throughout the summer her glossy images will hang in the Whitechapel Gallery for the delectation of all school-boys with an eye for tits and bums. The tits and bums, however, are not those of the popular newspaper, nor of the Renaissance masterpiece, but are more akin to the lurid illustrations of an ancient medical encyclopedia; a highly coloured nipple oozes milk, on a pair of ample buttocks every inch of skin is embellished with pustules of Vesuvian proportions, each yellow head about to burst and pour poison down its flanks, and what I take to be a detail of a face is so grotesquely enlarged that it is barely recogniseable as flesh and more resembles dilapidated sponge cake with too much jam.

This comparatively young woman, born in New Jersey in 1954, is now claimed to be one of the most influential American artists to have emerged in the last decade – to which the only possible response is that there is no accounting for the folly of gullible Americans where the appreciation of art is concerned. In the late Seventies, when with cosmetics and blonde wig she was able to affect the look of Baby Doll, she composed portraits of herself that closely resembled film stills from the days when Hollywood had starlets and B films were in black and white – Cindy in a bath towel playing the ingenue, Cindy the kitchen slut, Cindy the archetypal Baby Doll waiting, lips and legs apart, for her lover, Cindy the all-American sophomore who can just tell the difference between a book and a cookie jar, Cindy the hooker with a heart and a crucifix in her cleavage, Cindy in the city, Cindy on the shore. No imagination is required to recognise the cardboard characters and feeble plots, and yet these ordinary and obvious images have caused much speculation among her critics and have brought her much praise. The German author of the exhibition catalogue is inspired to ask 'What is she doing? What has she experienced? Why is she mournful? Why is she looking in a mirror? What are her thoughts? What does she want from us?' But as these film stills are all listed as *Untitled* and can be identified only by date and number, I feel inclined to scoff and quote Norman Rosenthal, eximious Exhibitions Secretary of the Royal Academy, who said of one of his recent exhibitions when quizzed by a foolish journalist 'There are only questions in art – no answers . . . the question is where are we now? But there's no answer.' If there really are no answers, then why should we bother with questions inspired by things as trivial as Cindy Sherman's photographs?

As for the more recent work, the nipples and the pimples, these too are photographs of herself, but with the added grotesquery of plastic parts that have the cast of preposterous prosthetic aids. Gross enlargement so changes the familiar texture of skin that it is not always possible to distinguish it from plastic, and only the crisp dividing line (when one can find it) offers a clue to unreality; yet even with such a line below another pair of buttocks, this time lacking spots but with an extraordinary pink band to emphasise the parting, one is unsure, for the thighs look even less real, as though Cindy's substantial legs are contained in some strange white plastic fetish garment (the dirty feet below are real enough). The image is not a pretty sight, and its small mystery should not detain us on aesthetic grounds, but willy-nilly we are held in wonderment by such a puzzle. This time, to give the lie to Rosenthal, the answer is immediately apparent – it is that Cindy deliberately uses the apparatus of pornography in such a way that it can have no effect and reverses images that should be erotic into those that only inspire aversion. Imagine the therapeutic effect of lifting a girl's skirts to discover, instead of peaches and cream, spots inflamed and large enough to match the celebrated syphilitic sores of the beggar in Grünewald's great altar of the Crucifixion.

Miss Sherman is interested in Old Masters and now that she is no longer in her first youth photographs herself in costumed poses that mimic paintings by Caravaggio, Holbein, Raphael and Leonardo. These too are without title – a matter for regret, for the differences between the originals and her reworkings are perhaps significant. Raphael's *Fornarina* is by tradition a portrait of his mistress, lushly beautiful and fresh for bed, but Miss Sherman uses the pose and nudity to reveal a pregnant woman, breasts pendulous with milk, eyes weary, face haggard with the ravages of morning sickness. That the breasts and stomach are not hers, but a plastic carapace tied on like an apron (can such things really be bought in New York joke shops, the ultimate extension of the false nose?), is here irrelevant, for the message seems to be that this is the after of a before and after morality tale, and a warning to women not to let themselves be used as the playthings of men. It is an ingenious promotion of the feminist message.

As for the photographs as works of art – they are large, bilious in colour, and closer to advertising than to art, but were one to devise an allegorical Olympus for kitsch, Miss Sherman would be somewhere near its peak as handmaiden to Jeff Koons and all his nastiness.

Evening Standard 1991

Kiki Smith

IF KIKI SMITH IS, AS THOSE WHO PROMOTE THE Whitechapel Gallery's current exhibition of her work would have us believe, 'one of the most exciting artists working in New York today', then on the basis of these amateur sculptures and feminine whimsies verging on the pretty, New York must be in the doldrums. The fine space and light of the gallery lend grace and majesty to utterly unworthy work often enough, but with Miss Smith it fails, and all we see is an empty theatrical presentation of the naked female figure in contrived attitudes and guises, offering far less aesthetic elevation and excitement than the shop windows of Knightsbridge.

This muted, trivial, disappointing exhibition is not the Kiki Smith that I expected, and my immediate thought was that, bearing in mind the public sources of the gallery's funds, and the nature and religious beliefs of its local Muslim audience, the Director must have asked Miss Smith to treat our sensibilities with far greater care than is her custom. I had hoped for an exhibition that allowed Miss Smith full licence as ambassador for the American school of artists obsessed with the body's business of emptying bowel and bladder, of bleeding and vomiting, and oozing tears, milk, semen, menstrual and other mysterious fluids, for it is a school of which we know very little in this country, though from time to time we are made aware of it by pale English imitators. Indeed, though it would undoubtedly cause outrage here, there is much to be said for mounting an encyclopedic exhibition of such material, not supported by the passionate eulogies of critics employed by the Arts Council (as was the case with Helen Chadwick's *Piss Flowers* and chocolate euphemisms for shit), but coolly, with no comments other than statements made by the artists themselves, so that we may judge, not only the works and images, but the intellectual arguments adduced by those who make them. In America — and you must forgive me for employing the vernacular that artists use to enhance the element of affront — shitting, pissing and cumming are well established fields of interest rooted, not only in the political correctitudes of feminism, sexual freedom, genital identity and Freud's concept of body-ego, but in the practices of abstract expressionist painting more than thirty years ago. In this particular context some may argue that as all painting is in some sense related to the infant's exploration of the waste matter of his body, the finger in the faeces so to speak, the adult is justified in rejecting the sophistications of art training and returning to the chamber pot to begin a new search for the meaning and practice of art — when all is said and done, penis and pencil have a common Latin source, every pointed paint brush is a phallic reference, and there is every reason to recognise the anus as the nozzle of a tube of paint.

Marcel Duchamp, with his upturned urinal of 1917, is the father figure for these artists, but where he joked with a visual pun and did not intend that it be treated with high seriousness, to artists of the Sixties Duchamp was a hero and no prankster, and his urinal became the grand authority for using urine and, by extension, faeces, as a medium. Papier maché painted to resemble excrement was first exhibited in New York in 1964, and the theme has remained constant ever since; a decade later, Andy Warhol adopted the arm-swing rhythms of Jackson Pollock's drip paintings when he and his catamites urinated on canvas coated with copper-based paint and let the random processes of oxydisation create the willy-nilly images. Inexorably the number of artists using urine and faeces multiplied, and as other body-waste materials came into use, so the imagery focused on their points of origin; artists who in the Sixties had been content to use the naked body as the instrument with which to smear paint onto canvas, and sometimes as the canvas itself, eventually saw it is a visual territory complete in itself, even to being its own source of paint. Miss Smith, for example, in her bolder presentations, has concentrated on man's reproductive functions, letting a nude male drip sperm while milk seeping from a woman's breasts runs down the belly to the thighs; she has explored the body's orifices and urogenital systems, let her imagination work on menstrual flux, and like a radiator on a wall, has installed a human digestive system in cast iron – her work, she claims, is 'like opening a can of worms – all life happens between the tongue and the anus'. It is perhaps worth observing that though Miss Smith has no formal training as an artist, she has qualified as a medical technician.

Miss Smith constructs her female figures in papier maché, stitched muslin, plaster and bronze, sometimes using her own body as a cast. Given such titles as *Siren*, *Mary Magdalen* and *Lilith*, they refer to a mythology of heroic women; dubbed *Scaffold Body*, *Blood Pool* or *Upside-Down Body*, they seem no more than a muted feminist lament. She thinks her own body a prison. Her 'sculptures', male or female, are scarcely competent, and were they made by a third-year art school student, none would deserve a second glance.

This is wretched stuff for a one-man show in one of London's most estimable galleries. Smith's work is no match for the nasty obscenities of Cindy Sherman, shown in Whitechapel in 1991, nor for the penile dementia of Robert Gober, revealed at the Serpentine in the same year, but it is of the same general ilk and obsession – indeed, she employs the same clichés of amputated limbs as Gober, and shares his taste for real pubic hair. Her present tendency to prettify her work with beads and pearls is a silly trick that quite undoes her message – but then her message is at best incoherent, at worst nonsensical. Within the large group of American artists who for a generation have used the human body and its secretions, emissions and evacuations as the vehicle for argument in favour of feminism, lesbianism, abortion, homosexuality, and all forms of sexual behaviour that some dub deviant, Smith is a woman of no importance, a latecomer with nothing to add. None of her images has the impact of Judy Chicago's exposure, way back in 1971, of the bloody realities of menstruation that lie behind television's demure advertisements for tampons, none is as repellent as Cindy Sherman's constructed photographs of human flesh, none is as surprising as Robert Mapplethorpe's cool and immaculate images of the extremes of homosexual pleasure.

We have had enough of this drip, drip business; if there is any merit, aesthetic or political, in their arguments, then let the Hayward or the Tate Gallery have the courage, shielding us from nothing, to show us the whole history of this American School of artists who with raw nature confront and abuse the cultural conventions of twenty centuries past. In the carcases of Damien Hirst, the frozen blood of Marc Quinn, the urine of Helen Chadwick and the chocolate smears of Anya Gallaccio, we have seen the work of British monkeys; let us now see what the American organ-grinders did and do.

Evening Standard 1995

Rabindranath Tagore

Astonishment was the only possible response to the announcement of an exhibition of the paintings and drawings of Rabindranath Tagore at the Barbican. To a generation of schoolboys perfectly capable of responding to Catholic confusions in the poetry of Francis Thompson, reconciling reason with the mysteries of Trans-substantiation and the Virgin Birth, and to whom Calvin, Luther and John Huss had been the commonplace of examination papers, Tagore remained a mystery. Not that his poetry was on the syllabus – but it was part of the mind-broad-ening exploration of literature encouraged by our masters, and, I suspect, a latter-day enthusiasm left over from their youth. To us he presented only impenetrable vagaries of thought, made to seem significant by a deliberate smog of language, and became Rabin-dranath the Bore.

He turned up later on the fringes of English art; William Rothenstein, a fine painter and a generous soul, but an erratic judge of character, was responsible for getting his poetry published in England; Eric Gill, who was pretty loony about sex, religion, life and art, responded to his philosophical maunderings with absurd enthusiasm; and Epstein made a portrait bust of him. In his autobiography Epstein pens a portrait more telling than the bust – to him Tagore was a man of arrogance and wrath, demanding the awe more properly given to a holy man, aloof and cold; like a king, he carried no money, and like a king, one word of command was enough for a disciple to service any need; when Epstein introduced to him a little Indian boy, the son of his model Sunita, Tagore enquired only if he were a Hindu, and on finding him a Muslim, snubbed him with silence. Yet this was the man who claimed to be '. . . he that sitteth among the poorest, the loneliest and the lost'. This was the man who proclaimed 'My religion is the reconciliation in my own individual being of the Super-personal Man, the Universal human spirit'.

He was a high caste Bengali Brahman, from a family that had been stinking rich, and was still wealthy enough to live in a palace and have country estates. He was comfortably isolated from the daily life of peasant Bengal – '. . . the Bengali with all his genius possesses little energy and character' – and was part of what I can best picture as the Bloomsbury Group of Calcutta, concerned with writing plays and poetry, publishing magazines, and performing music. With pre-pubertal precocity he joined in, and it was the beginning of twenty-six fat volumes of poetry and prose, and more than twenty of letters, to make no mention of his music, his painting, and an activity as philosopher, educationalist, lecturer and self-publicist that did not slow down until his death at the age of eighty in 1941.

But his international reputation had by then diminished. It had been mercifully brief and on a par with Beatlemania. It began at the age of fifty in 1911 with Rothenstein's interest, and was boosted two years later by the Nobel Prize for Literature – for which he beat Thomas Hardy (there's a measure of absurdity). In 1915 he was knighted. In 1922 the Germans claimed that he had wakened them to consciousness of their own German soul (he was always preaching Nationalism). In 1926 he was the welcome guest of Mussolini. In 1930 he traipsed round Russia on an official and misguided tour. And that was an end to it – by 1931 the great reputation was in tatters, and he returned to India to paint, in ten years of unrelenting activity, more than two thousand pictures.

He no longer trusted his writing – 'I sometimes wonder why I wrote so much in my life; just a few pieces would have done as well'. In a letter of 1939, again doubting the permanent value of literature, he wrote 'I have found, in my days of retirement, two stable havens of activity, song-writing and painting'.

Of the song-writing I can make no comment – but I doubt the value of a statement by a writer in the Exhibition catalogue that '. . . as a composer he has no equal, not even in the West – and I know Schubert and Hugo Wolf'.

Of the paintings equally absurd claims have been made – 'sound spatial judgment, chromatic freshness and textural variations of great subtlety' in which Impressionism, Expressionism, Romanticism, Naivety and Unconsciousness have all played their part. What seems to me to be the case is that the old bore trundled round the world poaching impressions of other people's pictures and drawings (including Epstein's), and in his dotage re-hashed them.

And hash is the word for it. They are abysmal. Never were scribble, scratch, scrawl and blot more industriously used to less effect. He has as much idea of spatial judgment as an infant reaching for the breast, his chromatic freshness is the muddied palette of primary ignorance, and 'textural subtleties' is critic's jargon for 'this is such a mess that I can't see what's what'. Never has the paraphernalia of the specious anniversary been put to more preposterous use.

Evening Standard 1986

Tate Gallery New Displays, 1995

Among the great treasures of the Tate Gallery are four bronze reliefs by Henri Matisse, all some six feet tall and four feet wide, all of a standing woman seen from the back. The original models, of plaster supplemented by clay, cover the period c1909 – c1930, and demonstrate the sculptor's progression from a naturalism that comfortably follows on the heels of Rodin, to a monumental simplification of form that is far more extreme than in any of his paintings – a woman turned into a pair of battered Doric columns.

They are not pretty. They are not desirable in the sense of many smaller bronzes by Matisse; nor, unlike those, do they excite in obvious connection with Cubism and parallels with Picasso; but in their heroic scale, their sense of the unlovely robust strength with which the long torso and short legs of Mediterranean women are endowed, and in images that revert to the primeval, they touch the core of womanhood that mattered most to those far ancient sculptors who turned woman into fecund fetish, made her a monster of wide child-bearing hips, and appointed her goddess of all earth's fertility. They used to hang in the octagon that breaks the length of the Tate's sculpture gallery, their shadows shifting with the times of day, their colour responding to the warm light of summer, but they are there no longer – indeed it is many months since they were last seen in London, for they are victims of the Tate's annual game of ring-a-ring-of-roses, and have been shipped to Liverpool, a fact of which visitors to Millbank, be they from Edinburgh or anywhere abroad, are unaware until they reach the gallery. Sending these bronzes to Liverpool may please a few Liverpudlians, but it is a grave national and international disservice.

This one act of folly is enough to demonstrate the damage that can be done by ill-considered business sponsorship, for it is money given by British Petroleum that enables the Director of the Tate, Nicholas Serota, to shift and shunt at whim the national collections in his cure. Every year now at the Tate we are presented, not with a national collection of masterpieces, but with a dog's dinner of art history in which works of art are forced to fit themes and notions conjured from very little by the Tate's curators. These pseudo-academic beds of Procrustes are given such whimsical titles as *Joie de Vivre*, *Existence and Expression*, and *The Search for the New Aesthetic* (an alternative to Hunt the Thimble?), reducing the Tate's rooms to a series of minor exhibitions for which its resources are often quite inadequate, and bringing about, simply because they fit the themes, the resurrection of minor pictures and sculptures of such secondary quality and interest that visitors from abroad must wonder why the Tate is hailed as a gallery of international importance. Indeed, no one whose purpose in visiting the Tate is to see a particular masterpiece illustrated in the catalogue, should do so without first checking that it is in the building, for it may well be in the far provinces or relegated to the stores in favour of some minor work of momentary interest.

The new hang is not even reliable art history. Consider the room given to *Allegory and Realism at Mid-Century*: decent paintings by Freud and Minton, but a wretched Lowry, a worse Jack Smith, an Ayrton, a poor small Balthus – are these the pictures with which to illustrate such a theme? – no Francis Gruber, no Bernard Buffet, and above all, no Nicholas de Stael, none of whom may seem important now, but they were in 1950, as were the CoBrA Group, represented in another room by one of its feeblest and most insignificant members.

From *Myth and Gesture in Mid-Century*, devoted to the grandees of American abstract art, does it make any sense to exclude the huge *Summertime* of Jackson Pollock, the most gestural and highly coloured of his paintings, at the very time when the gallery's spring exhibition is devoted to Willem de Kooning, and the kinship and rivalry of these two masters of gesture and colour is a major issue to consider? To place this important picture elsewhere, under the misleading title *Myth and Nature*, is an act of lunacy.

It is often argued that the Tate has far too little room to show all its thousands of possessions, as though such an aim were in any way desirable; the riposte must be that any national collection must to some considerable extent function as a reference library, a repository of the forgotten, the neglected, the arcane and the almost utterly negligible, and that these must stay in reserve until required for a particular purpose – such as the miserable exhibition at the Barbican (*Impressionism in Britain*) – like the rarely opened pages of an encyclopedia. The Tate defeats its own argument with this current hang, so meagre is it – Room 20 is some 75 feet long, yet one wall is occupied by only four paintings, of which the total width is 19 feet, and elsewhere, between a small Bacon and a smaller Kokoschka, lie 16 feet of blank wall, with 25 feet to keep apart a tiny Stephen Gilbert (why hang such a trifle?) and a modest Beckmann. With such prodigal wastes of wall space, the argument won't wash.

The Tate is not the personal instrument of its Director, though he clearly thinks it so; it is not the plaything of Londoners, an ever-changing freak show the success of which is to be measured, not by the quality of aesthetic and spiritual experience within its walls, but by an increase in the numbers climbing its front steps; the Tate owes instead a duty to the whole nation and to the international visitor, for it is part of the world's network of museums serving the world's heritage and not merely some little local interest. This purpose can only be served by a measure of permanence in its displays, assuring us all that its major works are constantly on view, supported by a rolling programme of small exhibitions from the Gallery's resources, occupying perhaps a tenth of the Tate's space.

To exhibit all its masterpieces would not put pressure on

demands for space, for the present ever-changing nonsense demonstrates with devastating clarity that as a national collection of international modern art, the Tate is meagre to the point of provincial wretchedness, pathetically weak in its holdings of Impressionist and Post-Impressionist painting, even feebler in its Expressionist resources, grossly inadequate as a storehouse of Surrealism, quite unable to demonstrate the emergence of Abstraction early in this century, and risible as a repository of Cubism.

If ever a Director of the Tate had a duty to fill these gaps before all else, it is Serota, and he should have directed the sponsorship of such supporters as BP towards acquisitions that would lend strength to the Gallery's international status, but we have instead the damaging idiocy of the annual merry-go-round, while huge funds from the Lottery are to be applied to the adaptation of the Bankside Power Station to a people's palace of absurdity. Serota writes of this as though it will change the whole economy of London, bring down the price of bread and wipe out the National Debt; it will, instead, embarrass us with the emptiness of its exhibits, its broken furniture, mechanical contraptions, feeble videos and all the other idioms of overblown and space-consuming contemporary art, with, no doubt, the emptyings of bowel and bladder that are now so popular with artists who suffer the creative urge, but have neither the brain nor skill to convert it into art – and, of course, their chocolate euphemisms. If Serota must be allowed to pillage the Lottery, let us at least not abuse old Tate's memory by giving his name to the Bankside Folly – let that be dubbed The Serota Gallery, his memorial alone. There is no doubt that if only as a holding operation while we think we need a gallery of contemporary art, though we need far more urgently an entirely separate gallery given to the years from Impressionism to Surrealism, and I am content to let Serota and his cronies accumulate as many pantomime pianos in the Power Station as they wish, and let posterity judge – but his choice is the work of artists whose perspectives of the past are cripplingly short, their obsessions and concerns mere trivial whims, all contact with the ancestral traditions of European art abandoned, and in the context of the Tate they are irrelevant.

Twice a year, with the Turner Prize and the re-hanging, Serota throws down a challenge, if not an affront. He responds to no criticism and counters all argument by pointing to an increasing flood of visitors. Freak shows and circuses bought precisely that kind of popularity in ancient Rome, the Rome of the Decline and Fall.

Evening Standard 1995

Cy Twombly

WRITE THE NAME OF THE ANCIENT ROMAN poet VIRGIL in rough irregular capitals with a soft pencil, lick your finger and smudge its wet tip across the script, and to all intents and purposes you have reproduced a work of art by Cy Twombly.

Begin a lesson in fractions on a blackboard, erase half and scribble a whirl of wild white lines over the rest, and you have Twombly number two.

For Twombly three, prime a canvas with creamy white paint and scribble on it with an assortment of soft graphite pencils while it is still wet; then let it dry hard and scribble again; some of the graphite will merely disturb the oil paint and be submerged in it, some will stay on top, darkening the peaks of paint, skipping the troughs.

Scribble odd notes on a sheet of paper; write one word on another, preferably a classical allusion, and stick it on the first; add an outline drawing of a crocus on a third; then scribble over all three.

Take an enormous canvas – fifteen feet wide or thereabouts – put some red and white paint on your palette, dip your brush into both, unmixed, and stir vigorously onto the canvas, either in small patches that will resemble a whirligig rhododendron (and about the same size), or rambling scrawls, or vaguely vertical scribbles. Add Naples yellow to the mix and do it again, taking care not to overlap anything already done. Make small unconnected jabs at the canvas in messy dark tones (Hooker's green and Vandyke brown make a suitably unpleasant combination) or bright white and yellow. Outline some of these marks in blue and black. In the wide spaces that remain, write words and figures with a pencil, making sure that they are either incomplete or difficult to read; draw small squares, circles and an erect penis of no particular distinction labelled Hercules. Then call this parade of smudges, blobs and jottings *The Triumph of Galatea*, conjuring the ghost of Raphael, and you declare that you have made a masterpiece.

Most of the work now on view in the Whitechapel Gallery, when not nameless, carries a title taken from the mythology of Greece and Rome. Twombly lives in Rome, a sixtyish American, heir to the empty gestures of Abstract Expressionism, claiming to draw new strength and vigour for it from the classical heritage of his chosen Mediterranean environment. The claim is insupportable twaddle.

His apologists see in his work the nocturnes of Whistler, the marine fantasies of Turner, the waterlilies of Monet, and the white on white abstractions of Malevich. He has only to write such a word as ANABASIS on a sheet of paper and they see in it the whole history of Alexander from Macedonia to Kashmir, or Xenophon's long march from Babylon to Armenia – though one of the paintings under this title resembles nothing so much as a baby's drawing of a baby's pram. In *Leda and the Swan* I see only what may be the damp and muddy print of a webbed foot – nothing of the peck and flutter of sexual conjugation between the naked princess and Zeus in one of his clammier disguises.

Were I a kindly critic I would try to see in this the art of the palimpsest – a re-used manuscript from which the first text has been inadequately erased and is still fragmentarily readable under the second; late Roman sculptors carving inscriptions on old stones sometimes adapted their spelling and spacing so as to employ letters from the earlier inscription – it is a fascinating game to piece together the earlier text from such scattered and disguised clues. But Twombly is responsible for all the layers and erasures that are consciously and deliberately part of the final effect, and his layers are not language but mere gesture.

The gesture often assumes the character of script, and conditions us to expect words and meaning; when the words are clear we are expected to react like Pavlov dogs to such triggers as we might recall from the tattered relics of a classical education – Proteus, Nike, Pan and Sabines raped.

I have never seen the point of Twombly's work. That he can paint is powerfully suggested by three mated seascapes called *Hero and Leander* that do indeed evoke the treacherous drowning waters of the Bosphorus, hinting at Turner and Monet – but the rest of it is arrogant in its assumption that we will recognise mastery in mere gesture and a written word, wilful rubbish by a painter who chooses not to paint.

I am alone in this view. The handsome catalogue quotes the opinions of seven sages who see him as Rembrandt and Raphael, quivering with life, penetrating to the depths, in wild sexual catharsis, as offering the space for events rather than the events themselves, primeval and innovative. These essays are masterpieces of the aesthetic self-deception and self-generating hyperbole that have done so much damage to the arts in the post-war years – the pseudo-intellectual hijack. The cynic will see Twombly's line liberated from subject repeated ad nauseam in any infants' school.

Evening Standard 1987

Euan Uglow

The Whitechapel Gallery CONFRONTED BY THIRTY PAINTINGS OF THE female nude, work covering more than thirty years of Euan Uglow's activity as a painter, two questions drift into the spectator's mind – does Uglow like the women whom he paints? – and, the more serious, does he like painting them? He treats them as objects on which to lavish rather less affection than might be given to a pound of pork sausages half unravelled on a kitchen slab; and the act of painting them emerges as the painful effort of a labour with which Uglow has scant sympathy, as though not a single stroke of paint is on the canvas as the consequence of instinct, impulse or skill, but is mere information derived from a computer, diligently applied by an uncomprehending clerk who would much prefer to be delving in his herbaceous border.

Born in 1932, Uglow is of that generation that had its first experience of painting pictures in the smudgy style so much the affectation of painters calling themselves the School of Euston Road – a group for which little is to be said in praise and much in condemnation, but at least they practised some small freedoms in the way they handled paint. Uglow has none. It was not always so – there was a time, in the mid-Sixties, when he produced small pictures in which the texture of the paint and the action of the brush were paramount, if tentative, as though Auerbach or Kossoff had briefly held his hand; ten years later he again toyed with the small painterly picture, though much more tightly drawn, but that was the last of his aberrant exercises in sensuous handling, and he became a one-eyed intellectual intent on significant form – I suspect that he would have fitted very well into the aesthetic atmosphere of Bloomsbury before the First World War. The format of his more characteristic and important pictures does not overwhelm – three feet may be one measurement of a perfect proportional relationship between height and width, but in large areas of colour that is bright and fashionable in the clothing industry, painted without modulation of tone or texture, not a brushstroke can be seen. The effect is harshly boring, and tends to compel the eye to seek relief in the varied flesh tones of the nudes.

Alas, even the nakedness of women elicits from him only an arid intellectual exercise, a coldly mathematical compromise between abstraction and realism of the narrowest appeal – and that certainly not to the loins. I am aware of the rage of eminent feminists that men should ever think of women as sexual objects, seeing no distinction between the booby bimbos of Page 3 and the smothering, billowing, dimpling, dumpling forms beloved by old Rubens – but they must surely object even more strongly to the neutering meted out by that enquiring pathologist, Mr Uglow. His emotions safely tucked in the refrigerator, he examines his woman as though she were a corpse. Such intellectual discipline, even dominance, might be forgivable were it impeccably accurate, but it is not; in spite of all the irritating ticks and measurements with which he maps his models, schedules the day's work, and pretentiously leaves to litter the canvas with distractions ('I don't really finish a painting, it stops'), many of his subjects are disgracefully ill-drawn and disproportionate, some so ludicrously inept that they would embarrass a first-year student at the Slade (and that is saying a great deal, by the present standards in that benighted School).

Uglow takes as many as five years to paint his pictures, and the interruptions to the labour are all too obvious, marked by abrupt changes of tone, colour and scale as he shifted his concentration in the tedious journey from sole of foot to dome of skull. When he sets his models in anything other than a full frontal pose, he utterly defeats himself as a draughtsman or constructor – the nude seated in a bentwood chair, painted in 1962–3, is remarkable for a preposterous ugliness of neck, shoulder and arm that is the consequence solely of Uglow's ineptitude as the very thing he claims to be, an observer of what is 'right', not 'like'; and the *Lugano Nude* of 1976 is so far from either right or like as to be contemptible on any count. He practises monocular vision, excluding all extraneous detail, but his total concentration on the parts destroys the whole.

I share the layman view expressed by Freud, that the subject of a painting often has a stronger immediate attraction than its formal and technical qualities, and that the intellectual response is secondary; I go further, and say it should be so, yet Uglow sterilises the first and gives primacy to the second. He paints unexpectedly but purposely unlovely women who challenge us to enjoy the mathematics of proportion, their images dubbed *Root Five Nude* or *Double Square, Double Square*, and compel us to forget that the subtle tones of skin and the softness of live flesh can, in another man's hands, mean troubling sensuality.

Uglow claims that his pictures are intended as aesthetic ideas, not ideals, but they emerge as statements, even polemics – 'I think one should behave morally with paint' – and the sexiest subject among all the nudes is his fashionable hip-thrusting toothbrush.

I have often argued that the retrospective exhibition is a disservice to the minor painter, revealing more weaknesses than strengths. The occasional appearance of a single painting by Uglow in mixed company has lent strength to a reputation that he scarcely deserves, for almost any study of the nude was a relief at the height of bucket and slosh, dominant a decade ago; now that bucket and slosh is in retreat and disarray, Uglow deserves some sort of good conduct medal for staying at his post for so long, but he has done nothing to merit the cruel reward of exposure in the bright summer light of the Whitechapel Gallery, where too many feeble pictures betray this very minor painter as a struggling bore inspired by little more than moral rectitude and muddled mathematics.

Evening Standard 1989

Jean-Luc Vilmouth

I HAVE FOR SOME YEARS BEEN ACCUMULATING the oddments that come my way as an art critic – the etchings that are occasionally sent as invitations, the envelopes so beautifully inscribed that they touch the postmen and are saved from the brutalities of franking, the dark brown willy-warmer sent by a furious feminist who works in chocolate, letters of abuse from those who would be famous, and handwritten notes (no copies to be found in files) scribbled by despairing souls in the Tate Gallery – and to these I must now add a tea-bag.

This small gift is from the Arts Council, an invitation to see its multiples and ready-mades in May. The packet bears the exhortation 'You are invited to the private view of Art Unlimited . . . please bring this invitation with you.' Just think of it – to turn up without your tea-bag means exclusion from this great event. 'No tea-bag, Minister? – Be off with you.' Duchesses will fumble in their reticules and Dukes in dinner jacket pockets, humbled by the doorman's 'I don't care if you are a Devonshire, sans tea-bag you have no business here.' No Dormouse, March Hare or Mad Hatter should attend without the tea-bag, for if they do they will be tossed into the treacle-well or compelled to join Lord Gowrie in the 'Twinkle, twinkle' chorus.

Not caring for private views, I took my tea-bag to the kitchen, there to discover that unlike the first bottle in Alice's adventures the legend on the tag read not 'Drink me,' but the very reverse, with 'Not suitable for consumption . . . the South Bank is a registered charity' – a non sequitur well worthy of Carroll's Wonderland.

And then I read the press release – a tale of artists in rebellion against the world of art, of Establishment's cheek reddened by the gauntlet's strike, of heroic efforts to make art accessible and cheap, of soap shaped like a Hepworth sculpture, and remembered Oldenburg's cast aluminium *Baked Potato*, and the flood of faked potatoes that soon followed, and all the other multiples of Pop Art. The fake tea-bag must be within this category and thus a work of art, the Arts Council's little gift an investment to be treasured, a pension for my dotage.

It was with this new enlightenment that I viewed the work of Jean-Luc Vilmouth in the Camden Arts Centre. My first inclination on seeing pot plants crowded on a table, watered by a noisy pump, was to see no more than that rather than a symbol of Creation. I was distracted by as many pot plants on the floor, but these Miss Lomax, prize-winning Directrice of the Centre, dismissed as rejects and bade me raise my eyes. For pot plants to be art they must be arranged by one who declares himself an artist – any old plant watered by any old body will not do. I suggested that 'Take me . . .' at the Serpentine Gallery preached the very contrary, but with a huff and puff and charming giggle she damned that exhibition as absurd, implying that there is an obvious intellectual distinction between pot plants on a trestle table and old clothes on the floor.

She took me to the café room where grossly enlarged photographs of house mites decorate the table tops and the light is lurid pink, and thence to the large room that tells us why the world is round. I could imagine the mistress of an infants' school telling her pupils that the world is not round but globular, charging them with the task of illustrating the distinction, and littering the walls with Vilmouth's photographs of eyeballs, apples, nipples, fossils and astral turbulence, as well as clocks and convex mirrors, with ball bearings, egg yolks and slices of salami if need be. For a while I found the ladder, brillo pad, plastic bag, door wedge and pink duster on the floor embellishments as intriguing as the lesser details in Dali's surreal dreams, but they proved irrelevant – 'If it ain't round, it ain't in the exhibition.' *In statu pupillari* I hinted to Miss Lomax that I sometimes have difficulty in knowing what is art and what is not, and with a disarming grin she trotted out the standard answer – 'Art is what is in an art gallery.' And so it may be, but I cannot see why, if we removed from the room all things circular, the remaining ladder, wedge and duster should not then immediately be art.

My puzzlement was compounded at the ICA, where wretched little paintings by Luc Tuymans, utterly conventional, are presented as more stretching of the boundaries when they are merely incompetent, unworthy even of the Royal Academy; and in the upper rooms, supported by the Arts Council and the Henry Moore Foundation, Abigail Lane 'upstages art' by papering the walls with the bloody palm prints of a New York murder victim. Worse confusion followed at the gallery of Anthony d'Offay, perhaps London's most dominant dealer in the avant-garde, where video projections dismay with deafening shriek and groan, and Rachel Whiteread offers twenty-five identical resin casts of the space beneath an office stool that look like jellied urine with a trace of ink – is there no limit to her profundities? Worse still was my dismay at the Camberwell Art Gallery, where Damien Hirst and his friends present a show called *Minky Manky*, though *Winky Wanky* suits it better with a splash of semen elegantly framed, and a life-size plaster arm masturbating a more than life-size candle poking through the pouch of jockey shorts.

I am encouraged to discard my scepticism and embrace as art the parent's loving video of squawking child, white noise, uncomely insect made a giant, palm tree rubbing shoulders with a rubber plant, wax model in gorilla suit, wax cast of severed head, mouth agape in terminal scream, raspberry pink to match the bloody wallpaper, and, of course, the Arts Council's tea-bag – and so I might, so overwhelming is the glut of this material, so persistent the propaganda in its favour, so many and so weighty the institutions and panjandrums that support it (the Whitechapel Gallery's new exhibition is of road maps painted on forty mattresses on double beds), were it not for one thing – if all this is art, I know no word that fits the work of Michelangelo and Titian.

Evening Standard 1995

Bill *Viola*

Whitechapel Gallery

THE WHITECHAPEL GALLERY HAS BEEN CON-verted into a cinema of sorts – though with too few seats for its potential audience if indeed visitors are expected to see every minute of the show. One enters, and is immediately confronted by a triple screen on which are performed, at length, the acts of birth and death, separated by a watery abstraction, accompanied by the screams of contraction and the rattle of Cheyne-Stokes breathing. The fashionable business of a father's presence at parturition, the sweat, the groans, the probing fingers of the rubber glove and such other details as the frightful red fingernails of an attendant woman, suggest that we are in the presence of poor whites in a cabin in the Adirondacks. It is far more demanding than the other wing, and throws the triptych out of balance. We watch, as it were, a home-made documentary as dull as any video of a holiday in Palma Nova, as technically incompetent as any nonsense submitted to the mercies of Jeremy Beadle, and as extended by longueurs as *Last Year in Marienbad*, but without its subtle beauties; it may, perhaps, be of some small interest to medical students – but I doubt it; it may, perhaps, have some small value as sex education for adolescents – but few could give it the necessary span of attention; it may, perhaps (and this is the only possible justification for showing it in an art gallery), have a contemplative element – but if so, it eluded me, for I could see nothing in it that is beautiful, pathetic or affecting, nothing that triggered an empathic response, nothing that shocked or disturbed (other than the frightful fingernails), nothing that lifted the wearisome business into art, nothing even that for me matched my having to insert my hand into a much-loved bitch to reverse a puppy pointing in the wrong direction.

Nor is the other wing any more elevating. Here we watch the death of an old woman, her lips and teeth sinking into the toothless skull, so frail and still that the moment of her passing is not perceptible; in contrast to the birth, the circumstances are clinical, the bed that of a hospital or nursing-home. She is watched by a middle-aged man who clumsily attempts to close her jaw, but does not know that he must tie it in place until rigor mortis holds it shut. All this too is done to the relentless whirring of one of Mr Sony's intrusive inventions, and the video is again presented as an art form – a self-portrait of the American artist Bill Viola at the dormition of his mother.

It is unfortunate for Viola that his exhibition follows that of Lucian Freud, and that Freud too dealt with the ageing and death of his mother. Freud brought to his single images a restrained intensity of emotion that is utterly absent from the multiple images of Viola's work; the painter distils his anguish, heightens his pathos, and holds the spectator with the age-old business of interpretation and the demand for empathy, and in this he stands in line with Goya and Velazquez, for whom the low technology of paint on canvas was enough to tell a tale that sears the soul; but with all the high technology of Mr Sony to assist him, Viola provides us with emotional interest as flat as cold bread pudding.

The centre panel of this triptych is devoted to images of water and floating and drowning; later on the same day I saw the film *The Piano*, in which water again plays its part, compelling me to see Viola's work as amateur and incompetent, not only in a technical sense, but as an artist – indeed his claims to be an artist are inexcusably pretentious, and the support of his apologists is quite absurd. His wretched video films have nothing to do with the arts of painting and sculpture. It may be clever to put video screens in steel drums of scummy water, to put television tubes face to face so that the images are all but impossible to see, and to invent a rapidly revolving screen that seems both to receive images and to reflect them on the audience, but the experience is no more than a meagre entertainment, the poor relation of the cinema and disco club. Viola's work has no place in an art gallery – it simply isn't art; if it has a place at all, then it is in the cinema – but in that context it is no more than the wretched stuff of peripheral experiment and jiggery-pokery, and Viola's claim to be a 'video visionary' producing work that is 'visually ravishing' is risible. That he sees himself as both in the artistic tradition of European avant-garde painting and as the single-handed maker of a new Renaissance striding into the future is self-esteem of overweening vanity.

He claims to be interested in sound, to sense it as a perceptual field, but his use of it is utterly commonplace and not in the least inventive – indeed the monotony of his intoning, 'The one who stains, the one who converges, the one who investigates, the one who rapes, the one who masturbates [such word-images are now almost mandatory], the one who paints . . .' was old-fashioned a decade ago among the painters of Berlin. Sound as a support for his visual images is as unpleasant and unconvincing as the sound in many a cinema where things seen on the screen are disconcertingly heard from left or right, and a disruptive intellectual effort must be made to relate the information derived by different senses.

To exhibit Viola's work is an abuse of the purposes of the Whitechapel Gallery – but then, in its proper place, the Odeon, it would get the short shrift that it merits. It is in high fashion in America – but we should not necessarily be led by transatlantic fools looking for art forms that are no more than novel and ingenious, and that fit the politically correct fads of Abject Art – the stuff of bowels, body functions and the deliberate use and abuse of body fluids – without being quite so nasty. The video camera has given licence to countless imbeciles to pretend that they are Eisenstein reborn, but Viola thinks himself a new Michelangelo; that this absurd notion, though perhaps excusable now that self-delusion is the primary activity of 'artists', should be supported by influential curators, must cause us to question their competence. The triptych of birth, death and watery confusion is soon to be presented to the Tate Gallery by the Patrons of New Art.

Evening Standard 1993

Andy Warhol

I HAVE ONLY A BLURRED RECOLLECTION OF MY first awareness of the work of Andy Warhol, way back in 1963 – not a picture, print or drawing, but an interminable film peopled by ghastly girls whose only act of any interest was to bandage the penis of the hero. Nothing was amiss with it – no Cape Cod fishwife had filleted it, no surgeon, rabbi or mullah had circumcised it – and it needed neither bandage for bleeding nor splint for erection. This very Sixties episode, half-heartedly outrageous, neither titillating nor pornographic, too extended to be amusing, seemed random, whimsical and pointless – but then the Sixties were the years in which the old indulged the young, and the young, not knowing what to do with the indulgence, frittered away their new freedoms. Warhol enjoyed being bored – 'When you just sit and look out of a window, that's enjoyable. It takes up time. Yeah. Really. My films are just a way of taking up time.' He became the Billy Graham of boredom, and sought to convert us all to the mindless pleasures of the intellectually numb. I have seen no Warhol film since.

My experience of New York in the Sixties was limited to the piranha pool of art dealers and a few respectable collectors, scholars and curators whose public pose was proprietorial and proper; in their cups, however, their circles widened to embrace an unlikely crew of kept boys and unkempt girls whose moral sense was moribund, who fed them Acid on small cubes of sugar and sat them down in rings with the saliva-sodden stumps of home-made cigarettes combusting home-grown cannabis. Time passed, Warhol-style, and the participants in these ineffectual orgies fell into vaguely sexual conjunctions, but, undone by drugs, unmanned, incapable, struck only impotent attitudes, half sleeping, half awake, in a limbo of sapped energy, careless of the public eye, serene in the security of folly shared. Warhol's Factory, as, significantly, he called his studio on 47th Street, was the setting for many such nights, on a grand and crowded scale, with Warhol the Marschallin voyeur, maintaining an endless levée of hairdressers, shoemakers and Italian tenors, never quite identifying his Octavian in the hallucinating haze.

Warhol is most celebrated for his images of Marilyn Monroe, Elvis Presley, Chairman Mao and Mona Lisa, silkscreened onto canvas, neither proper print nor proper painting, repeated ad nauseam, as spiritually uplifting as a sheet of postage stamps, and for his images of tins of Campbell's soup, meticulously enlarged to gross billboard scale. Neither of these genres has anything to commend it as art in any sense of the term as I understand it – mulligatawny is no match for Michelangelo, nor black bean soup for Botticelli, and the grain of the screenprint is crude vulgarity when tested against the delicate glazes of Leonardo's Lisa, obscured though they are by discoloured varnish. With the help of studio assistants (or factory workers), Warhol reproduced images from popular magazines and papers without significantly changing them, repeated small in serried ranks, or writ large and single on separate canvases, more or less identical; the *more or less* must be observed and credited, for though the screenprint work was inevitably identical in scale, it was greatly varied in intensity and tone, and Warhol not only deliberately intervened to provoke the accidental effects of blur, smudge and misprint that offer some small support to those who argue that each item from this mass production is an individual work of art, but was wholly responsible for the often ghastly and irrelevant colour.

In pretending to the status of artist, Warhol's one idea was not enough – this presentation of the common and familiar object unaltered in detail, but on the unfamiliar scale and in the number of the dream and nightmare, the single can six feet instead of six inches high, or two hundred in ten unvarying ranks, an implacable phalanx as the apotheosis of tomato soup or Coca-Cola. It was a formula not only to be adapted to portraits and the Mona Lisa but to the car crash, to tins of infected tuna and the dead victims of their botulism, to the electric chair, boys' bottoms and the circumcised penis – this last on a canvas more than sixteen feet long.

For twenty years he exploited this single idea, and no amount of changing the colour from apple green to knicker pink, no amount of sloshing paint on the parts of no importance, could add significance to the central images, or make them individual, original, diverse – the upturned car, the race riot, the all-American man, remain resolutely banal, and it matters not at all that the photographs are printed on grounds of orange, red or lavender. If the idea of repetition ever had any power, the very repetition must swiftly exhaust it, destroying all visual immediacy; if, with the shock of recognition, the first exercise takes fifteen seconds of attention, the second might take five, but the third and all others can be absorbed at a brisk trot, ticking off the identities as though they are a shopping list and the gallery a branch of Sainsbury's – one large tin of tomato soup, one turquoise Marilyn, one red Elvis, two hundred and ten Coca-Colas, two large kisses, one double torso, ten Mick Jaggers, one Beethoven, four chandeliers and sixty Last Suppers – and ring them up in dollar signs at 25,000 for each repetition of each repetition. Warhol was a very, very rich man, and his studio well named The Factory.

The ideas of the soup can and the repeated images have been credited to one of Warhol's friends in joking mood, but they were taken seriously – 'Andy has fought by repetition to show us that there is no repetition really, that everything we look at is worthy of our attention. That's been a major direction for the twentieth century.' They have been claimed as the evidence of a serious and deliberate aesthetic revolution, a response to the need to escape the loose, rough quality of paint that conformed to the aggression of Abstract Expressionist painting, an attempt to re-popularise art by making it indistinguishable from the poster and the magazine front cover, though it is difficult at this late stage to divine whether Warhol's sybilline statements about art inspired his work or were inspired by it, reflecting a need to offer a rational explanation of an idiom that was so alien to the established norms of art as we moved into the Sixties. To me, the repeated images and grotesque enlargements are so hallucinatory yet so keyed to trivial realities that they can only be a response triggered by LSD.

Born in 1928, Warhol was rather older than most of the brilliant children of the Sixties (Roy Strong, for example), and it has slipped our memories that he was already celebrated as a commercial artist in demand by *Harper's Bazaar, Vogue* and Tiffany's when that indulgent decade began. He was a brilliant designer of footwear, a Shilling of the shoe, and in pure line drawing could match the delicacy, sympathy, wit, tenderness and sexuality of Cocteau, and the cold precision of Hockney; he could illustrate with precision, replacing all extraneous detail with elegant grace-notes of his own invention. His early work is obedient to his commissioners' commands, informing and instructing, setting the spectator at an emotional distance, asking him to make a judgement between this shoe and that, this hat and the other – a formula that finds an echo in the later repetitious work – between this pretty boy and the next. The skill, elegance and economy of his drawing at this stage is immaculate, and I suspect that it and his ideas stem from access to French pattern books dating back to the 17th and 18th centuries, as well as to the work of French etchers and the engravers of the 1920s; I am convinced that he knew the drawings made by Jean Cocteau to illustrate *Le Livre Blanc* and *Dessins d'un Dormeur*, and the untitled collection reproduced in a paperback book in 1923, for without them, Warhol's elegantly concise and linear studies of pretty boys, thirty years later, are too remarkable a coincidence.

Little of this delicacy appears in his earliest paintings. These are based on crass commercial posters, translating the megaphone messages of the rupture appliance and the corn plaster from printed paper to painted canvas, with a hint of Dada in the abuse of type faces and the occasional use of extended cuttings from real newspapers – trite and unremarkable. He tried his hand at painting the characters of strip cartoons – Popeye, Batman, Superman – and at enlarging to eight feet the front pages of sensational newspapers. He drew dollar bills and Do-it-yourself-by-Numbers paintings, dance diagrams for the waltz and tango, and the mouth organ noses of preposterous Cadillacs, and inexorably the commonplace commercial draughtsman was seized by the notion that he was both great artist and great proselytiser, that it was his destiny to turn art into pop culture, and that he could re-popularise it by making it indistinguishable from the poster and the cover of the glossy magazine. This he did, and in the doing, both reduced the Renaissance heritage to nothing and so elevated commercial art to the status of an aesthetic instrument of Mammon, class, and fashion that critics and art historians have ever since, like timorous puppies, rolled on their backs and peed on their own bellies.

It is suddenly the Andy Warhol season, and exhibitions devoted to this first-generation Czech American, lately deceased, erupt all over London like the plague sores in the groin of Saint Roch. The V&A is host to Nat Finkelstein's photographs of the man, picking his teeth, picking his nose, wiping a drip, signing his name, groping a boy – all those little intimacies that may be exploited by a shrewd observer who can then say of his god that he was, after all, human and a nice guy like one of us (a warning to every famous man not to keep company with a parasite carrying a Pentax). At the National Film Theatre, Warhol's tedious films, random, whimsical, pointless, witless, endless records of the fatuities of his fans and catamites, the longueurs of *Last Year in Marienbad* translated to New York and played by tramps of both sexes, are revived to remind us of how limp and listless were the Swinging Sixties. At the Serpentine and Hayward Galleries, everything that Warhol ever made is on view in such an atmosphere of veneration that I am inclined to quote the Creation chapter of Genesis and Saint John's perfect précis of it – 'All things were made by him; and without him was not anything made that was made.' When, in June 1968, he was shot by the drugged and demented Valerie Solanis, his liver, lungs, stomach, spleen and gullet perforated by the bullets, all his vital functions died away on the operating table, and he was, for a considerable time, dead; with his revival, there was talk of Lazarus and that other, grander, Resurrection; Warhol observed only that living had become an extended extra-corporeal experience, a variant of watching himself on television.

He was homosexual and made a virtue of the flamboyance that often accompanies that affliction, his life-style itself a work of art, a non-stop happening – 'Publicity is like eating peanuts. Once you start, you can't stop' (peanuts, I observe, leave a nasty sludge in the deep recesses of the mouth). I suspect that, like Hockney, he was a pasticheur always in desperate need of external stimulus, but, lacking Hockney's interpretive ability and his capacity for serious intellectual revision, Warhol merely repeated what was under his nose. His humour darkened to embrace the car crash and the electric chair, to mimic police photography; Botticelli, Munch, Chirico and Tischbein joined Leonardo as a source of images; in homosexual obsession Cocteau's elegance gave way to the phallocentric rough stuff of graffiti; and at the very end, the ageing and indulgent head of *The Factory* camouflaged his face and let Jean-Michel Basquiat, a pretty and seductive parasite, wreak havoc on his pictures. Few able men have had a more destructive influence on art, reducing it to the mechanical processes of the production line; few men have so far dulled the standards of aesthetic achievement on the one hand and aesthetic judgement on the other that any vulgar fool with access to a camera and a print shop can pretend to be an artist; no man has so exploited the business of self-publicity that simply *being* an artist has become more important than any work that an artist may produce. That it is now possible for any witless schoolboy to declare himself an artist, though he cannot draw, cannot paint, cannot sculpt, is illiterate, inarticulate, ignorant and has no skills of any kind, is largely Warhol's work, his donation to posterity. He was, as Carl André observed, 'the perfect glass and mirror of his age, and certainly the artist we deserved'. Of himself he said, 'If you want to know all about Andy Warhol, just look at the surface of my paintings, and there I am. There's nothing behind it' – yet we persist in finding what was never there.

Tatler 1989

Carel Weight: A War Retrospective

Carel Weight, darling of the Royal Academy each summer, belongs to those peculiar genres of painter so much loved in England, the professional amateur and the amateur professional whose genuine incompetence is redeemed by madness, mysticism or eccentricity – a line that began with Blake and continued in this century with Alfred Wallis, L.S. Lowry, Stanley Spencer, Cecil Collins and their kind. Sane men abandon reason in the presence of their pictures; in the case of Weight, whose work bridges both categories, their eyes are blind to the coarse handling of paint, crude drawing, violent colour, erratic perspective and disrupted space, their imaginations instead touched uncannily by some lurking element of disaster as yet unformed, by things Satanic in suburbia, by Battersea uneasily bewitched, by Wandsworth in the grip of warlocks, and by Clapham clouded by the flight of phantoms. Confronted by Weight's paintings one is compelled either to surrender to their sinister mood and cast aside the conventions of connoisseurship, or to conclude that those who have so strenuously admired them – with Lord Clark of Civilisation and Lord Gowrie of the Arts Council among their number – took leave of their sense when they did so, adult men who should be sceptical still spellbound and seduced by the nightmares of childhood.

Had Marc Chagall been born in Balham and died at the age of eight, we might have discovered a cache of childish paintings akin to those of Carel Weight at eighty, for there is spiritual kinship in their blazing skies, stunted figures, grotesqueries and narratives. *The Poet Reclining*, Chagall's masterpiece in the Tate Gallery since 1942, could easily provide the setting for one of Weight's evocations of mysterious presences (I observe, in passing, that this beautiful picture has not been on view in Millbank since 1987 – in Mexico, Japan and Germany, but not in London – a scandalous abuse). Weight has never been averse to the influence of older masters – Munch shrieks over his shoulder, Bonnard's clumsy hand holds his and both fumble with the brush, Vuillard taught him how to make a figure hunch and shrink into a corner, and he has kept the company of old Pieter Brueghel's peasants; his claim that as a student he 'learned a lot from Poussin', seems less credible.

Very little of Weight's early work survives, for his attic studio in Shepherd's Bush was destroyed by a bomb in the spring of 1941, but a small self portrait of 1933 suggests belated Bloomsbury and the influence of Duncan Grant. By 1941, however, he had developed the style that is immediately recogniseable as his, with faults that seem quite astonishing for a man of thirty-three earning his living as a teacher in an art school – in a painting of a German bomber over Wimbledon, all his favourite emotions, alarms and excursions are made to seem ridiculous by a stunted trolleybus and the scrambling gnomes that were its passengers.

He wanted to be a War Artist, but was not officially appointed until May 1945, just as the war ended, and was then despatched to Italy. As a war artist without a war to paint, and more or less at ease and freedom in a land that had been at peace for a year or so, Weight found himself in astonishing new worlds of opera, music, great art and architecture, and of the museums and churches of Naples, Rome, Perugia, Pisa, Rimini and Verona, with even the great treasures of the Vatican open to him – only in Florence, where precuations against loss and damage had not been reversed, was he disappointed. If he had work to do, it was not under the stress of battle.

His responses to baroque and Renaissance architecture, bombed or intact, were quite uncluttered with the suburban myths of his London work, though the influence of the London painters of the Euston Road school is obvious; the figures are strongly drawn in strokes of black paint as though by Geoffrey Tibble, one of its few deservedly influential members, with whom Weight by necessity (Tibble by choice) shared a palette dominated by khaki and ochre. Perhaps compelled to kow-tow to the conventional taste of army officers, Weight's sense of structure in these pictures too is more orderly, the townscapes almost topographical, the figures far from caricatural, and the perspective rarely on the wayward tilt. It was not that the characteristics emerging in Weight's work in 1940 were entirely suppressed, but that in pictures more or less commissioned for archival purposes, there were fewer opportunities for such mannered diversions; when he moved on to Vienna in the winter of 1945–6, and thence to Greece, he painted such dull and faithful pictures of the view that they could easily be mistaken for the now forgotten Hanslip Fletcher or Adrian Daintrey in their prime, or another dozen of the ilk.

It must be argued that the disciplines imposed on the War Artist brought into being some of Weight's finest pictures, his familiar panoramic view of Holborn Circus in 1947 his masterpiece, embracing skills and subtleties of drawing and transparent paint of which there had been no evidence in 1940, and which were utterly dispersed within a decade. To see all his war paintings, both those that date from his years of official appointment, 1945 and 1946, and those that were occasionally commissioned, with two major post-war pictures to point the way thereafter, gathered in an exhibition in the Imperial War Museum, is to see Weight's rise and fall encapsulated; it is a melancholy sight, less for the occasional melancholy of subject – as in the roofless Tempio Malatestiana in Rimini, the rain pouring on the raised umbrella of the priest, the floor of the famous church awash – than for the falling-off into the deliberate dramatic whimsy that is now the stuff of popular expectation, unremittingly repeated.

Contemplation of Weight's work is remorselessly interrupted by broadcast announcements, abrasive and intrusive – 'Ding-dong,' and then a patronising female voice urges us 'to experience Operation Jericho . . .' 'Ding-dong' for the umpteenth time and one wishes the walls of the Museum to come tumbling down. 'Ding-dong . . . we have no barriers round the exhibits . . . do not climb on them . . . or else . . .' 'Ding-dong,' and one thinks of the V&A, to which the Director of the Imperial War Museum soon transfers his notions. The Museum has a new room for its pictures, unsympathetic, bleak and poorly lit, calculated to make them dull and drab, the hanging miserably thin. The Museum charges a hefty entrance fee. These are matters to make us tremble for South Kensington.

Evening Standard 1995

Whistler

J OHN RUSKIN WAS A FOOL TO ABUSE WHISTLER for the 'pot of paint' flung in the public's face that represented a rocket tumbling earthwards over Cremorne Gardens. Though self-appointed as Turner's apologist, his touch with other contemporary artists was quite unsure, and among those of the past he preferred the winsome Virgins of Perugino to the heroic nudes of Michelangelo; an amateur artist himself, a social reformer of risible eccentricity, and a lover of pre-pubertal girls in private fancy, he was quite demented by 1878 when Whistler sued him for his insult, had been so since 1861, and was eventually to become literally barking mad, woof-woofing over his garden wall. The folly of the insult, however, did not lie in melancholy, nervous debility, depression, mania and other euphemisms for his mental malady, but in its revelation of his utter incompetence as a critic, his ignorance of Whistler's work and eyes blind to Whistler's workmanship, for the sparks of the falling rocket are no accident, not paint flung at the canvas, but paint brushed on it with exquisite precision, touched in with the bristles' point, the paint varying in hue and density to suggest explosive heat and dying ember.

Had Ruskin known anything of Whistler, indeed, had he known anything of art, he should surely have recognised that this now notorious *Nocturne* was comfortably within a tradition of night painting that in this country stemmed from Wright of Derby, Loutherbourg, and the painters of the Industrial Revolution. That having spent so many months in Venice since 1849 he should have been in total ignorance of the smokey, misty nocturnes of Ippolito Caffi, heir, as it were, to the night scenes of Canaletto, whose work of the 1850s remarkably anticipates many of Whistler's crepuscular pictures, is an indictment of the critic's narrow mind, obsessed with the far Venetian past rather than its present. Had Ruskin paid attention to Whistler twenty years earlier, he might have recalled

that lamplit night scenes had been among the painter's earliest
interests and had continued to occupy him with their subtleties,
together with subjects painted in the half light of evening, their tone
consistently darkening until he felt able to conceive and control a
night scene that owed nothing to the dying sun or rising moon, or
to the drama of pitch darkness, and everything to colour and
impression. Whistler should not have sued Ruskin when he could
have destroyed his reputation by pointing to his critic's ignorance
and wilful blindness, and told the ranter's audience that they listened
to a lunatic.

The critic should have fired his Ruskinade at Whistler five years
earlier, in 1872, when the celebrated portrait of the painter's mother
was exhibited at the Royal Academy, but his mind and body were
elsewhere. Whistler's Mother has become one of the most famous
pictures in western art, the Mona Lisa of the 19th-century, praised
far beyond its merits, though it did not at once find favour. Its
eventual and extraordinary popularity was due partly to the
sentimentality of Victorian and vulgar attitudes to the subject –
any man who painted his mother with such evident respect must be
a good egg – and partly to the sympathy of late 19th-century
methods of monochrome reproduction, for in photogravure the
contrasts of the blacks against the lighter tones is much less
ponderous than in the paint, and the composition softens into
the *Arrangement in Grey and Black* that is its other title, the edges
gentled, the leaden darkness of the sitter's dress muted into
luminous shadow, the stark whites softened by the paper and
the printing tone. Had it been possible in Victoria's day to
reproduce the picture in colour, the title would have made little
sense to ordinary mortals, for reproductions introduce a strong
blue-green into the greys and none of the seductive subtleties of
monochrome come into play; in colour, this image of stern piety
would never have been so favoured by seaside landladies and
parlourmaids.

It is a wretched picture, ill-balanced, haphazard and clumsy,
disturbed by evidence of much correction and revision; there are

nice touches in the curtain and the hands, but the thin painting of the black dress defeats the modelling; the placing of Whistler's framed etchings on the wall is meaningless in terms of composition, and the comparatively abrupt brightness of white mounts destroys the sense of space; the dark curtain is so assertive in its mass that it draws attention away from the portrait head that is tucked into the top right corner. Cut in half, the picture makes much better sense, both as portrait and abstract *Arrangement*.

It served its purpose, however, as foreplay for the far superior portrait of Carlyle, painted a year or so later, in 1872-3. In this, another *Arrangement in Grey and Black*, the sitter's silhouette is much more lively, the supporting chair more evident, giving logic to the pose. Here the framed prints are deliberately used as a counterpoise to Carlyle's head, and the frames are gold and brown in tone, their white mounts toned down too so that they do not disrupt the space within the picture. The tone of wall and floor are much the same, divided by a dark dado that serves to anchor the figure (one of Whistler's favourite devices); the only startling fracture in the overall tone is the white of Carlyle's collar, a device that serves to draw attention to the head.

The French critics who thought Whistler's Mother 'a poor woman abandoned in a room with a smoking chimney' (they also thought it the portrait of a corpse), could easily have said much the same of Carlyle's portrait, for it is even smokier – but this is the very quality that makes it so impressive. There is no doubt that without the fumblings with his Mother, Whistler would not have made a masterpiece of Carlyle (though it too was much amended in execution, the lessons learned in placing, balance, tone and pictorial space all skilfully applied – and yet this portrait, surely one of the best painted in the later 19th century, overshadowed by the sentimental taste of philistines, has not half the reputation that it should.

These two paintings make another point – that Whistler was always an uneven artist, his touch often both sure and unsure within a single picture, often wasting time on failures without realising it, success and disaster often hand in hand within the same genre or subject. The balance of good work and concurrent bad is most obvious in the portraits of the 1880s, but in the 1890s it became imbalance, fudged, messy and unfinishable portraits far preponderent as his small genius evaporated. Whistler has been promoted as a great painter, but he was nothing of the kind, merely a minor figure given to an excess of refined taste and ingenuity, reflecting the widespread revival of interest in Frans Hals and Velasquez but never their match, the friend of Fantin-Latour, Courbet and Degas but never their equal, never quite Impressionist (they invited him to join their number), never quite Symbolist, never more than a mirror of his time and often not even that, no match even for Tissot. Had he not advertised himself with as much wit, spite and arrogance as Oscar Wilde, he would long ago have slipped into obscurity.

Evening Standard 1994

Christopher Wood

Nothing enhances a painter's reputation faster than his suicide. Christopher Wood's leap onto the railway track at Salisbury station on 21 August 1930 ensured, if not a shortage, the abrupt end to an over-abundant supply, defined the whole development, closed the critical eye to clumsy things of wretched quality, hinted at romantic hopes never to be realised, and introduced melancholy notes of guilt and regret that patronage, now all too willing, came too late. This last, of course, was remedied by those who posthumously paid the prices to which Wood had long aspired.

Christopher Wood, Kit to his friends, was twenty-nine when his mortal remains were recovered from beneath the wheels of the Atlantic Coast Express, the youthful genius cut off in his prime. He is remembered as remarkably handsome, endowed with the well-trimmed good looks of the public schoolboy, the flannelled fool of cricket, the prefect on whom adolescents have a crush, the luxurious catamite in silk pyjamas; mild polio gave him a slight limp, a flaw that made the rest of him seem the more perfect, adding to sexual attraction a tug at the strings of sympathy. At nineteen his appeal to older men was perhaps unconscious, his exploitation of their willingness to give quite innocent and unaware, but at twenty he knew it to be the instrument that opened doors to security, comfort and louche society. There were women in his life, but his relationships with them were romantic follies, flirtatious or convenient camouflage, and his mother was the woman who mattered far the most to him. All the evidence suggests that he was a pretender in heterosexual matters, even a silly snob collecting Duchesses, and far more at his ease in the company of rich and influential homosexual men.

These are matters that inform much of his work as painter and draughtsman, but most of his friends, and the writers and admirers who knew him, conspired to cast over them an obscuring gloss of wistful melancholy as they polished his halo and made a myth of him. Lucy Carrington Wertheim, the devoted dealer who supported him in his last months, still in the Sixties, in her dotage, burned tiger bright with her recollections of the golden boy. Even as recently as 1979, Winifred Nicholson, then eighty-six, could conjure him as a sailor riding the dark depths of the oceans of the mind, a painter understood only by those 'who enjoy the regions between poetry and art', her enthusiasm undimmed since 1926, when she had described him as 'England's first painter. His vision is true, his grasp is real, his power is life itself.' Eric Newton, a serious art critic, wrote of his Cornish and Breton landscapes as haunted by the Holy Grail, claimed for him the sunshine of Fra Angelico and the thunder of El Greco, opined that among the five hundred surviving pictures none was pretentious, monotonous or trivial, and in the pantheon of British painters, put him as high as Hogarth. Twenty years later, in 1959, Jean Cocteau, perhaps once his lover, in an excess of sentimentality, claimed eternal youth for the angelic boy who 'walked with a limp because he had only one foot on the earth'. Even now, sixty-five years after the dramatic death, an old crone of his acquaintance speaks of Kit as 'a brighter light than any known in England'.

Brighter than Augustus John and Sickert, Gainsborough and Palmer? The work, even at its best, does not support the claim. With most of his adult life spent in Paris, enjoyment the purpose there, smoking opium and doing his sexual duty at least as important as the sour virtue of slavery at his easel, it was inevitable that in one way or another he would mix with celebrated painters and benefit from their ideas and influence, but that he should be seen as England's Fra Angelico and the nation's first great painter is preposterous. His experience of the Parisian avant-garde nourished his work, but intellectually he was far behind; it was to Picasso's early Pink and Blue Periods that he turned, not to his Cubism; Utrillo, long in decline, influenced his street scenes and perspective, Modigliani his figures, and Vlaminck lent him the dramatic tricks of stormy black and white; he borrowed card-players from Cézanne, and from Kisling's figures the unblinking stare; Cocteau taught him the value of the clean, unhesitating line, and Picasso urged the exchange of soft red chalk for hard black pencil; from Christian Bérard, much given to high-buttocked sailors, whom he regarded as 'the best of young French painters', he derived a simple formula for the male nude, half way between the real and the erotic. In Alfred Wallis, primitive, self-taught, a genuine illiterate of mephitic influence, he found a perfect exemplar of a naive theory of modern art that he had once propounded to his mother – that it is the thing seen through the eyes of the smallest child, refined by the painter's experience. All this absorbed, and encouraged by Frank Dobson, he had the vanity to see himself as usurping an exhausted Augustus John (whom he once greatly admired) – 'John is finished . . . it rests with me to carry on and go further.'

In the last year of his life, deliberate naivety largely abandoned but still attached to what Gwen Raverat dismissed as 'fashionable clumsiness', he produced his best pictures, of which *The Yellow Man* is perhaps the most remarkable combination of influences and origins. Picasso figures from the pink and blue Saltimbanques are imposed on a clumsy backdrop of an English village street, out of scale, the perspective incoherent. The acrobat's yellow costume, framed by a black cloak, is startling among the low tones and cold greys scratched and scraped. Light falls from a hidden moon. The heads, as grey as leaden death masks, seeming as heavy, wear expressions that offer no clue to the narrative – and yet the narrative element is overwhelming and in a peculiar mood of elusive mystery, as though Wood illustrates a haunting episode from Alain-Fournier's *Grand Meaulnes* (1912). It is a picture that in spite of its Picasso mountebanks, the weak connections with Surrealism and de Chirico, the hints of Vlaminck in the light and tone, and even the vile Ripolin enamel thinned with turpentine with which it is painted (and which contributes much to its uneven surface), has nothing in common with the School of Paris in the Twenties. In retrospect its connections are entirely English, and it is in this that Wood seems most remarkable, standing alone as the first Neo-Romantic painter, anticipating by half a generation the work of Burra, Minton, Vaughan and Ayrton, seeming to direct them to the soul weighed down and the uneasy dream.

A new biography of Wood gives all the facts known and recently discovered, his character inexorably less likeable as he moves towards the suicide that still cannot be explained – opium perhaps the cause, or the Wall Street Crash that overnight impoverished his friends and patrons, and wrecked the market for his pictures just as he showed signs of lyric genius.

Evening Standard 1995

Jack Butler Yeats

'JACK YEATS WAS, WITHOUT DOUBT, THE greatest Irish artist of the first half of the twentieth century.' This bold statement by the eximious authors of a recent (and speedily remaindered) encyclopedic tome on Irish painters, though perhaps admirable for its gutsy tub-thumping, deserves questioning scrutiny rather than mute acceptance, for it may seem to depend on the assumption that unfinished canvases, unresolved ideas, and often unlovely smudges and smears of paint are the marks of unarguable superiority.

Smudges and smears are plentiful in the Whitechapel Gallery's exhibition of forty-five later and late paintings by this younger brother of the celebrated poet, William Butler Yeats, so much so that the thought at once occurred to me that the Gallery, having just exhibited the bleached and blasted, blobbed and buttered absurdities of the preposterous American Albert Pinkham Ryder, perhaps proposes that Ireland too could produce a famous rotten painter – and that the logic of the one exhibition immediately following the other is that both painters had work hung in the *Exhibition of Modern Art* at the Armory in New York in 1913 (the most important event in the history of modern art in America), both were on the late and lunatic fringe of Romanticism with a poetic slant, and both were writers as well as painters. The pity is that Yeats did not accompany his pictures to New York and thus did not encounter the dirty and reclusive dotard who is now regarded as the father of Abstract Expressionism, for if ever that term could be applied to a painter earlier than Pollock, de Kooning and their ilk, it is to Jack Yeats in his declining years.

Two less irreverent thoughts followed – that the selectors had chosen almost entirely the wrong pictures, and that Yeats is, though an interesting curiosity, so minor a painter that it makes no sense to mount with so much fanfarrado an exhibition of so few late paintings, when an exhibition of a hundred or so, embracing all his work, would have answered the inevitable (and justifiable) questions about his roots and his development. The earliest picture on view dates from 1922, when Yeats, at 51, was well-known from an exhibition history of almost thirty years; it implies a narrative of some kind – that of the *Punch* cartoon or the travel poster – and one is tempted to supply balloons of low conversation on the subject of the slack G-string. The last painting dates from 1956, the year before Yeats's death at the age of 85, and is a pantomime queen of sorts, an operatic Dido prancing before the fishy eye of a monster worthy of late Turner. Between them runs a string of landscapes and figure subjects bearing such poetic titles as *The Violence of Dawn*, *Humanity's Alibi*, *The Golden Age*, and *Drift*.

We should perhaps question the wisdom of mounting a Yeats exhibition in London in the very year when Dublin has been appointed the Cultural Capital of Europe, for none of the Whitechapel pictures is borrowed from the National Gallery of Ireland, where last year I stood enchanted by what seemed to me small masterpieces. I am, moreover, convinced that in the thirty years since Victor Waddington (the first and most kindly of Cork Street dealers, now dead) took me aside and showed me similar small treasures, I have seen many paintings in the market place far better than most of those included in this show. This is not to suggest that the choice is uniformly weak; a large and splashy seascape painted in 1950 is fresh enough in its attack, and I suspect was bought by the Scottish National Gallery for its resemblance to the windsweepings of MacTaggart, and Waddington's *Come* says in the compass of nine by fourteen inches all that can be said of unnerved horse and gentling man, with the paint as wild as the one and the tone and structure as controlled as the other; this, in truth, is masterpiece enough to arouse the cupidity of any man who cares for painting, but it makes the point, as does a strange little thing called *The Shadowed Hour* (all slanting light and monotone, its Topolski figures suggesting threatened violence), that Yeats was much more successful with emotional intensity when he was least ambitious in scale.

This is not a comfortable exhibition; too many of the compositions seem to be ill-recollected borrowings from other painters, from Millet, Constable, John Martin, Puvis, Roussel and Dufy (an astonishingly catholic range), though I am at a loss to explain the kinship of *A Place of Islands* with Caspar David Friedrich's *Wanderer*, the handling of paint, allied to imagery, often suggests Ensor, Munch and Kokoschka, without the competence of any of them (Kokoschka, in whose admiration of Yeats is recognition of a fellow messy painter, may indeed have been recognising his own influence); but the greatest discomfort comes from a sense that Yeats was either not quite sane (though not quite mad) or, like Wyndham Lewis, was as blind as a bat and painted as he did because he could not see – I wonder if an autobiographical clue lies in his play *The Silencer*, where Charlie Weston was a man who would not wear his glasses until the level of rye whiskey was up between his eyes. We must not forget that Jack Yeats was almost as much a literary man as his brother William, that his early influential friendships were with J.M. Synge, John Masefield and Lady Gregory, and that James Joyce and Samuel Beckett bought his paintings: I am tempted to recall that Strindberg too was both writer and painter, and of his lunacy there is no doubt.

The exhibition catalogue, an extravagantly expensive babble of blarney, reveals more of the inadequacies of its too many contributors than of Yeats, who is described as the 'third son and youngest of six'; 1915 marked the 'Beginning of illness and depression', but of these we hear no more, though both, if they became chronic conditions, must surely offer some clue to his mannerisms of style and subject.

Yeats began as a competent illustrator of a kind all too common in the magazines of circa 1900, absorbed something of the strengths of James Pryde and William Nicholson, Orpen and Augustus John, and then began to beg, borrow, mix and mismatch from any source that intrigued him. Most of the late and supposedly Expressionist paintings are overworked and smudged to mud, and if they have any vitality it is in the discordant high notes of raw bright pigment taken straight from the tube, to which we have too primitive a response. Once in a while he left well alone at an early stage and the colour stayed clean and clear; once in a while he evoked the wide wild mystery of a world landscape that could hang with old Brueghel's *Tower of Babel*; once in a while he produced a painting of marvellous beauty that was not accident; but much of what now hangs in Whitechapel is as crude in drawing, colour and construction as any daub wet from the easel of almost any haggis-fingered scion of the Second School of Glasgow in the past quinquennium.

Evening Standard 1991